VEGAN

AIR FRYER COOKBOOK

300+ Easy and Delicious Plant Based Air Fryer Recipes to Heal Your Body and Live A Healthy Lifestyle

Author Name:
Jennifer Roast

© Copyright 2021 - All rights reserved.

Table of Contents

Introduction:

Lots of people decide to go vegan for ethical reasons. They feel empathy for animals and do not want to eat meat. Some people don't consider milk and eggs to be fit for consumption, but many do. Once they decide to go vegan, they confront the fact that they will still, through necessity, be adversely affected by the use of animals. Most, at that point, won't pursue it any further.

For those who do continue being vegan, they get into it for environmental reasons. Meat, specifically beef, is too energy-intensive. Grass-fed beef requires 23 calories worth of plant matter for every calorie of beef produced. Research has shown that animals are harmful to the environment even when they aren't eaten. They are dangerous because they consume fertilizer and food that could be used to grow plants for humans. Animal agriculture causes a disproportionate amount of greenhouse gas emissions when compared to other domestic industries. The UK alone produces 20-25% of greenhouse gas emissions, and farming accounts for 71% of those emissions.

From an ethical and environmental perspective, being vegan seems like the only clean option.

So why do people become vegan? The answer is simple. As soon as you decide to go vegan, you no longer live in a safe and comfortable reality that you had previously. You now must consider what you're going to wear, the products you use, where your electricity comes from and if you need to drive to where you're going. The vegan reality is one of being responsible for yourself.

And here's where it gets interesting. When someone decides to become vegan, they often do so wrongly too. For instance, I know many people who get into the lifestyle without the necessary understanding of nutrition. They hear the word "vegan" and think: "Hey, that sounds good. Let me give it a go." But most people don't have enough information to make such a big jump. Knowing what foods to eat and avoid, how to sleep, and the amount of water to consume are some of the first things to learn because being vegan is demanding, and it needs to be done correctly to avoid adverse side effects.

I can only presume that perhaps is why people are choosing to become vegan. The current generation is concerned more with personal well-being than any other. We are all responsible for our actions.

I find it romantic that although we are more aware of the consequences of our actions than ever before, we are still willing to change our way of life to be better people. And that's never a bad thing.

What is the Vegan Diet?

I was vegan once upon a time. And I enjoyed it immensely. You see, I never intended to go vegan. But after a few months on a diet, I grew to love it. And for the last two years, I haven't eaten any animals.

As a vegan, you eat what the name implies you should. You eat vegetables. And maybe some fruit and nuts. Vegan diets are commonly misconceived as a diet of crackers and tofu. That is not the case at all. A vegan diet is a diet of vegetables as long as you eat the right vegetables.

The most abundant vegetables on the planet are soya beans, rice, wheat, potatoes, corn etc. These are the base of the vegan diet. The quantities of these foods are relatively small when compared to carb-rich foods like bread. But, in many cases, what these foods lack in quantity, they make up in quality. They are high in fiber and low in calories.

The ethical choice to avoid animal products extends to clothing, cosmetics and other goods that we consume every day. Veganism is more of a choice for lifestyles than anything else.

But you have to be careful. If you want to eat a healthy vegan diet, you need to remember that meat alternatives may taste good, but like all processed foods, they have almost twice the saturated fat and twice as much sugar as the same amount of meat. So you must be able to work around it and take this into account when planning your diet.

Cooking your meals is your first step. Air fryers are easy and quick ways of cooking vegan dishes. You can make fries, fries, crepes, cakes and many other words that will make you very happy. The only thing harder than being vegan is being a vegan chef. Knowing what goes with what and using enough spices to keep it interesting is tricky.

The amount of vegan food out there is spectacular and growing all the time. Your imagination limits your diet. But remember: as a vegan, you need to know the food you are eating. A lot of types of food that seem like they could be vegan are not.

Lastly, the thing I miss the most is the kindness of strangers. As a vegan, you open your heart to so many people, and everyone is friendly. Better still, they ask you how you've been doing and what you think about all of this. These people are curious and almost always have a very positive effect on you. The world is a more pleasant place being vegan, and at first, I found it very hard to accept and notice this. I am always attracted to new people and see them in new ways. Veganism has been one of the best choices I have ever made in my life.

If you're very concerned with starting a vegan diet, you should educate yourself on nutrition—some of the base foods needed in a vegan diet like lentils, beans, rice and similar. Also, contain a lot of healthy vitamins. A well-balanced diet includes different vitamins and minerals.

The other factor is how you sleep. After a day of hard work, the naked truth is that the last thing you want is to be tired when you go to bed.

It's essential when you eat a healthy vegetarian diet every day. Also, if you're considering changing your diet, it's necessary to evaluate your health. Remember, the only way to stay healthy is by exercising at least once per day. That makes it easier to digest the food that you eat.

If you're healthy, you're eating the right foods. It's the best way to go.

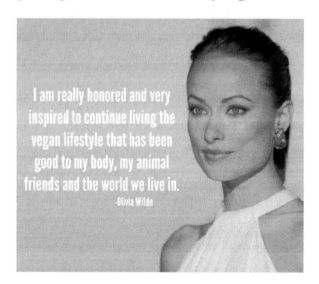

I am really honored and very inspired to continue living the vegan lifestyle that has been good to my body, my animal friends and the world we live in.
-Olivia Wilde

Why Air fryer is best for Vegan recipes?

Air fryer been in the market for a while. It comes with advanced and innovative technology that rivals any other products. It significantly reduces the use of oil in food, as compared to use of deep fryers which have a high oil content.

Vegan recipes such as French fries is a great example of why people are switching to air fryers over deep fryers. They are so easy to make and consume less oil. They are also easy to store as there are more space where it can be placed.

One of the effects of air fryers is that the end product doesn't taste as oily as deep fried ones. This is because it uses less oil in the cooking process. The end product does not contain excess salt although it can be used to salt the food before it is placed in the air fryer.

Some air fryers have more safety features than others. That is if they have overheating sensors. This is due to the fact that air fryers use a lot of electrical power to make the food. So the sensors are there to prevent equipment failure in case the coil is overheated.

The temperature controls on air fryers are another great feature, especially when cooking frozen foods. Most people don't have a good time cooking frozen foods with conventional ovens that used a lot of gas. The controls on the air fryers allow it to cook frozen foods from scratch or totally frozen. They also contain timers which start counting down when the food is first put in. The finish time can be easily seen from a nearby place. This is an excellent way of managing time.

What are some of the best and easy healthy vegan air fryer recipes?

Tomatoes Salad is the most popular vegan healthy recipe so far and it is also the easiest. Zucchini and Squash Salad is one of our favorites, too. Okra and Eggplant Stew is delicious with nice spicy flavor.

Look at the recipe right below. You can also check our vegetarian food category for easier healthy vegan recipes.

Vegan recipes are healthy, cheap and also easy. Lots of people might think that a vegan diet is a difficult diet to follow as it does not include meat. This is not real as there are many choices and it is not restrictive as some people think.

The best part of vegan diet is that you get to eat healthy and at the same time lose weight. They do not have side effects and this is really amazing. The fact that you are able to lose weight without much effort is something which makes many people chooses this lifestyle.

Fruit is a very good part of any diet. You should try the fruits as they are not fattening but give you necessary nutrients required for the body. They contain antioxidants and also vitamins which are very important for the body.

Normal diet plan includes drinking fresh fruits juice and eating fruits. Fruits have the ability to make your brain more active and give a lot of energy for different activities. One can also drink fruit juice in winter to make the vitamin intake in your body much better.

Last but not least, there are some places in the world where fruits are abundant. You should go to such parts of the world and find the fruits there which are not available in your area and make them part of your diet. Choosing healthy vegan recipes is a must if you decide to be a vegan.

CHAPTER 5:

Advantages Of Using The Air Fryer

Basic Operation and Benefits of the Air Fryer

It is an appliance that cooks food by circulating hot air around it and gets rid of the oil to fat. It circulates hot air around food from outside of the fryer to inside of the fryer using an extraction fan and getting food's surface crisp.

Most of range air fryers use convective heat and infrared heat. This means that air is blowing and radiation is applied to food at the same time. A range air fryer is a combination of the technology of a convection oven and a griddle. Convective heat is applied to the surface of food because the hot air is travelling the food's length. As for infrared heat, it is blown right to the surface of food because the source of infrared heat radiation is a red hot steel coil. When airflow and infrared heat are combined, food can roast on the inside and crisp on the outside at the same time. The heat also circulates inside the appliance, blown by a fan, and continuously heats inside and outside the fryer to cook food evenly.

Nutritional Benefits Of Air Fryer Recipes

A lot of people are not aware of the several benefits Air-fryer offers. There are several meals out there, but Air-fried meals have become popular over the years for the numerous services. One of the most popular questions on Google is "How do I know if cooking with an Air fryer is healthy?" Since so many people are curious about the many benefits of air fryer, I have decided to include Air Fryer Recipes' services. What exactly is Air-fryer? An air fryer is a gadget that helps you fry your meals by circulating air around the meal. Many people are used to consuming fried meals. However, you know that a high intake of deep-fried meals may be disastrous to your health. It is funny that your brain keeps clamouring for these 'dangerous' meals. Aside from the fact that you may suffer the risk of obesity, there are other disadvantages of deep-fried meals which no one would ever tell you. To help you enjoy your favourite fried meals without the fear of becoming obese or people with diabetes, air-fryer has been designed to help you get the same taste and flavour.

Benefits of Air-Fried Meals

- Air-Fryers Help You Reduce Fat Content: One reason Air fryers are better than deep-fryers is that it helps cut down the fat content. How is this possible? When deep-frying your meals, the fat content in your food is very high because it requires the process of immersing your entire food in oil. However, air fryers allow you to fry your food with little oil (or a tablespoon of oil). This helps you reduce the fat content in your meal.
- Helps you lose weight: One other reason you need to consider going for air-fried meals is that air-fryers are good for weight loss. Aside from lowering the fat content in your feed, air fryers also help you reduce your calorie intake. What do I mean by this? Do not assume that an air fryer is a machine that helps reduce calorie intake automatically. The point here is that air fryers require very little oil, which makes your food crispy and crunchy. Thereby reducing your calorie intake.
- Air fryer reduces your consumption of harmful compounds: Deep fried foods contain a chemical called acrylamide content. This chemical is hardly ever present in Air-fried meals. However, you

must know that some people are very skeptical about the healthiness of air-fried meals. Some of them fear the risk of cancer. While there are no proofs about these, you should always remember that Air-fried meals are much better than deep-fryers and healthier. If you desire to eat healthy meals, join the number of people who have made Air-fried meals their lifestyle.

- Eating Air-fried foods can help you reduce disease risk: Not everyone is aware that too much oil damages the body system. People who consume excess fat are prone to several diseases. This is precisely what deep-fried food does to you. To avoid this risk, you are advised to make air-fried meals a lifestyle.

CHAPTER 6:

Practical Tips for Veganism

Going vegan might seem expensive, impossible, or less practical. Well, it is not. The minute you put your mind to and make small, subtle changes to your diet and way of thinking, a lot can change over a few days to a month.
Starting the journey also does not mean that you need to jump into it and never look back; the idea is to gradually begin until it becomes the only way of eating, which will happen.

Tips and Tricks to Try

- Meat-free Monday: Choose to leave out all animal products from your diet on a Monday.
- Knit-one, slip one: Like a meat-free Monday, every alternate day, you leave out animal products from your diet or leave out animal products from your diet for every alternate meal time.
- Read up on veganism: Do your research, read-up online, and visit your library. Purchase a few vegan recipe books to help you realize that there is more to veganism than munching on a salad, day in and day out.
- Read the packaging: Always remember to read the back of the packaging if you are unsure about anything regarding the making of the item.
- Visit your whole-foods aisle: Never be afraid of the unknown; not sure what a product is, pick up the packaging and read up on preparing it.
- Begin by swapping out your milk: That is right; make a simple move by swapping your regular dairy milk for an alternative like almond or coconut milk.
- Saying good-bye: Do not toss all your animal products out in one go; instead, throw away the ones that you won't miss as much before going full tilt.
- Stay positive: We are all bound to fail in some instances, and that is ok!

There are Air fryer Vegan recipes that have helped to contribute to the popularity of this machine. Dehydrating fruits and vegetables can yield some of the tastiest treats that will make you forget about the conventional deep fryer.
Moreover, you can even start making your homemade snacks from home that are packed with rich nutrients.
Nothing's more exciting than finding a small piece of 'gold' in the form of an Air Fryer Vegan recipe that can save you from a critical situation.
A great dish like Greek Potato Mix, Zucchini, Squash Salad, Blooming Potato, Potato, and Broccoli with Tofu Scramble, Air Fryer, and Lemon Cream Bars can be enough to make your mouth water for days.
You can still enjoy all those savoury snacks and delicacies on the go when you are on the move.
You can even whip up a healthy snack for your little ones.
It uses less oil and even stops the oil from reaching the food while cooking.
The machine combines the microwaves with a convection process to make the food juicy with a crispy outer layer.
Air Fryer Vegan recipes are gaining popularity day by day.

Say No, Too

A vegan diet means that the items you consume contain no animal products; that means that an individual should say no to the following:

- Animal-based products such as whey, gelatin, shellac, casein, and omega-3 fatty acids sourced from fish
- Eggs from any animal
- All dairy products such as milk, cream, yogurt, butter, cheese, and ice-cream
- All seafood
- Bee product such as honey, royal jelly, and beeswax
- Meat
- Poultry

Supplements to Consider

Supplements and added vitamins are worth considering if you are a vegetarian or vegan. Always consult with a doctor before you undertake to administer any of the below-mentioned vitamins.

Getting enough fortified foods into your diet can be difficult, and by taking these, you guarantee that your body is getting all that it needs to function at capacity and its best.

- Zinc
- Calcium
- Vitamin B12
- Vitamin D
- Iodine
- Iron

Make sure that each meal is varied and contains a mixture of fresh fruits, vegetables, seeds, nuts, and legumes.

CHAPTER 7:

Benefits And Nutritional Tables Of Correspondence Of Vegan And No GMO Controlled Filira Foods.

What Is Nutritious Vegan Food?

Foods to Eat on the Vegan Diet

This list includes plant and plant-based products such as:

Types of Food	Nutrition
Fruits and vegetables	Vitamins and minerals. Such as magnesium, vitamins A (beta-carotene), C and E, phosphorous, zinc, and folic acid.
Whole grains, cereals, and pseudo-cereals such as spelt, quinoa, and teff	These are high-protein options that are also excellent sources of complex carbs, B vitamins, and several minerals such as zinc, iron, potassium, to name a few, and fibre.
Fermented and sprouted plant foods	This includes pickles, kimchi, Ezekiel bread, miso, natto, and tempeh.
Nutritional yeast	This is an excellent protein supplement you can include in dishes as a substitute for cheese, given its cheesy flavour.
Seeds such as chia seeds, flax seeds, and hemp seeds	Which are good sources of protein and omega-3 fatty acids
Nuts and nut butter	Great sources of fibre, magnesium, zinc, selenium, vitamin E, and iron. The unroasted and unblanched varieties are best
Legumes such as lentils, beans, and peas	Great protein sources and increase nutrient absorption
Plant-based protein replacements	This includes tofu, tempeh, and seitan. They make great replacements for meat, fish, poultry, and eggs in recipes
Calcium-fortified plant milk and yogurts	These are an excellent replacement for milk and yogurt and help provide the recommended daily supplement of calcium. Try to get versions that have been fortified with vitamin B12 and D when possible

Some vegans find it difficult to ensure that they get adequate supplies of all nutrients required daily. Therefore, supplements can be taken to fortify the vegan diet. Accessories include EPA and DHA, which are omega-3 fatty acids that can be sourced from algae oil, Iron, vitamin D, vitamin B12, calcium, zinc, and iodine-supplemented by adding 1/2 teaspoon of iodized salt to your diet.

Eating Out on a Vegan Diet

Eating out on any diet can be challenging, and the same can be said for eating out as a vegan. The way to make this as stress-free as possible for you is to plan. To make this process easier for you, here are a few tips that you can employ while eating out:

- Try to find the restaurant menu online beforehand to determine if there are any vegan options available.
- You may try calling ahead to arrange a special vegan dish with the chef.
- At the restaurants, you can simply ask the staff about any vegan options available before you get seated so that you can know if this restaurant is the right choice for you.
- Try ethnic restaurants such as Mexican, Thai, Indian, Middle-Eastern, and Ethiopian cuisine because they tend to have several natural vegan-friendly options.
- At a restaurant, try to identify the vegetarian options on the menu and ask if any dairy or egg products can be removed to make the vegan-friendly dish.
- If there are no vegan meal options, order vegan side dishes or several vegan appetizers to make up a meal.
- Also, check out the new vegetarian and vegan restaurants within your neighbourhood. With the widespread awareness of leading a plant-based lifestyle gaining traction each day, there are always more recent pure vegan and vegetarian restaurants also popping up everywhere you go!

Foods to Avoid on the Vegan Diet

On a vegan diet, you should avoid consuming any animal foods or foods containing ingredients derived from animals. The list of foods to avoid on a vegan diet include:

- Poultry and meat. This includes organic meat, chicken, duck, quail, beef, lamb, pork, turkey, veal, wild meat, etc.
- Eggs. This can be from any animals, including chickens, fish, ostriches, etc.
- Fish and Seafood. This includes all types of fish and seafood, including shrimp, squid, crab, lobster, mussels, anchovies, scallops, etc.
- Dairy products. This includes cheese, butter, cream, yogurt, milk, etc.
- Bee products. This includes honey, royal jelly, bee pollen, etc.
- Animal-based products. This list includes fish-derived omega-3 fatty acids, animal-derived vitamin D3, whey, lactose, egg white albumen, gelatin, shellac L-cysteine, casein, etc.

This list is pretty extensive, but some surprising foods you may not realize are not vegan friendly. This list includes:

- Milk chocolate. Cocoa itself is vegan, but milk, milk products, whey, and casein are often added to chocolate.
- Wine and beer. A gelatin-based substance derived from fish is often used as a clarifying agent in the manufacture of wine and beer.
- Sugar. Table sugar, which is made from sugar beets or sugarcane, is both wonderful to use. However, some sugars are processed with bone char, used in the refining process to help whiten sugar. Bone char is not vegan-friendly.
- Sugary snacks. Some of your favourite candies like gummies and marshmallows contain gelatin, derived from animals, and hence not vegan-friendly.
- Red, processed foods. Some foods such as yogurt, fruit juices, soda, and candy contain an ingredient called carmine (otherwise known as a red dye) derived from an insect.
- Non-dairy creamers. Some of these contain a milk-based derivative called sodium caseinate.

- Worcestershire sauce. Traditional recipes for this include anchovies. Note that there are vegan-friendly options available.
- Bread. Many common bread options include egg, butter, milk and other animal byproducts in the ingredient list. Luckily, there are bread recipes available which do not contain such ingredients.
- Omega-3 fortified products. Ensure that the packaging for your omega-3 fortified purchases do not contain fish-based ingredients like sardines, anchovies, and tilapia.

CHAPTER 8:

Vegetable

1. Greek Potato Mix

Preparation time: 10 minutes
Cooking time: 20 minutes
Servings: 4
Ingredients:
1½ pounds potatoes, peeled and cubed
Two tbsp. olive oil
Salt and black pepper to taste
One tbsp. hot paprika
2 ounces coconut cream
Directions:
Put potatoes in a bowl and add water to cover.
Leave them aside for 10 minutes.
Drain them and mix with half of the oil, salt, pepper and paprika and toss them.
Put potatoes in your air fryer's basket.
Cook at the set temperature 360 degrees F for 20 minutes.
In a bowl, mix coconut cream with salt, pepper and the rest of the oil and stir well.
Divide potatoes between plates.
Add coconut cream on top. Serve and enjoy!
Nutrition:
Energy (calories): 203 kcal
Protein: 4 g
Fat: 7.17 g
Carbohydrates: 32.22 g

2. Tasty Mushroom Cakes

Preparation time: 10 minutes
Cooking time: 2 Hours 8 Minutes
Servings: 8
Ingredients
Ounces mushrooms, chopped
One small yellow onion, chopped
Salt and black pepper to the taste
¼ tsp. nutmeg, ground
Two tbsp. olive oil
One tbsp. breadcrumbs
14 ounces of coconut milk
Direction
Over medium-high heat, cook and heat half of the oil in a pan...
Add onion and mushrooms.
Stir and cook for 3 minutes.
Add the coconut milk, salt, nutmeg and pepper, and stir.
Take off heat and leave aside for 2 hours.
Mix the rest of the oil in a bowl, with breadcrumbs and stir well.
Take one tbsp. mushroom filling, roll in breadcrumbs and put them in your air fryer basket.
Repeat with the rest of the mushroom mix and cook cakes at 400 degrees F for 8 minutes.
Divide mushroom cakes between plates. Serve and enjoy!
Nutrition:
Energy (calories): 46 kcal
Protein: 0.64 g
Fat: 3.53 g
Carbohydrates: 3.3 g

3. Green Salad

Preparation time: 10 minutes
Cooking time: 10 minutes
Servings: 4
Ingredients
One tbsp. lemon juice
Four red bell peppers
One lettuce head, cut into strips
Salt and black pepper to taste
Three tbsp. coconut cream
Two tbsp. olive oil
1 ounces rocket leaves
Direction
Place bell pepper in your air fryer's basket.
Cook at the temperature of 400 degrees F for 10 minutes.
Transfer to a bowl and leave them aside to cool down.
Peel, cut them into strips and put them in a bowl.
Add rocket leaves and lettuce strips and toss.
In a bowl, mix oil with lemon juice, coconut cream, salt and pepper and whisk well.
Add over the salad, toss to coat divide between plates. Serve and enjoy!
Nutrition: Energy (calories): 130 kcal
Protein: 2.71 g Fat: 11.07 g
Carbohydrates: 7.54 g

4. Tomatoes Salad

Preparation time: 10 minutes
Cooking time: 20 minutes
Servings: 2
Ingredients
Two tomatoes halved
Cooking spray
Salt and black pepper to taste
One tsp. parsley, chopped
One tsp. basil, chopped
One tsp. oregano, chopped
One tsp. rosemary, chopped
One cucumber, chopped
One green onion, chopped
Direction
Spray tomato halves with cooking oil.
Season with salt and pepper. Place them in your air fryer's basket.
Cook for 20 minutes at 320 degrees F.
Transfer tomatoes to a bowl.
Add parsley, basil, oregano, rosemary, cucumber and onion,
Toss, serve and enjoy!
Nutrition:
Energy (calories): 55 kcal
Protein: 2.59 g
Fat: 0.67 g
Carbohydrates: 11.62 g

5. Savoury French Mushroom Mix

Preparation time: 10 minutes
Cooking time: 25 minutes
Servings: 4
Ingredients
2 pounds mushrooms, halved
Two tsp. herbs de Provence
½ tsp. garlic powder
One tbsp. olive oil
Direction
Over a medium heat, heat a pan with the oil.
Add herbs and heat them for 2 minutes.
Add mushrooms and garlic powder and stir.
Introduce pan in your air fryer's basket and cook at 360 degrees F for 25 minutes.
Divide between plates. Serve and enjoy!
Nutrition:
Energy (calories): 81 kcal Protein: 7.07 g
Fat: 4.15 g Carbohydrates: 7.69 g

6. Zucchini and Squash Salad

Preparation time: 10 minutes
Cooking time: 25 minutes
Servings: 4
Ingredients
Six tsp. olive oil

1 pound zucchinis, cut into half-moons

½ pound carrots, cubed

One yellow squash, cut into chunks

Salt and white pepper to taste

One tbsp. tarragon, chopped

Two tbsp. tomato paste

Direction

In your air fryer pan, mix oil with zucchinis, carrots, squash, salt, pepper, tarragon and tomato paste.

Cover and then cook at 400 degrees F for 25 minutes.

Divide between plates. Serve and enjoy!

Nutrition:

Energy (calories): 116 kcal

Protein: 4.18 g

Fat: 7.4 g

Carbohydrates: 10.99 g

7. Tasty Squash Stew

Preparation time: 10 minutes

Cooking time: 30 minutes

Servings: 8

Ingredients

Two carrots, chopped

One yellow onion, chopped

Two celery stalks, chopped

Two green apples, cored, peeled and chopped

Four garlic cloves, minced

2 cups butternut squash, peeled and cubed

6 ounces canned chickpeas, drained

6 ounces canned black beans, drained

7 ounces canned coconut milk

Two tsp. chilli powder

One tsp. oregano, dried

One tbsp. cumin, ground

2 cups veggie stock

Two tbsp. tomato paste

Salt and black pepper to taste

One tbsp. cilantro, chopped

Direction

In your air fryer, mix carrots with onion, celery, apples, garlic, squash, chickpeas, black beans, coconut milk, chilli powder, oregano, cumin, stock, tomato paste, salt and pepper.

Stir, cover and cook at 370 degrees F for 30 minutes

Add cilantro and stir.

Divide into bowls and serve hot.

Nutrition:

Energy (calories): 112 kcal

Protein: 3.28 g

Fat: 2.37 g

Carbohydrates: 21.99 g

8. Chinese Green Beans Mix

Preparation time: 10 minutes

Cooking time: 30 minutes

Servings: 6

Ingredients

1 pound green beans, halved

1 cup maple syrup

1 cup tomato sauce

Four tbsp. stevia

¼ cup tomato paste

¼ cup mustard

¼ cup olive oil

¼ cup apple cider vinegar

Two tbsp. coconut aminos

Direction

In your air fryer, mix beans with maple syrup, tomato paste, stevia, tomato paste, mustard, oil, vinegar and amino.

Stir, cover and cook at 365 degrees F for 35 minutes.

Divide into bowls and serve hot.

Nutrition:

Energy (calories): 301 kcal

Protein: 2.92 g Fat: 9.94 g

Carbohydrates: 51.5 g

9. Black Beans Mix

Preparation time: 10 minutes

Cooking time: 25 minutes

Servings: 6

Ingredients

One yellow onion, chopped

One tbsp. olive oil

One red bell pepper, chopped

One jalapeno, chopped

Two garlic cloves, minced

One tsp. ginger, grated

½ tsp. cumin

½ tsp. allspice, ground

½ tsp. oregano, dried
30 ounces canned black beans, drained
½ tsp. stevia
1 cup of water
A pinch of salt and black pepper
3 cups brown rice, cooked
Two mangoes, peeled and chopped
Direction
In your air fryer's pan, combine onion with the oil, bell pepper, jalapeno, garlic, ginger, cumin, allspice, oregano, black beans, stevia, water, salt and pepper.
Stir, cover and cook at 370 degrees F for 25 minutes.
Add rice and mangoes
Toss and divide between plates. Serve and enjoy!
Nutrition:
Energy (calories): 79 kcal
Protein: 2.14 g Fat: 4.58 g
Carbohydrates: 9.28 g

10.   Okra and Eggplant Stew

Preparation time: 10 minutes
Cooking time: 25 minutes
Servings: 10
Ingredients
2 cups eggplant, cubed
One butternut squash, peeled and cubed
2 cups zucchini, cubed
10 ounces tomato sauce
One carrot, sliced
One yellow onion, chopped
½ cup veggie stock
10 ounces okra
1/3 cup raisins
Two garlic cloves, minced
½ tsp. turmeric powder
½ tsp. cumin, ground
½ tsp. red pepper flakes, crushed
¼ tsp. sweet paprika
¼ tsp. cinnamon powder
Direction
In your air fryer, mix eggplant with squash, zucchini, tomato sauce, carrot, onion, okra, garlic, stock, raisins, turmeric, cumin, pepper flakes, paprika and cinnamon

Stir, cover and cook at 360 degrees for 5 minutes.
Divide into bowls. Serve and enjoy!
Nutrition:
Energy (calories): 39 kcal
Protein: 1.4 g
Fat: 1.17 g
Carbohydrates: 7 g

11.   Savory White Beans Stew

Preparation time: 10 minutes
Cooking time: 20 minutes
Servings: 10
Ingredients
2 pounds white beans, cooked
Three celery stalks, chopped
Two carrots, chopped
One bay leaf
One yellow onion, chopped
Three garlic cloves, minced
One tsp. rosemary, dried
One tsp. oregano, dried
One tsp. thyme, dried
A drizzle of olive oil
Salt and black pepper to the taste
28 ounces canned tomatoes, chopped
6 cups chard, chopped
Direction
In your air fryer's pan, mix white beans with celery, carrots, bay leaf, onion, garlic, rosemary, oregano, thyme, oil, salt, pepper, tomatoes and chard.
Toss, cover and cook at 365 degrees F for 20 minutes.
Divide into bowls and serve.
Nutrition:
Energy (calories): 58 kcal
Protein: 2.43 g Fat: 1.66 g
Carbohydrates: 10.31 g

12.   Spinach and Lentils Mix

Preparation time: 10 minutes
Cooking time: 15 minutes
Servings: 8
Ingredients
10 ounces spinach
2 cups canned lentils, drained

One tbsp. garlic, minced

15 ounces canned tomatoes, chopped

2 cups cauliflower florets

One tsp. ginger, grated

One yellow onion, chopped

Two tbsp. curry paste

½ tsp. cumin, ground

½ tsp. coriander, ground

Two tsp. stevia

A pinch of salt and black pepper

¼ cup cilantro, chopped

One tbsp. lime juice

Direction

In a pan that suites your air fryer, mix spinach with lentils, garlic, tomatoes, cauliflower, ginger, onion, curry paste, cumin, coriander, stevia, salt, pepper and lime juice.

Stir, introduce in the air fryer and cook at 370 degrees F for 15 minutes.

Add cilantro and stir.

Divide into bowls. Serve and enjoy!

Nutrition:

Energy (calories): 68 kcal

Protein: 4.23 g Fat: 1.9 g

Carbohydrates: 11.62 g

13.   Cajun Mushrooms and Beans

Preparation time: 10 minutes

Cooking time: 15 minutes

Servings: 4

Ingredients

Two tbsp. olive oil

One green bell pepper, chopped

One yellow onion, chopped

Two celery stalks, chopped

Three garlic cloves, minced

15 ounces canned tomatoes, chopped

8 ounces white mushrooms, sliced

15 ounces canned kidney beans, drained

One zucchini, chopped

One tbsp. Cajun seasoning

Salt and black pepper to the taste

Direction

In your air fryer's pan, mix oil with bell pepper, onion, celery, garlic, tomatoes, mushrooms, beans, zucchini, Cajun seasoning, salt and pepper.

Stir, cover and cook on at 370 degrees F for 15 minutes.

Divide the veggie mix between plates. Serve and enjoy!

Nutrition:

Energy (calories): 192 kcal

Protein: 5.01 g

Fat: 13.12 g

Carbohydrates: 15.83 g

14.   Corn and Cabbage Salad

Preparation time: 10 minutes

Cooking time: 15 minutes

Servings: 4

Ingredients

One small yellow onion, chopped

One tbsp. olive oil

Two garlic cloves, minced

One and ½ cups mushrooms, sliced

Three tsp. ginger, grated

A pinch of salt and black pepper

2 cups corn

4 cups red cabbage, chopped

One tbsp. nutritional yeast

Two tsp. tomato paste

One tsp. coconut aminos

One tsp. sriracha sauce

Directions

In your air fryer's pan, mix the oil with onion, garlic, mushrooms, ginger, salt, pepper, corn, cabbage, yeast and tomato paste.

Stir, cover and cook at 365 degrees F for 15 minutes.

Add sriracha sauce and amino, stir, divide between plates. Serve and enjoy!

Nutrition:

Energy (calories): 387 kcal

Protein: 10.9 g Fat: 7.57 g

Carbohydrates: 73.28 g

15.   Wintergreen Beans

Preparation time: 10 minutes

Cooking time: 16 minutes

Servings: 4

Ingredients

One small yellow onion, chopped

One tbsp. olive oil

Two garlic cloves, minced

One and ½ cups mushrooms, sliced

Three tsp. ginger, grated

A pinch of salt and black pepper

2 cups corn

4 cups red cabbage, chopped

One tbsp. nutritional yeast

Two tsp. tomato paste

One tsp. coconut aminos

One tsp. sriracha sauce

1½ cups yellow onion, chopped

1 pound green beans, halved

4 ounces canned tomatoes, chopped

Four garlic cloves, chopped

Two tsp. oregano, dried

One jalapeno, chopped

Salt and black pepper to taste

1½ tsp. cumin, ground

One tbsp. olive oil

Direction

Preheat your air fryer at 365 degrees F temperature.

Add oil to the pan; also add onion, green beans, tomatoes, garlic, oregano, jalapeno, salt, pepper and cumin.

Cover and cook for 16 minutes.

Divide between plates. Serve and enjoy!

Nutrition:

Energy (calories): 503 kcal

Protein: 13.31 g

Fat: 15.3 g

Carbohydrates: 84.48 g

16. Green Beans Casserole

Preparation time: 10 minutes

Cooking time: 20 minutes

Servings: 4

Ingredients

One tsp. olive oil

Two red chillies, dried

¼ tsp. fenugreek seeds

½ tsp. black mustard seeds

Ten curry leaves, chopped

½ cup red onion, chopped

Three garlic cloves, minced

Two tsp. coriander powder

Two tomatoes, chopped

2 cups eggplant, chopped

½ tsp. turmeric powder

½ cup green bell pepper, chopped

A pinch of salt and black pepper

1 cup green beans, trimmed and halved

Two tsp. tamarind paste

One tbsp. cilantro, chopped

Direction

Prepare baking dish that fits your air fryer combines the oil with chillies, fenugreek seeds, black mustard seeds, curry leaves, onion, coriander, tomatoes, eggplant, turmeric, green bell pepper, salt, pepper, green beans, tamarind paste and cilantro.

Toss and put in your air fryer.

Cook at 365 degrees F temperature for 20 minutes.

Divide between plates. Serve and enjoy!

Nutrition:

Energy (calories): 57 kcal

Fat: 1.7 g

Carbohydrates: 10.21 g

17. Savoury Chinese Cauliflower Rice

Preparation time: 10 minutes

Cooking time: 20 minutes

Servings: 4

Ingredients

Four tbsp. coconut aminos

½ block firm tofu, cubed

1 cup carrot, chopped

½ cup yellow onion, chopped

One tsp. turmeric powder

3 cups cauliflower, riced

1½ tsp. sesame oil

One tbsp. rice vinegar

½ cup broccoli florets, chopped

One tbsp. ginger, minced

Two garlic cloves, minced

½ cup peas

Direction

In a bowl, mix tofu with two tbsp. coconut aminos, ½ cup onion, turmeric and carrot.

Toss to coat and then transfer into your air fryer.

Cook at 370 degrees F for 10 minutes, shaking halfway.

In a bowl, mix cauliflower rice with the rest of the coconut aminos, sesame oil, garlic, vinegar, ginger, broccoli and peas.

Stir and add to the tofu mix from the fryer.

Toss and cook everything at 370 degrees F for 10 minutes.

Divide between plates. Serve and enjoy!

Nutrition:

Energy (calories): 111 kcal

Protein: 6.56 g Fat: 5.44 g

Carbohydrates: 11.34 g

18.   Tasty Artichokes Dish

Preparation time: 5 minutes

Cooking time: 12 minutes

Servings: 4

Ingredients

Four big artichokes

Salt and black pepper to taste

Two tbsp. lemon juice

¼ cup olive oil

Two tsp. balsamic vinegar

One tsp. oregano, dried

Two garlic cloves, minced

Direction

Season artichokes with salt and pepper.

Now rub them with half of the oil and half of the lemon juice.

Next, put them in your air fryer and cook at 360 degrees F for 7 minutes.

In a bowl, mix these ingredients the remaining oil, the lemon juice, with vinegar, salt, pepper, garlic and oregano and stir very well.

Divide artichokes between plates.

Drizzle the vinaigrette all over and serve them as a side dish.

Nutrition:

Energy (calories): 207 kcal

Protein: 5.68 g Fat: 13.8 g

Carbohydrates: 19.74 g

19.   Beet Salad

Preparation time: 10 minutes

Cooking time: 14 minutes

Servings: 4

Ingredients

Four beets, trimmed

Two tbsp. balsamic vinegar

A bunch of parsley, chopped

Salt and black pepper to the taste

One tbsp. extra-virgin olive oil

One garlic clove, chopped

Two tbsp. capers

Direction

Put beets in your air fryer's basket and cook them at 360 degrees F for 14 minutes.

In a bowl, mix parsley with garlic, salt, pepper, olive oil and capers and stir very well.

Leave beets to cool down.

Now peel them, slice and put them in a bowl.

Next, add vinegar and the parsley mix.

Toss, divide between plates and serve as a side dish.

Nutrition:

Energy (calories): 33 kcal

Protein: 0.87 g

Fat: 1.68 g

Carbohydrates: 3.83 g

20.   Creamy Brussels Sprouts

Preparation time: 3 minutes

Cooking time: 11 minutes

Servings: 4

Ingredients

1 pound Brussels sprouts, trimmed

Salt and black pepper to taste

One tbsp. mustard

Two tbsp. coconut cream

Two tbsp. dill, chopped

Direction

Put Brussels sprouts in your air fryer's basket.

Cook them at 350 degrees F for 10 minutes.

In a bowl, mix the cream with mustard, dill, salt and pepper and whisk.

Add Brussels sprouts and toss.

Divide between plates and best to serve as a side dish.

Nutrition:

Protein: 4.48 g

Fat: 3.09 g

Carbohydrates: 11.94 g

21. Yellow Lentil Mix

Preparation time: 10 minutes
Cooking time: 15 minutes
Servings: 2
Ingredients
1 cup yellow lentils, soaked in water for 1 hour and drained
One hot chilli pepper, chopped
The 1-inch ginger piece, grated
½ tsp. turmeric powder
One tsp. garam masala
Salt and black pepper to taste
Two tsp. olive oil
½ cup cilantro, chopped
1½ cup spinach, chopped
Four garlic cloves, minced
¾ cup red onion, chopped
Direction
In a pan that suites your air fryer, mix lentils with chilli pepper, ginger, turmeric, garam masala, salt, pepper, olive oil, cilantro, spinach, onion and garlic.
Toss, introduce in your air fryer.
Cook at 400 degrees F temperature for 15 minutes.
Divide lentil mix between plates. Serve and enjoy!
Nutrition:
Energy (calories): 115 kcal
Protein: 5.56 g
Fat: 5.01 g
Carbohydrates: 15.78 g

22. Veggie Lasagna

Preparation time: 10 minutes
Cooking time: 20 minutes
Servings: 4
Ingredients:
300 g / 0.66 lbs. zucchini
One carrot
200 g / 0.44 lbs. tomatoes
200 g / 0.44 lbs. tofu
100 g / 0.4 cup water
Four tsp. soy milk
One tsp. black pepper
One tsp. chilli pepper
One tsp. cilantro

One tsp. oregano
One yellow onion
Directions
This veggie lasagna tastes even better than the lasagna with ground meat. Try it once, and you will want to eat it again and again. Remove the skin from the tomatoes. Take the bowl with hot water and put the tomatoes in it for 1 minute. Then remove the tomatoes from the water and peel them. Slice the tomatoes. Chop the tofu cheese. Peel the carrot and slice it. Peel the onion and chop it very roughly. Slice the zucchini with the help of a hand slicer. Preheat the air fryer to 190 C / 380 F. Take the big vessel and make the lasagna. Put the sliced zucchini in the bottom of the vessel, and then add little-chopped tofu. Then put the layer of tomatoes. Then add chopped onion. Then cover the mixture with the tofu again. Sprinkle the lasagna with oregano, cilantro, chilli and black peppers. Transfer it to the air fryer and close the lid. Cook it for 15 minutes. Serve it immediately.
Nutrition:
Caloric content 79 kcal
Proteins 6.2 grams
Fats 2.5 grams
Carbohydrates 10.4 grams

23. Onion Pie

Preparation time: 10 minutes
Cooking time: 35 minutes
Servings: 4
Ingredients:
150 g / 0.33 lbs. flour
50 g / 0.2 cup almond milk
One tsp. salt
50 g / 0.2 cup water
300 g / 0.66 lbs. onion
One tsp. olive oil
100 g / 0.22 lbs. tofu
50 g / 0.2 cup soy milk
Four tomatoes
Directions
Peel the onion and then chop it into tiny bits. Transfer the chopped onion to the big mixing bowl and sprinkle it with salt. Then chop the tofu cheese and add it to the mixing bowl too.

Stir it gently till you get a homogenous mass. Take small tomatoes for this dish and cut them into two parts. Then leave the mixture with chopped onion and take another bowl and sift the flour in it. Add soy milk and almond milk. Take the hand mixer and mix the mass very carefully. Preheat the air fryer and set at 200 C / 390 F temperature. Meanwhile, take the pie tray and spray it with olive oil. Knead the dough very carefully. Then put it on the tray and make it flat. Transfer the onion mixture to the dough and add tomato halves. Take another vessel and pour water into it. Transfer the vessel with water to the air fryer and put the tray with pie in it. Close the lid and decrease the temperature to 180 C / 360 F and cook the pie for 20 minutes. Then open the lid and leave it for 10 minutes more. Enjoy!

Nutrition:

Caloric content 252 kcal

Proteins 8.5 grams

Fats 6.1 grams

Carbohydrates 42.3 grams

24.   Veggie Pizza

Preparation time: 10 minutes

Cooking time: 20 minutes

Servings: 4

Ingredients:

100 g / 0.4 cup water

One tsp. dried yeast

One tsp. sugar

Three tomatoes

100 g / 0.22 lbs. black olives

One yellow zucchini

200 g / 0.44 lbs. tofu

100 g / 0.22 lbs. spinach

Two tsp. dill

Two tsp. parsley

One tsp. tomato paste

One sweet red pepper

One onion

200 g / 0.44 lbs. flour

Directions

Firstly make dough for pizza: take the big bowl and combine warm water with dried yeast. Stir it carefully till the yeast is dissolved. Then sprinkle the mass with sugar and stir it again. Sift the flour and add half of it to the mixture and stir it gently. Cover the mass with a towel and leave it in a warm place. Meanwhile, slice black olives and chop the tofu cheese. Slice the tomatoes and chop the red sweet pepper. Then peel the onion and chop it into small pieces. Chop the parsley and dill and combine them in the mixing bowl. Slice the zucchini. Preheat the air fryer and set to 200 C / 390 F. Meanwhile, remove the towel from the dough and stir it again gently. Add the other half of the dough and knead it. Then make the flat circle and transfer it to the tray. Put the tofu cheese in the bottom of the dough. Add sliced zucchini and onion. Then put red sweet pepper and tomatoes. Sprinkle the pizza with a mix of chopped parsley and dill. Transfer the pizza to the air fryer and cook it for 18 minutes. Remove the cooked pizza from the air fryer and serve it immediately. Enjoy!

Nutrition:

Caloric content 305 kcal

Proteins 12.7 grams

Fats 5.8 grams

Carbohydrates 53.0 grams

25.   Festive Vegetable Stew

Preparation time: 10 minutes

Cooking time: 30 minutes

Servings: 4

Ingredients:

300 g / 0.66 lbs. tomatoes

200 g / 0.44 lbs. zucchini

One onion

Two sweet green peppers

One sweet yellow pepper

100 g / 0.22 lbs. tomato paste

100 g / 0.4 cup almond milk

One tsp. cilantro

One tsp. chilli pepper

100 g / 0.22 lbs. leek

100 g / 0.22 lbs. lentils

300 g / 1.2 cup vegetables stock

Directions

Chop the tomatoes into tiny pieces. Then slice the zucchini and cut it into two parts more. Remove the seeds from the sweet pepper and cut it into strips. Then cut each strip into two parts more. Chop the leek. Take the big bowl and combine all ingredients in it. Stir it gently. Then add lentils to it and sprinkle the mass with the cilantro, chilli pepper, and tomato paste. Stir it carefully and leave it. Preheat the air fryer set at 200 C / 390 degrees F. Meanwhile, peel the onion and chop it roughly. Combine vegetable stock with almond milk and stir it. Then pour the liquid into the air fryer and add vegetable mass. Stir it gently with the help of the wooden spoon. Close the lid and cook it for 20 minutes. The lentils should absorb all water. Then remove the stew, chill it little and serve it immediately.

Nutrition:

Caloric content 247 kcal

Proteins 11.2 grams

Fats 7.1 grams

Carbohydrates 38.0 grams

26.   Spinach Dish

Preparation time: 10 minutes

Cooking time: 0 minutes

Servings: 4

Ingredients:

200 g / 0.44 lbs. oatmeal flour

150 g / 0.6 cup water

½ tsp. baking soda

200 g / 0.44 lbs. spinach

100 g / 0.22 lbs. oatmeal

One onion

One tsp. olive oil

One tsp. oregano

One tsp. dill

Directions

Firstly this dish will amaze you with its view, and then you will be surprised by its delicious taste. Take the bowl put oatmeal flour in it together. Add dill and oregano. Stir it. Take the bowl and pour warm water into it. Add baking soda and stir it till baking soda is dissolved. Combine oatmeal flour with liquid and knead the dough. Put it in the fridge. Meanwhile, chop the spinach and combine it with oatmeal. Take the tray and spray it with olive oil. Then take the dough and grate dough on it. Add spinach mass and stir it with the help of hands very gently. Preheat the

air fryer and set at 180 C / 360 degrees F and transfer the tray with the mixture in it. Close the lid and then cook it for 15 minutes. Serve it immediately! Enjoy!

Nutrition:

Caloric content 319 kcal

Proteins 11.7 grams

Fats 6.3 grams

Carbohydrates 55.6 grams

27.   Baked Veggie Salad

Preparation time: 10 minutes

Cooking time: 20 minutes

Servings: 4

Ingredients:

Two red sweet peppers

One sweet green pepper

One red onion

100 g / 0.22 lbs. tofu

Two tsp. lemon juice

50 g / 0.2 cup soy sauce

One red apple

100 g / 0.4 cup water

200 g / 0.44 lbs. tomatoes

50 g / 1.76 oz. chopped chives

50 g / 0.2 cup soy milk

10 g / 0.35 oz. garlic

One tsp. rice flour

50 g / 1.76 oz. quinoa

Directions

Get the seeds from the sweet peppers and chop the pepper. Put it in the big bowl and sprinkle the vegetables with chopped chives and soy sauce. Stir it. Then chop the tomatoes and apples. Peel the onion and chop it too. All the vegetables should be chopped at the same size. Add them to the bowl with pepper mixture and stir it. Add rice flour, quinoa, and garlic. Stir the mass. Chop the tofu roughly and add it to the bowl too. Preheat the air fryer to 200 C / 390 F. Then pour soy milk into it and transfer the vegetable mixture to the air fryer. Cover with the lid and cook it for 10 minutes, not more. Open the lid and remove the salad from it. Sprinkle the salad with lemon juice and serve it immediately. Enjoy!

Tips: do not cook the salad for more than 10 minutes. Otherwise, the vegetables become soft and not delicious.
Nutrition:
Caloric content 159 kcal
Proteins 7.4 grams Fats 2.6 grams
Carbohydrates 28.4 grams

28.   Fragrant Quinoa

Preparation time: 10 minutes
Cooking time: 30 minutes
Servings: 4
Ingredients:
200 g / 0.44 lbs. quinoa
300 g / 1.2 cup vegetable stock
One tsp. chilli pepper
One tsp. rosemary
One tsp. basil
One tsp. turmeric
One tsp. cilantro
100 g / 0.4 cup spinach
10 g / 0.35 oz. fresh mint
200 g / 0.44 lbs. tomatoes
One red sweet pepper
One tsp. black pepper
Directions
Take the small bowl and combine chilli pepper, rosemary, basil, turmeric, cilantro, and spinach. Stir the mixture very carefully. Then remove the seeds from the sweet pepper and chop it. Sprinkle the chopped peppers with the black pepper and stir it gently. Chop the tomatoes and mint. Take the big bowl and transfer all ingredients to sprinkle the mass with the spice mixture then and stir it carefully. Leave it. Meanwhile, preheat the air fryer to 200 C / 390 F. Transfer the mixture to the air fryer and pour it with vegetable stock. Mix it using a wooden spoon. Close the lid and reduce the air fryer's heat to 180 C / 360 F. Cook the quinoa for 15 minutes or till it absorbs all water. Close the lid and remove the dish from the air fryer. Serve it immediately. Tips: you can sprinkle the final dish with the mix of chopped dill and parsley.
Nutrition: Caloric content 219 kcal
Proteins 9.0 grams Fats 3.5 grams
Carbohydrates 38.7 grams

29.   Delicious Festive Broccoli

Preparation time: 10 minutes
Cooking time: 20 minutes
Servings: 4
Ingredients:
400 g / 0.88 lbs. broccoli
100 g / 0.4 cup soy milk
100 g / 0.22 lbs. mushroom
One yellow onion
10 g / 0.35 oz. almond flakes
One tsp. white pepper
100 g / 0.22 lbs. grated tofu
30 g / 1 oz. chopped dill
Directions
Take only fresh broccoli for this dish. Make the florets from the broccoli and sprinkle them with white pepper. Then take the big bowl and combine almond flakes and chopped dill in it. Add soy milk and stir the mass very gently. Then chop the tofu cheese and slice the mushrooms. Peel the onion and then chop it into tiny pieces. Combine chopped ingredients and stir it. Preheat the air fryer to 190 C / 380 F and put the broccoli florets in it. Then pour it with liquid mass and add chopped vegetable mass. Stir it with the help of the wooden or plastic spoon and close the lid. Cook it for 15 minutes. Remove the air fryer's dish and serve it immediately: firstly, put the broccoli on the plate, then pour it into a liquid mixture. Enjoy!
Nutrition:
Caloric content 116 kcal
Proteins 8.8 grams
Fats 3.5 grams
Carbohydrates 17.1 grams

30.   Baked Eggplant's Halves

Preparation time: 10 minutes
Cooking time: 30 minutes
Servings: 4
Ingredients:
Four eggplants
Two yellow onions
100 g / 0.4 cup soy milk
One carrot
200 g / 0.44 lbs. tofu
One tsp. olive oil

100 g / 0.22 lbs. soy cheese
One tsp. black pepper
One tsp. basil
One tsp. oregano
50 g / 1.76 oz. parsley
50 g / 0.2 cup water
One tsp. salt
Directions
Wash the eggplants and cut them into two parts. Then rub it with salt and leave it. Meanwhile, peel the yellow onions and chop them. Peel the carrot and grate it. Combine chopped the onion and grated carrot together. Sprinkle it with black pepper, basil, oregano and stir it carefully. Take the eggplants and remove the meat from them. Chop the meat and combine it with carrot and onion. Stir it. Chop the parsley and then put into the mixture too. Stir it again. Grate the tofu cheese. Preheat the air fryer to 190 C / 380 F. Pour the soy milk and water into the air fryer and stir it with the help of a wooden spoon. Fill the eggplants with the vegetable mass and sprinkle each half with grated tofu cheese. Transfer all eggplant's halves to the air fryer and close the lid. Cook it for 20 minutes. Then remove the dish from the air fryer and chill it a little. Enjoy!
Nutrition:
Caloric content 248 kcal
Proteins 12.0 grams
Fats 6.2 grams
Carbohydrates 43.2 grams

31.   Super Vegetable Burger

Preparation time: 10 minutes
Cooking time: 15 minutes
Servings: 4
Ingredients
1/2-pound (227 g) cauliflower, steamed and diced, rinsed and drained
Two tsp. coconut oil, melted
Two tsp. minced garlic
¼ cup desiccated coconut
½ cup oats
Three tbsp. flour
One tbsp. flaxseeds plus three tbsp. water divided

One tsp. thyme
Two tsp. parsley
Two tsp. chives
Salt and ground black pepper, to taste
1 cup bread crumbs
Directions
Preheat and set the temperature at 390 F (199 C)
Combine the cauliflower with all the ingredients, except for the bread crumbs, incorporating everything well
Using the hands, shape eight equal-sized amounts of the mixture into burger patties. Coat the patties in bread crumbs before putting them in the air fryer basket in a single layer
Place the basket of air fryers on the baking pan and move into position 2 of the rack. Select Air fry and set time to 12 minutes, or until crispy
Serve hot
Nutrition:
Energy (calories): 117 kcal
Protein: 4.97 g
Fat: 3.65 g
Carbohydrates: 21.58 g

32.   Sweet Potatoes with Zucchini

Preparation time: 20 minutes
Cooking time: 20 minutes
Servings: 4
Ingredients
Two large-sized sweet potatoes, peeled and quartered
One medium zucchini, sliced
1 Serrano pepper, deseeded and thinly sliced
One bell pepper, deseeded and thinly sliced
1 to 2 carrots cut into matchsticks
¼ cup olive oil
1 ½ tbsp. maple syrup
½ tsp. porcini powder
½ tsp. fennel seeds
One tbsp. garlic powder
½ tsp. fine sea salt
¼ tsp. ground black pepper
Tomato ketchup, for serving
Directions
Preheat the air fryer oven set at 350 F (177 C) degrees.

Put the sweet potatoes, zucchini, peppers, and carrot into the air fryer basket. Coat with a drizzling of olive oil

Place the air fryer basket on the baking pan and move into rack position2, pick the air fryer and set the time for 15 minutes.

In the meantime, prepare the sauce by vigorously combining the other ingredients, except for tomato ketchup, with a whisk

Lightly grease a baking dish

Transfer the cooked vegetable to the baking dish, pour over the sauce and coat the vegetable well

Set the temperature at 390 F (199 C) and air fry the vegetable for an additional 5 minutes

Serve warm with a side of ketchup

Nutrition:

Energy (calories): 247 kcal

Protein: 3.05 g

Fat: 13.84 g

Carbohydrates: 29.74 g

33.   Ratatouille

Preparation time: 20 minutes

Cooking time: 25 minutes

Servings: 4

Ingredients

One sprig basil

One sprig flat-leaf parsley

One sprig mint

One tbsp. coriander powder

One tsp. capers

½ lemon, juiced

Salt and ground black pepper, to taste

Two eggplants sliced crosswise

Two red onions, chopped

Four cloves garlic, minced

Two red peppers sliced crosswise

One fennel bulb cut crosswise

Three large zucchinis sliced crosswise

Five tbsp. olive oil

Four large tomatoes, chopped

Two tsp. herbs de Provence

Directions

Blend the basil, parsley, coriander, mint, lemon juice and capers, with a little salt and pepper. Make sure all ingredients are well incorporated

Preheat and set the temperature at 400 F (204 C)

Coat the eggplant, onion, garlic, pepper, fennel, and zucchini with olive oil.

Transfer the vegetable into the baking dish and top with the tomatoes and herb puree. Sprinkle with more salt and pepper, and the herbs de Provence

Place the baking dish into rack position 1, select convection bake and set time to 26 minutes

Serve immediately

Nutrition:

Energy (calories): 358 kcal

Protein: 6.99 g

Fat: 19.36 g

Carbohydrates: 45.8 g

34.   Potato and Broccoli with Tofu Scramble

Preparation time: 15 minutes

Cooking time: 30 minutes

Servings: 3

Ingredients

2 ½ cups chopped red potato

Two tbsp. olive oil, divided

One block tofu, chopped finely

Two tbsp. tamari

One tsp. turmeric powder

½ tsp. garlic powder

½ cup chopped onion

4 cups broccoli florets

Directions

Preheat and set the temperature at 400 F (204 C)

Toss together the potatoes and one tbsp. of the olive oil, then transfer to a baking dish

Place the baking dish into Rack position 1, select convention Bake and set time to 15 minutes. Stir the potatoes once during cooking

Combine the tofu, the remaining one tbsp. of the olive oil, turmeric, onion powder, tamari, and garlic powder, stirring in the onions, followed by the broccoli

Top the potatoes with the tofu mixture and bake for an additional 15 minutes

Serve warm

Nutrition:

Energy (calories): 220 kcal

Protein: 11.88 g

Fat: 11.41 g

Carbohydrates: 20.77 g

35.   Lush Summer Rolls

Preparation time: 15 minutes

Cooking time: 15 minutes

Servings: 4

Ingredients

1 cup shiitake mushroom, sliced thinly

One celery stalk, chopped

One medium carrot, shredded

½ tsp. finely chopped ginger

One tsp. soy sauce

One tsp. nutritional yeast

Eight spring roll sheets

One tsp. corn water

Two tbsp. water

Directions

Preheat and set the temperature at 400 degrees F (204 C)

In a bowl, combine the ginger, soy sauce, nutritional yeast, carrots, celery, mushroom, and sugar

Mix the cornstarch and water to create an adhesive for the spring rolls

Scoop a tbsp. full of the vegetable mixture into the middle of the spring roll sheets. Brush the edges of the sheets with the cornstarch adhesive and enclose around the filling to make spring rolls. Arrange the rolls in the air fryer basket

Place the air fryer basket on the baking pan and move into position 2 of the rack; choose Air Fry and set the time to 15 minutes or until crisp.

Serve hot

Nutrition:

Energy (calories): 250 kcal

Protein: 8.99 g

Fat: 3.47 g

Carbohydrates: 45.04 g

36.   Super Veg Rolls

Preparation time: 20 minutes

Cooking time: 10 minutes

Servings: 6

Ingredients

Two potatoes, mashed

¼ cup peas

½ cup mashed carrots

One small cabbage, sliced

¼ cups beans

Two tbsp. sweet corn

One small onion, chopped

½ cup bread crumbs

One packet spring roll sheets

½ cup cornstarch slurry

Directions

Preheat and set the temperature at 390 F (199 C)

Boil all the vegetables in water over low heat. Rinse and allow drying

Unroll the spring roll sheets and spoon equal amounts of vegetables onto the center of each one. Fold into spring tools and coat each one with the slurry and bread crumbs. Transfer to the air fryer basket

Place on the baking pan the air fryer basket and slide into rack position2; pick Air Fry and set the time to 10 minutes

Serve warm

Nutrition:

Energy (calories): 202 kcal

Protein: 5.1 g

Fat: 0.69 g

Carbohydrates: 45.4 g

37.   Sweet Potatoes with Tofu

Preparation time: 15 minutes

Cooking time: 35 minutes

Servings: 8

Ingredients

Eight sweet potatoes, scrubbed

Two tbsp. olive oil

One large onion, chopped

Two green chillies, deseeded and chopped

8 ounces (227 g) tofu, crumbled

Two tbsp. Cajun seasoning

1 cup chopped tomatoes

One can of kidney beans, must drained and rinsed

Salt and ground black pepper, to taste

Directions

Preheat and set the temperature at 400 F (204 C)

With a knife, pierce the skin of the sweet potatoes and transfer them to the air fryer basket

Place the air fryer basket onto the baking pan and slide into Rack position 2. Select air fry and set time to 30 minutes, or until soft.

Remove from the oven, halve each potato, and set to one side

Over medium heat, fry the onions and chillies in the olive oil in a skillet for 2 minutes until fragrant

Add the tofu and Cajun seasoning and air fry for a further 3 minutes before incorporating the kidney beans and tomatoes. Sprinkle some salt and pepper as desire

Top each sweet potato halves with a spoonful of the tofu mixture and serve

Nutrition:

Energy (calories): 127 kcal

Protein: 5.45 g

Fat: 9.16 g

Carbohydrates: 7.22 g

38.   Rice and Eggplant Bowl

Preparation time: 15 minutes

Cooking time: 10 minutes

Servings: 4

Ingredients

¼ cup sliced cucumber

One tsp. salt

One tbsp. sugar

Seven tbsp. Japanese rice vinegar

Three medium eggplants, sliced

Three tbsp. sweet white miso paste

One tbsp. mirin rice wine

4 cups cooked sushi rice

Four spring onions

One tbsp. toasted sesame seeds

Directions

Coat the cucumber slices with the rice wine vinegar, salt, and sugar

Put a dish on top of the bowl to weight it down completely

In a bowl, mix the eggplants, mirin rice wine, and miso paste. Allow marinating for half an hour

Preheat and set the temperature at 400 F (204 C)

Slice the eggplant and put in the air fryer basket

Place the air fryer basket onto the baking pan and slide into rack position 2, select air fry and set time to 10 minutes

Fill the bottom of a serving bowl with rice and top with the eggplants and pickled cucumbers

Add the spring onions and sesame seeds for garnish. Serve immediately

Nutrition:

Energy (calories): 516 kcal

Protein: 20.82 g

Fat: 26.82 g

Carbohydrates: 88.75 g

39.   Cauliflower, Chickpea, and Avocado Mash

Preparation time: 10 minutes

Cooking time: 25 minutes

Servings: 4

Ingredients

One medium head cauliflower, cut into florets

One can chickpeas, drained and rinsed

One tbsp. extra-virgin olive oil

Two tbsp. lemon juice

Salt and ground pepper, to taste

Four flatbreads, toasted

Two ripe avocados, mashed

Directions

Preheat and set the temperature at 425 F (218 C)

In a bowl, mix the chickpeas, cauliflower, lemon juice and olive oil. Sprinkle salt and pepper as desired. Transfer to the air fryer basket

Place the air fryer basket onto the baking pan and slide into Rack position 2, select air fry and set time to 25 minutes

Spread on top of the flatbread with the mashed avocado. Sprinkle with more pepper and salt and serve

Nutrition:

Energy (calories): 285 kcal

Protein: 7.96 g

Fat: 18.04 g

Carbohydrates: 28.03 g

40. Mushroom and Pepper Pizza Squares

Preparation time: 10 minutes
Cooking time: 10 minutes
Servings: 10
Ingredients
One pizza dough, cut into squares
1 cup chopped oyster mushrooms
One shallot, chopped
¼ red bell pepper, chopped
Two tbsp. parsley
Salt and ground black pepper to taste
Directions
Preheat and set the temperature at 400 F (204 c)
In a bowl, combine the oyster mushrooms, shallot, bell pepper and parsley. Sprinkle some salt and pepper as desired
Spread the mixture on top of the pizza squares, and then transfer to a baking pan
Slide the baking pan into Rack position 1, select convection bake and set time to 10 minutes
Serve warm.
Nutrition:
Energy (calories): 161 kcal
Protein: 7.8 g
Fat: 5.28 g
Carbohydrates: 20.85 g

41. Balsamic Brussels Sprouts

Preparation time: 5 minutes
Cooking time: 13 minutes
Servings: 2
Ingredients
2 cups Brussels sprouts, halved
One tbsp. olive oil
One tbsp. balsamic vinegar
One tbsp. maple syrup
¼ tsp. of sea salt
Directions
Preheat and set the temperature at 375 F (191 C)
Evenly coat the brussels sprouts with olive oil, balsamic vinegar, maple syrup, and salt. Transfer to the air fryer basket
Place the air fryer basket onto the baking pan and slide into Rack position 2, select air fry and set time to 5 minutes

Give the basket a good shake, increase the temperature to 400 F (204 C) and continue to air fry for another 8 minutes
Serve hot.
Nutrition:
Energy (calories): 131 kcal
Protein: 3.02 g
Fat: 7.02 g
Carbohydrates: 15.94 g

42. Green Beans with Shallot

Preparation time: 10 minutes
Cooking time: 10 minutes
Servings: 4
Ingredients
1 ½ pound (680 g) French green beans, stems removed and blanched
One tbsp. salt
½ pound (227 g) shallots, peeled and cut into quatres
½ tsp. ground white pepper
Two tbsp. olive oil
Directions
Preheat and set the temperature at 400 F (204 C)
Coat the vegetables with the rest of the ingredients in a bowl. Transfer to the air fryer basket
Place the air fryer basket onto baking pan and slide rack position 2, select air fry and set time 10 minutes, making sure the green beans achieve a light brown colour
Serve hot
Nutrition:
Energy (calories): 166 kcal
Protein: 3.91 g
Fat: 7.16 g
Carbohydrates: 22.49 g

43. Black Bean and Tomato Chili

Preparation time: 15 minutes
Cooking time: 23 minutes
Servings: 6
Ingredients
One tbsp. olive oil
One medium onion, diced
Three garlic cloves, minced
1 cup vegetable broth

Three cans of black beans must drained and rinsed

Two cans of diced tomatoes

Two chipotle peppers, chopped

Two tsp. chilli powder

One tsp. dried oregano

½ tsp. salt

Directions

Over medium heat, fry the garlic add onion in the olive oil for 3 minutes

Add the remaining ingredients, stirring constantly and scraping the bottom to prevent sticking

Preheat and set the temperature at 400 F (204 C)

Take a dish and place the mixture inside. On top put a sheet of aluminum foil.

Place the dish into Rack Position 1, select convection bake and set time to 20 minutes

Serve immediately

Nutrition:

Energy (calories): 362 kcal

Protein: 1.27 g

Fat: 38.95 g

Carbohydrates: 6.52 g

44. Herbed Pita Chips

Preparation time: 5 minutes

Cooking time: 6 minutes

Servings: 4

Ingredients

¼ tsp. dried basil

¼ tsp. marjoram

¼ tsp. ground oregano

¼ tsp. garlic powder

¼ tsp. ground thyme

¼ tsp. salt

¼ tsp. salt

Two whole 6-inch pitas, whole grain or white cooking spray

Directions

Preheat and set the temperature at 330 F

Mix all the seasoning

Cut each pita half into four wedges; break apart wedges at the fold

Mist one side of pita wedges with oil. Sprinkle with half of the seasoning mix.

Turn pita wedges over, mist the other side with oil, and sprinkle with remaining seasoning. Place the pita wedges in a baking pan

Slide the baking pan into rack position 1, select convention bake and set time to 4 minutes. Shake the pan in the middle of cooking time

If needed, bake for 1 or 2 more minutes until crisp. Serve hot

Nutrition:

Energy (calories): 485 kcal

Protein: 17.9 g

Fat: 4.74 g

Carbohydrates: 100.36 g

45. Lemony Pear Chips

Preparation time: 15 minutes

Cooking time: 12 minutes

Servings: 4

Ingredients

Two firm bosc pears, cut crosswise into 1/8-inch-thick slices

One tbsp. freshly squeezed lemon juice

½ tsp. ground cinnamon

1/8 tsp. ground cardamom

Directions

Preheat and set the temperature at 380 F

Separate the smaller stem-end pear rounds from the large rounds with seeds. Remove the core and seeds from the large slices. Sprinkle all slices with lemon juice, cinnamon, and cardamom

Put the smaller chips into the air fryer basket

Place the air fryer basket onto the baking pan and slide into rack position 2; select air fryer and set time to 5 minutes, or until light golden brown. Shake the basket once during cooking. Remove from the oven.

Repeat with the larger slices, air frying for 6 to 8 minutes, or until light golden brown, shaking the basket once during cooking

Remove the chips from the oven, cool and serve or store in an airtight container at room temperature up for two days

Nutrition:

Energy (calories): 62 kcal

Protein: 0.36 g

Fat: 0.1 g

Carbohydrates: 14.99 g

46. Artichoke Pesto Pasta With Air-Fried Chickpeas

Preparation time: 10 minutes
Cooking time: 15 minutes
Servings: 4
Ingredients
8 ounces vegan pappardelle or other pasta
One packed cup (1 ounce) fresh basil leaves
Six jarred artichoke hearts drained and squeezed slightly to remove excess liquid
2 Tbsp. shelled pumpkin seeds (pepitas)
Juice of half a lemon (~1 Tbsp.)
One clove garlic
½ tsp. white miso paste
One tsp. extra virgin olive oil (optional)
One batch air-fried or roasted chickpeas
Directions
Cook the pasta according to package directions.
While pasta is cooking, you can combine basil leaves, artichoke hearts, shelled pumpkin seeds, lemon juice, garlic, and white miso paste in a food processor until it is thoroughly combined. Scrape down the sides, as needed, and then continue processing until the pesto is mostly smooth.
If the pasta is already cooked, drain in a colander. Then transfer the noodles to a larger bowl and add extra virgin olive oil to keep them from sticking together (optional). Spoon over the pasta with the artichoke pesto, and toss until evenly mixed.
Serve pasta topped with chickpeas which are air-fried or roasted.
Nutrition:
Energy (calories): 196 kcal
Protein: 7.96 g
Fat: 3.38 g
Carbohydrates: 38.74 g

47. Fishless Tacos With Chipotle Crema

Preparation time: 10 minutes
Cooking time: 20 minutes
Servings: 4
Ingredients
For the tacos:
6 Gardein fishless filets
Six soft corn tortillas
1 ½ cups chopped green leaf lettuce or Romaine
3 Tbsp. chopped onions
Two avocados, pit removed and sliced
Cilantro, chopped (garnish)
One lime, sliced (for serving)
For the chipotle crema:
½ cup + 1 Tbsp. raw cashews
¾ cup of water (plus extra for soaking, if not using a high-speed blender)
Two chipotle peppers in adobo sauce (from 7 oz. can)
One tsp. adobo sauce from a can
One tsp. agave syrup
½ tsp. lemon juice
1/8 tsp. salt
Directions
To make the tacos:
Cook the Gardein fishless filets see directions on the package.
In a prepared skillet, warm the corn tortillas one at a time for about 1 minute on each side on medium heat. If each tortilla has been warmed on both sides, move it to a plate and then cover with a clean dish towel to keep them pliable until serving.
Once the filets are fully cooked, remove them from the oven and slice them into four pieces on a bias. Put a sliced filet in each tortilla and stuff with green leaf lettuce, onions, sliced avocado, and a sprinkling of cilantro. Drizzle each taco with chipotle crema and then serve with lime slices.
To make the chipotle crema:
If you don›t have a high-speed blender, soak the cashews in water for several hours, and then drain. If you will use a high-speed blender, you can skip this step.
Put the cashews, ¾ cup water, chipotle peppers, adobo sauce, agave syrup, and lemon juice in a blender. Blend until smooth. For 24 hours, it'll be the best. (If you are helping the crema right away and don't have time, try reducing the amount of water by a tbsp...)
Nutrition:
Energy (calories): 465 kcal
Protein: 8.64 g Fat: 33.76 g
Carbohydrates: 39.9 g

48. Easy Vegan Falafel

Preparation time: 10 minutes
Cooking time: 15 minutes
Servings: 4
Ingredients
One 15-ounce (425 g) can chickpeas, rinsed, drained and patted dry
1/3 Cup (15 g) of chopped fresh parsley (or sub cilantro)
Four cloves garlic, minced
Two shallots, minced (3/4cup, 65 g | or sub white onion)
2 Tbsp. (17 g) of raw sesame seeds or you can use (sub finely chopped nuts, such as pecans)
1 ½ tsp. cumin, plus more to taste
¼ tsp. sea salt
black pepper
Optional: A Healthy pinch each cardamom and coriander
3-4 Tbsp. (24-31 g) all-purpose flour (or use as sub oat flour or gluten-free blend with varied results)
3-4 tbsp. (45 - 60 ml) of grapeseed oil for cooking (or use any neutral oil with a high smoke point)
Optional: Panko bread crumbs for coating (see pacakge for instructions)
Garlic Dill Sauce for serving
Directions
In a food processor or blender, add the chickpeas, parsley, sesame seeds, shallot, garlic, cumin, salt, pepper (and coriander and cardamom if used) and mix/pulse to combine, scraping down the sides as needed until thoroughly combined.
Add one tbsp. of flour at a time and pulse/mix until the dough is no longer wet, and you can shape the dough into a ball without sticking to your hands - I used 4 Tbsp. Taste the seasonings and change them as needed. I added a little more salt, pepper, and a splash of coriander and cardamom.
To firm up, move to a mixing bowl, cover and refrigerate for 1-2 hours. You can skip this step if you're in a rush, but they'll be a little more delicate when cooking.

Once chilled, scoop out rounded tbsp. amounts (30 g in weight / I used scoop) and gently form into 11-12 small discs.
Optional: Sprinkle with panko bread crumbs and press to stick gently - turn and repeat. This is going to create a crispier crust, but this is optional.
Heat a large skillet over medium heat and add enough oil to coat the pan - about 2 Tbsp. generously. Swirl to coat.
If the oil is hot, add only as many falafels as will fit very comfortably in the pan at a time - about
Cook for 4-5 minutes in all, flipping when deep golden brown is on the underside. The deeper golden brown they are, the crispier they will be, repeat until all falafel is browned. When slightly cooled, they will also firm up further.
Serve warm with garlic-dill sauce or hummus, inside a pita with desired toppings or atop a greens bed.
Best when fresh, while leftovers can be kept covered for several days in the refrigerator. Freeze after that for up to 1 month to remain new.
Nutrition:
Energy (calories): 347 kcal
Protein: 10.54 g
Fat: 18 g
Carbohydrates: 37.48 g

49. Thai-Style Vegan Crab Cakes

Preparation time: 10 minutes
Cooking time: 15 minutes
Servings: 4
Ingredients
600g / 4 cups diced or about four medium potatoes
7-8 individual / 1 bunch green onions
One lime, zest & juice
1½ inch knob of fresh ginger
One tbsp. Tamari, or soy sauce
Four tbsp. Thai Red Curry Paste
Four sheets nori
220g / 1 can heart of palm; the long tubular shaped ones work best
100g / ¾ cup canned artichoke hearts
pepper, to taste

salt, to taste

Two tbsp. oil for pan-frying, optional

Directions

The potatoes are peeled and cubed, then added to a pan. Cover and fork-tender with water and simmer, then rinse, mash and set aside.

When the potatoes are boiling, add a food processor with the green onions, lime juice, lime zest, ginger, tamari and curry paste. Break the nori sheets into manageable pieces and place them with the other ingredients in the food processor. Process until a paste is made. The nori appears to remain a little bit more chunky than everything else, and that's all right.

Drain the hearts of palm, either grate them or shred them with a fork, then drain the artichokes and roughly chop.

When the potatoes are sufficiently cooled to handle, add the pasta and mix well so it is evenly distributed, then add the shredded palm hearts and the chopped artichoke and gently stir through.

Shape them into patties and put them as you go on a tray with some baking parchment. You can either pan-fry them for cooking, bake them in the oven or cook them on a griddle. As they grow a lovely golden crust, they are best pan-fried.

To pan-fry

Warm a couple tbsp. of oil in a pan at set medium-high heat. Once really hot, add the crab cakes carefully. To allow a dense, golden crust to develop, leave them well alone for about 4 minutes, then turn over and do the same on the other side. To absorb excess oil, remove it from the pan and rest it on some kitchen paper. Your pan can not be large enough to cook all of them at once, so have the oven low and pop the cooked ones in there to keep the others warm while you cook.

To griddle

Warm your griddle to medium-high heat. When hot, carefully place the crab cakes on the griddle and cook for 4-5 minutes on each side.

To oven bake

Place on a tray on baking parchment and bake at 400°F for around 25 minutes. Turn over halfway through.

Nutrition:

Energy (calories): 477 kcal

Protein: 11.6 g

Fat: 8.96 g

Carbohydrates: 94.02 g

50. Almond-Crusted Cauliflower Bites with Avocado Ranch Dip

Preparation time: 10 minutes

Cooking time: 15 minutes

Servings: 4

Ingredients

Avocado Ranch Dip

1 cup heaping mashed avocado

Two tbsp. unsweetened non-dairy milk

One tbsp. white vinegar

One tbsp. lemon juice

½ tsp. onion powder

½ tsp. dried parsley

½ tsp. nutritional yeast

¼-½ tsp. sea salt to taste

¼ tsp. garlic powder

¼ tsp. agave nectar

Pinch of dried dill

Almond-crusted Cauliflower Bites

One piece large head cauliflower florets chopped into bite-sized

½ cup unsweetened non-dairy milk

Six tbsp. vegan mayo soy-free

¼ cup chickpea flour

¾ cup almond meal

¼ cup cornmeal

One tsp. onion powder

One tsp. garlic powder

One tsp. of sea salt

½ tsp. paprika

Pinch of black pepper

Directions

Avocado Ranch Dip

Directions:

Place all ingredients in a prepared mixing bowl and mash together until combined and mostly smooth. Refrigerate until ready to serve.

Almond-crusted Cauliflower Bites

Preheat oven at temeprature of 400F and line a large baking sheet with parchment paper or a silicone mat.

Whisk together the non-dairy milk, vegan mayo and chickpea flour in a medium mixing bowl until smooth and thick enough to cover a spoon. Mix the almond meal, cornmeal, onion powder, garlic powder, salt, paprika and pepper in another mixing bowl until mixed.

Take each piece of cauliflower and first dunk it into the wet mixture, let excess drip off, then press into crumb mixture, covering evenly and shaking off loose bits; place onto the a baking sheet. Repeat until all pieces are coated and then on the baking sheet.

Coat cauliflower bites lightly with cooking oil spray and place in oven. Bake for 15 minutes, flip pieces over and lightly spray with oil again, bake for an additional 15 minutes or until golden. The cool baking sheet on a rack for 5 minutes before serving with avocado ranch dip!

Nutrition:

Energy (calories): 485 kcal

Protein: 7.67 g

Fat: 41.41 g

Carbohydrates: 25.66 g

51.   Simple Vegan Spring Rolls

Preparation time: 10 minutes

Cooking time: 15 minutes

Servings: 4

Ingredients

Extra virgin olive oil

Four cloves of garlic

One onion

Two carrots

Four leaves of cabbage

1 ounce or 30 grams soy sprouts

Two tbsp. tamari or soy sauce

Eight sheets spring roll pastry

Water

Sweet and sour sauce

Directions

In a wok, heat extra virgin olive oil (1 tbsp. is sufficient), add the vegetables (garlic, julienne, carrots, cabbage, and soy sprouts) and the tamari sauce. Cook over a medium-high heat for around 5 minutes...

You can see how to make the vegan spring rolls in the sixth photo of this post. You only have to

place the wrapper like a diamond, place two tbsp. of filling near a corner, tightly roll the wrapper, fold over the left side, fold over the right side, paint a little water along the edge and close it up.

In the wok, heat a lot of extra virgin olive oil, and when it's scorching, add the spring rolls and cook for around 1 minute or until golden brown on both sides.

Nutrition:

Energy (calories): 285 kcal

Protein: 9.66 g

Fat: 4.72 g

Carbohydrates: 50.6 g

52.   Vegan Popcorn

Preparation time: 10 minutes

Cooking time: 15 minutes

Servings: 4

Ingredients

2 cups dried soy chunks

3 cups vegetable broth

Two cloves of garlic, mashed

1 tsp. salt

1-inch cube of ginger, grated

½ cup flour

¾ cup vegetable broth

½ cup cornstarch

1 cup bread crumbs

1 tbsp. garlic powder

1 tbsp. lemon pepper

½ tsp. salt

For the dip:

1 tbsp. chopped fresh dill

1/3 Cup sour cream (use sour soy cream to keep it vegan)

dash of salt and pepper

Directions

Combine soy chunks, ginger, mashed garlic, 1 tsp. of salt, and fill the bowl with vegetable broth in a wide bowl until the soy chunks are coated. Soak until the bits are soft, or about 20 minutes. Heat a pot with an inch of oil on medium-high heat.

Mix ½ cup flour and ¾ cup vegetable broth from the soaking soy chunks and whisk until no lumps remain—divide between two bowls.

Squeeze the excess fluid from the soy chunks gently and coat in one of the bowls of the flour mixture until the chunks are soft and soaked.

Using 1/2 cup cornstarch to move the chunks to a Ziploc bag. Shake until coated, then move to the second bowl of flour mixture, cover, and then place the garlic powder, bread crumbs, lemon pepper, and salt in another ziploc container.

In batches, fry the chunks in oil until golden. To fry both sides, you can need to shift them around because they seem to like to float in one direction.

Remove and drain on a sheet of paper towel.

In a food processor, blend the dill, sour cream, salt and pepper to make the dip.

Serve the fried chunks with dip and enjoy!

Nutrition:

Energy (calories): 1676 kcal

Protein: 15.79 g

Fat: 166.67 g

Carbohydrates: 45.24 g

53. Stuffed Baby Eggplant

Air Fryer Stuffed Baby Eggplant is a delicious Indian dish made with baby eggplants packed full of aromatic and flavorful spices. This dish makes the perfect appetizer or first course for an elegant dinner.

Preparation time: 8 minutes

Cooking time: 12 minutes

Servings: 4

Ingredients:

For the eggplant:

Eight baby eggplants rinsed and patted dry

2 tsp. olive oil

For the spice stuffing:

1 tsp. Ground cumin

¾ tbsp. Coriander powder

¾ tbsp. Dry mango powder

½ tsp. Ground turmeric

½ tsp. Kashmiri red chilli powder

½ tsp. garlic powder

1 tsp. salt

To Garnish:

1 tbsp. cilantro leaves to garnish

Directions:

In a small bowl, stir all the stuffing spice together.

Take the eggplants and leaving the stems intact. Slit in the center from the bottom until just above the branch, careful not to split the eggplant into two pieces.

Now turn the eggplant at 90 degrees and add another slit from the center. The eggplant should in 4 but still held together by the stem.

Mix a tsp. of oil in the spices, and with a small spoon, fills the spice paste into each slit of the eggplants.

In the air fryer, put the eggplants in a single layer and brush oil on each eggplant, ensuring that both sides are coated...

Cook the air fryer at 360 degrees Fahrenheit for 8-12 minutes.

The colour will change when they are cooked. At 8 minutes, check the eggplant, and cook for additional time as needed.

Garnish with cilantro, and enjoy!

Nutrition:

Calories: 106 kcal.

Total Carbohydrates 20g

Protein 3g

Total Fat 3g

Potassium 679mg

54. Sweet Potato Air Fried Hash Browns

Crispy Air Fryer Hash Browns is a quick, 5-ingredient recipe that is easy, paleo-compatible and Whole-30 compatible. That is a great vegan, low-fat recipe that packs a punch in terms of a flavorful side.

Preparation time: 10 minutes

Cooking time: 20 minutes

Servings: 4

Ingredients:

Four sweet potatoes, peeled

Two garlic cloves, minced

1 tsp. smoked paprika

1 tsp. ground cinnamon

2 tsp. olive oil

Salt and pepper, to taste

Directions:

Grate the sweet potatoes using the largest side of the cheese box grater.

Place the sweet potatoes in a bowl of cold water and soak for 20-25 minutes. Soaking the sweet potatoes in cold water helps remove starch from the potatoes, which will make them crunchier.

Drain the potatoes and pat dry using kitchen paper.

Place the potatoes in a dry bowl and then add the olive oil, paprika, garlic, salt and pepper. Stir to combine.

Add the potatoes to the air fryer and then cook at 400 degrees Fahrenheit for 10 minutes.

Shake the potatoes at this stage and then cook for a further 10 minutes.

Cool and serve.

Recipe Notes:

Cook times will vary depending on the brand of an air fryer. Check-in on the hash browns after they have cooked for 15 minutes to ensure they do not overcook.

Nutrition:

55. Kale Salad Sushi Rolls

Delicious, crunchy and filling, these Kale Salad Sushi Rolls are easy to make. They're also healthy and flavorful and perfect for entertaining!

Preparation time: 70 minutes

Cooking time: 10 minutes

Servings: 3

Ingredients:

For the Kale Salad Sushi Rolls:

One batch Pressure Cooker sushi rice cooled to room temperature

½ a Haas avocado, sliced

Three sheets of sushi nori

For the Kale Salad:

1½ cups chopped kale, de-stemmed

¾ tsp. soy sauce

¾ tsp. toasted sesame oil

½ tsp. rice vinegar

¼ tsp. ground ginger

1/8 tsp. garlic powder

1 tbsp. sesame seeds

For the Coating:

½ cup panko breadcrumbs

For the Sriracha Mayo:

¼ cup of your favourite vegan mayonnaise

Sriracha sauce to taste

Directions:

To make the Kale Salad:

In a prepared large bowl, combine the kale, sesame oil, vinegar, garlic powder, ginger and soy sauce.

Using clean hands, you can massage the kale until it turns bright green and slightly wilted and then stir in the sesame seeds. Set aside.

To make the Sushi Rolls:

Layout a sheet of nori on a clean and dry surface With slightly damp fingertips, grab a handful of sushi rice and spread it onto the nori. Try to get a thin layer of rice to cover almost the entire sheet of nori.

Along one edge, leave about ½-inch of naked seaweed; this is the flap that will seal the sushi roll shut.

On the other end of the seaweed, layout 2 - 3 tbsp. of the kale salad, and top with a couple of avocado slices.

Starting with the filling, roll up the sushi roll, pressing gently to get a tight roll.

When in the end, use the naked bit of seaweed to seal the roll shut.

If needed, get your fingertips wet, and then moisten that bit of seaweed to make it stick.

Repeat the steps above to make three more sushi rolls.

To make the Sriracha Mayo:

In a small bowl, whisk together the vegan mayo together with the Sriracha.

Start by adding one tsp. of Sriracha, and keep adding more, half a teaspoon at a time, until the desired spice level is reached.

To fry and slice:

Pour the breadcrumbs into a shallow bowl.

Grab the first sushi roll, and coat it evenly in the Sriracha mayo and then in the breadcrumbs. Repeat for all the sushi rolls.

Place the rolls into the air fryer basket and cook at 390 degrees Fahrenheit for 10 minutes, shaking gently after 5 minutes, to enable them to cook evenly.

When the rolls are cool, take a sharp knife and gently slice them into 6-8 pieces.

When slicing, think of gently sawing and not pressing hard with the knife.

Serve with soy sauce for dipping.

Nutrition:

Energy (calories): 154 kcal

Protein: 2.88 g

Fat: 14.36 g

Carbohydrates: 5.04 g

56.   Jackfruit Taquitos

Air Fryer Jackfruit taquitos are only made of four ingredients, so they are quick and easy to make. What's even better, they only take about half an hour to complete.

Preparation time: 10 minutes

Cooking time: 20 minutes

Servings: 4

Ingredients:

Four 6-inch corn or whole wheat tortillas

1 cup of cooked or canned red kidney beans, drained and rinsed

1 14-oz. can water-packed jackfruit, drained and rinsed

¼ cup of water

½ cup Pico de Gallo sauce

Canola oil or extra-virgin olive oil cooking oil spray

Directions:

In a medium saucepan, combine the beans, jackfruit, Pico de Gallo and water.

Heat the jackfruit, beans and Pico de Gallo mixture over medium-high heat until it begins to boil.

If you cook on the stovetop, reduce the heat, cover and simmer for 20 - 25 minutes.

If using a pressure cooker, cover it to bring to pressure, cook at low pressure for 3 minutes, and then do a natural release.

Mash the cooked jackfruit with a potato masher to shred the jackfruit to a meaty texture.

Preheat the air fryer at temperature of 370 degrees Fahrenheit for 3 minutes.

Put a tortilla on a clean and dry work surface and spoon a quarter cup of the jackfruit mixture onto the tortilla.

Roll up tightly, putting back any of the mixtures that fall out back into the tortilla.

Repeat this process to make four taquitos in total.

Coat the air fryer basket with the cooking oil spray. Also, spray the tops of the tortillas.

Place the rolled tortillas into the air fryer basket and cook for 8 minutes.

Serve immediately and enjoy!

Nutrition:

Energy (calories): 895 kcal

Protein: 26.8 g

Fat: 26.56 g

Carbohydrates: 140.64 g

57.   Ginger Tofu Sushi Bowl

Ginger Tofu over sushi rice is the perfect low-calorie, a low-fat dish for clean eating. It will fast become your soon-to-be favourite sushi roll fillings.

Preparation time: 10 minutes

Cooking time: 40 minutes

Servings: 4

Ingredients:

2-inch piece of fresh ginger

One clove garlic

2 tbsp. real maple syrup

1 tbsp. toasted sesame oil

2 tbsp. soy sauce

1 tsp. rice vinegar

1 tbsp. cornstarch (or potato starch)

One block extra firm tofu pressed and cut into 1-inch pieces

For the Sushi Bowls:

One batch Pressure Cooker sushi rice or 3 cups of cooked rice.

One green onion, sliced

¾ cup cucumber sliced into ¼-inch thick half-moons

½ cup carrot sticks

1 Haas avocado, sliced

One 0.16-oz packet roast seaweed snacks cut into thirds

½ cup roasted cashews

¼ cup pickled ginger

Directions:

To make the tofu:

To make the marinade, combine the garlic, ginger, maple syrup, soy sauce, sesame oil, and vinegar in a blender or food processor. Puree on high speed until smooth.

In a large deep bowl, toss together the tofu and the marinade. Set aside and allow to marinate for 10 minutes, then drain any excess marinade.

In the same tub, toss the marinated tofu with the cornstarch. Pour those into the basket of the air fryer and cook at 370 degrees Fahrenheit for 15 minutes. After 8 minutes of cooking time, shake to make sure they cook evenly.

To make the sushi bowls:

Divide the sushi rice between two bowls.

Top with tofu, green onion, avocado, cucumbers, carrots, seaweed snack pieces and pickled ginger.

Sprinkle on the cashews, and then garnish with the sliced green onion.

Serve immediately.

Nutrition:

Energy (calories): 597 kcal

Protein: 21.45 g

Fat: 43.2 g

Carbohydrates: 47.62 g

58. Cauliflower Chickpea Tacos

Cauliflower Chickpea Tacos are a healthy, fresh and flavorful dinner for all the family. It's quick to get to the table, vegan, easily made and gluten-free.

Preparation time: 10 minutes

Cooking time: 20 minutes

Servings: 4

Ingredients:

19-oz. can of chickpeas drained and rinsed

4 cups of cauliflower florets, cut into bite-sized pieces

2 tbsp. taco seasoning

2 tbsp. olive oil

To Serve:

Eight small flour tortillas

4 cups cabbage, finely shredded

2 Haas avocados, sliced

Coconut yogurt, for drizzling

Directions:

Preheat the air fryer at temperature of 390 degrees Fahrenheit.

In a prepared large bowl, toss the chickpeas and cauliflower with taco seasoning and olive oil.

Put them into the basket of the air fryer and cook in the air fryer for 20 minutes. Make sure to check often to ensure the cauliflower and chickpeas are evenly cooked through.

Serve in tacos with cabbage, avocado slices, and coconut yogurt drizzled on top.

Nutrition:

Energy (calories): 760 kcal

Protein: 22.84 g

Fat: 30.87 g

Carbohydrates: 103.75 g

59. Spicy Cauliflower Stir Fry

Spicy Cauliflower Stir-Fry is fast, healthy and straightforward. It's so gratifying and works well as a new and exotic side dish for your family to enjoy.

Preparation time: 5 minutes

Cooking time: 25 minutes

Servings: 4

Ingredients:

One head cauliflower, cut into florets

Five cloves garlic, finely sliced

¾ cup Spanish onion, thinly sliced

1½ tbsp. tamari, gluten-free tamari or light soy sauce

1 tbsp. Sriracha or any other of your favourite hot sauces

1 tbsp. rice vinegar

½ tsp. coconut sugar

To Garnish:

Two scallions, sliced

Directions:

Place the cauliflower in the air fryer. (If the air fryer has holes in the bottom, you'll need to use an additional air fryer insert).

Preheat the air fryer at temperature of 350 degrees Fahrenheit and cook for 10 minutes.

Open the air fryer, remove and shake the insert and slide back into the compartment.

Add the sliced white onion, stir and cook for a further 10 minutes.

Attach the garlic, then stir and cook for an additional five minutes.

In a small bowl, mix the rice vinegar, soy sauce, coconut sugar, Sriracha hot sauce, salt and pepper.

Add the mixture to the cauliflower in the air fryer and stir—Cook for a further 5 minutes. The insert will keep all of the juices inside.

Transfer to a serving bowl and then sprinkle the sliced scallions over the top to garnish.

Nutrition:

Calories: 93 kcal.

Carbohydrates 12g

Total Fat 3g

Protein 4g

Sodium 510mg

Potassium 519mg

60. Eggplant Parmesan

This easy Italian vegetarian dish, Eggplant Parmesan, is the perfect light weekday dinner. And made in the air-fryer, it couldn't be easier!

Preparation time: 10 minutes

Cooking time: 20 minutes

Servings: 6

Ingredients:

One large eggplant, sliced and de-stemmed

½ cup almond milk

½ cup flour

2 tbsp. vegan Parmesan, grated

½ cup Panko bread crumbs

Garlic powder, to taste

Onion powder, to taste

Salt and pepper, to taste

For the Topping:

1 cup of Marinara sauce, plus more for serving

Vegan Parmesan, grated

½ cup Vegan Mozzarella Shreds

To Serve:

4 oz. spaghetti or any other pastas your desired, cooked al dente (to serve two people)

Vegan Parmesan, grated

Italian parsley, chopped

Directions:

Wash, dry, de-stem the eggplant and slice lengthways.

Season the Panko breadcrumbs with vegan parmesan, garlic powder, onion powder, salt and pepper.

Dip the sliced eggplant into the flour, and then the almond milk and finally, the seasoned Panko bread crumbs.

Spray the eggplant lightly with cooking oil spray and place into the air fryer basket at 390 degrees Fahrenheit for 15 minutes. Check the eggplant flipping halfway through cooking, flip over and spray the second side lightly with cooking oil spray.

Nutrition:

Energy (calories): 146 kcal

Protein: 7.2 g

Fat: 3.13 g

Carbohydrates: 23.71 g

61. Stuffed Potatoes

Scrumptious and filling! This baked potato filled with a cheesy mash and re-baked will have your family asking for more. The air fryer can make the whole cooking process go faster and crisping up the potato even more. Try it out today!

Preparation time: 10 minutes

Cooking time: 90 minutes

Servings: 4

Ingredients:

Two large Russet baking potatoes

1 - 2 tsp. olive oil (you may leave the oil out if you want the recipe oil-free)

1 cup spinach or kale, chopped

2 tbsp. nutritional yeast

¼ cup unsweetened almond milk

¼ cup unsweetened vegan yogurt

½ tsp. salt

¼ tsp. pepper

For Topping (Optional):

Smoked salt and black pepper, to taste

Chopped chives, parsley or any other of your favourite fresh herbs

¼ cup unsweetened vegan yogurt

Directions:

Rub the skin of each Russet potato with oil on all sides.

Preheat the air fryer at the temperature of 390 degrees Fahrenheit unless the brand doesn't require it.

Once it's hot, add the potatoes to the air fryer basket.

Cook the potatoes for 30 minutes, and when the time is up, flip the potatoes over and cook for 30 more minutes.

Depending on the potatoes' size, they may need to cook for a further 10 - 20 minutes. The potatoes will be fork tender when it is already cooked. Set them aside to cool.

Slice each potato into half lengthwise and then scoop out the flesh while leaving enough to create a stable shell of the potato skin.

Mash the scooped potato flesh, almond milk, vegan yogurt, nutritional yeast, pepper and salt until smooth. Then stir in the chopped spinach and fill the potato shells. Cook the filled potatoes again at 350 degrees Fahrenheit for 5 minutes.

Serve with the toppings you really enjoy!

If you don't have an air fryer to use, you can do this all in the oven at 400 degrees Fahrenheit. Cooking times may vary since the air fryers use a convection type cooking method.

While the eggplant is cooking, for the meantime cook the pasta. Once golden on both sides, spoon some of the marinara sauce on top of the eggplant and top with a combination of the vegan Parmesan and mozzarella cheeses. Cook just until the cheeses just begin to melt. Serve with the pasta, extra Marinara. Garnish with fresh parsley and perhaps another sprinkle of the vegan parmesan. Enjoy!

Nutrition:

Energy (calories): 211 kcal

Protein: 7.64 g Fat: 3.24 g

Carbohydrates: 38.47 g

62.   Golden Turmeric Cauliflower Steaks

These healthy, meaty and delicious golden turmeric Cauliflower Steaks are loaded with flavor and full of spice. Perfect for a light lunch or dinner.

Preparation time: 10 minutes

Cooking time: 15 minutes

Servings: 2

Ingredients:

1-2 medium heads cauliflower, stems intact

2 tbsp. coconut oil or coconut spray Oil

1 tsp. ground turmeric

¼ tsp. ground ginger

1/8 tsp. ground cumin

1/8 tsp. salt

A pinch of black pepper

To Serve:

Mixed steamed greens

Tahini

White Sesame Seeds

Directions:

Cut the cauliflower head down the middle, leaving the stem intact. Trim off any green leaves.

On either side of the half, cut 1-inch steaks taking care not to make them too thin. Reserve any fallen florets for use at a later date.

Coat the steaks with coconut oil or coconut oil spray and rub the spices into all of the cauliflower cracks and crevices.

These recipes can be prepared in the oven or an air fryer. Cook at 390 degrees Fahrenheit for about 15 minutes, turning over the steaks halfway through the cooking time.

Serve the mixed greens on a bed, drizzled with tahini. Garnish with white sesame seeds, if desired.

Nutrition:

Energy (calories): 185 kcal

Protein: 4.46 g

Fat: 14.29 g

Carbohydrates: 13.26 g

63.   Golden Turmeric Falafel

Preparation time: 15 minutes

Cooking time: 20 minutes

Servings: 4

Ingredients:

For the falafel:

1 cup canned chickpeas, drained and rinsed

2 tbsp. tahini

2 tbsp. white onion, diced

½ tsp. fresh garlic, minced

2 tbsp. lemon juice

2 tbsp. fresh parsley

1 tsp. ground turmeric

½ tsp. ground cumin

¼ tsp. salt

1/8 tsp. black pepper

For the tzatziki dipping sauce:

¼ cup cucumber, finely diced

One container vegan almond milk yogurt

2 tsp. lemon juice

1 tsp. dill

Salt & Pepper, to taste

Garlic powder, to taste

For the couscous tabbouleh:

¼ cup chickpeas that remain from the falafel preparation 1 cup cooked quinoa or couscous

2 tbsp. cucumber, diced

2 tbsp. tomato, diced

One green onion, diced

2 tbsp. fresh parsley

Salt & pepper, to taste

Directions:

Preheat the air fryer at temperature of 370 degrees Fahrenheit or, if using an oven, 375 degrees Fahrenheit.

In a food processor, now combine all the falafel ingredients and carefully pulse until all the ingredients are coarsely chopped but mixed well.

Coat the air fryer basket with vegan cooking oil spray.

Using an ice cream scoop, scoop four balls of the mixture and flatten them into patties in your hands

Air fry (or bake in the oven) for 15 minutes. Halfway through cooking, flip them over to ensure even cooking.

While the falafel is cooking, prepare the couscous salad and tzatziki using all the ingredients.

Serve garnished with a few lemon wedges and fresh parsley.

Nutrition:

Energy (calories): 165 kcal

Protein: 7.39 g

Fat: 5.81 g

Carbohydrates: 23.37 g

64. Cherry Tomato Salad

Preparation time: 5 minutes

Cooking time: 25 minutes

Servings: 6

Ingredients:

Eight small beets, trimmed, peeled and cut into wedges

One red onion, sliced

One tbsp. balsamic vinegar

Salt and black pepper to taste

1 pint mixed cherry tomatoes, halved

2 ounces pecans, chopped

Two tbsp. olive oil

Directions:

Put the beets in your air fryer's basket, and add the salt, pepper, and one tbsp. of the oil.

Cook at the temperature of 400 degrees F for 15 minutes.

Transfer the beets to a pan that fits your air fryer, and add the onions, tomatoes, pecans, and remaining one tbsp. of the oil; toss well.

Cook at 400 degrees F for ten more minutes.

Divide between plates and serve.

Nutrition:

Calories 144

Fat 7g

Fiber 5g

Carbs 8g

Protein 6g

65. Broccoli and Scallions

Preparation time: 5 minutes

Cooking time: 7 minutes

Servings: 4

Ingredients:

One broccoli head, florets separated

Salt and black pepper to taste

Six cherry tomatoes, halved

¼ cup scallions, chopped

One tbsp. olive oil

Directions:

Put the broccoli florets in your air fryer's basket, and add the salt, pepper, and ½ tbsp. of the oil; toss well.

Cook at 380 degrees F for 7 minutes.

Transfer the broccoli to a bowl, and add the tomatoes, scallions, salt, pepper, and the remaining ½ tbsp. of oil.

Toss and serve.

Nutrition:

Calories 111

Fat 4g

Fiber 4g

Carbs 9g

Protein 2g

66.   Balsamic Red Cabbage

Preparation time: 5 minutes

Cooking time: 8 minutes

Servings: 4

Ingredients:

One red cabbage head, shredded

One tbsp. olive oil

One carrot, grated

¼ cup balsamic vinegar

Salt and black pepper to taste

Directions:

Place all ingredients in a pan that fits your air fryer, and mix well.

Put the pan in the fryer and cook at 380 degrees F for 8 minutes.

Divide between plates and serve.

Nutrition:

Calories 100

Fat 4g

Fiber 2g

Carbs 7g

Protein 2g

67.   Garlic Beans Mix

Preparation time: 5 minutes

Cooking time: 6 minutes

Servings: 4

Ingredients:

1 pound green beans, trimmed

Two tbsp. olive oil

Three garlic cloves, minced

Salt and black pepper to taste

One tbsp. balsamic vinegar

Directions:

Place all the ingredients in a prepared bowl, except the vinegar, and mix well.

Put the beans in your air fryer and cook at 400 degrees F for 6 minutes.

Divide the green beans between plates, drizzle the vinegar all over, and serve.

Nutrition:

Calories 101

Fat 3g

Fiber 3g

Carbs 4g

Protein 2g

68.   Oregano Eggplants Mix

Preparation time: 5 minutes

Cooking time: 15 minutes

Servings: 4

Ingredients:

Four eggplants, roughly cubed

Two tbsp. lime juice

Salt and black pepper to taste

One tsp. oregano, dried

Two tbsp. olive oil

Directions:

Place all of ingredients together in a pan that fits your air fryer and mix/toss well.

Put the pan into the fryer and cook at 400 degrees F for 15 minutes.

Divide the eggplants between plates and serve.

Nutrition:

Calories 125

Fat 5g

Fiber 2g

Carbs 11g

Protein 5 g

69.   Coconut Mix

Preparation time: 5 minutes

Cooking time: 8 minutes

Servings: 8

Ingredients:

1 pound brown mushrooms, halved

One small yellow onion, chopped

Salt and black pepper to taste

Two tbsp. olive oil

14 ounces of coconut milk

Directions:

Add all ingredients to a pan that fits your air fryer and mix well.

Place the pan in the fryer and cook at 400 degrees F for 8 minutes.

Divide between plates and serve.

Nutrition:

Calories 202

Fat 4g

Fiber 1g

Carbs 13g

Protein 4g

70. Artichokes with Coconut

Preparation time: 5 minutes

Cooking time: 15 minutes

Servings: 2

Ingredients:

Two artichokes, washed, trimmed and halved

Two garlic cloves, minced

¼ cup coconut, shredded

Juice of 1 lemon

One tbsp. coconut oil, melted

Directions:

In a bowl, mix the artichokes with the garlic, oil, and lemon juice; toss well.

Put the artichokes into your air fryer and cook at 360 degrees F for 15 minutes.

Divide the artichokes between plates, sprinkle the coconut on top, and serve.

Enjoy!

Nutrition:

Calories 213

Fat 8g

Fiber 6g

Carbs 13g

Protein 6g

71. Asparagus and Prosciutto

Preparation time: 5 minutes

Cooking time: 5 minutes

Servings: 4

Ingredients:

Eight asparagus spears, trimmed

8 ounces prosciutto slices

A pinch of salt and black pepper

Directions:

Wrap the asparagus in prosciutto slices and then season with salt and pepper.

Put all in your air fryer's basket and cook at 400 degrees F for 5 minutes.

Divide between plates and serve.

Nutrition:

Calories 100

Fat 2g

Fiber 5g

Carbs 8g

Protein 4g

72. Cajun Asparagus

Preparation time: 5 minutes

Cooking time: 5 minutes

Servings: 4

Ingredients:

One tsp. extra virgin olive oil

One bunch asparagus, trimmed

½ tbsp. Cajun seasoning

Directions:

In a prepared bowl, mix the asparagus with the oil and Cajun seasoning; coat the asparagus well.

Put the asparagus in your air fryer and cook at 400 degrees F for 5 minutes.

Divide between plates and serve.

Nutrition:

Calories 151

Fat 3

Fiber 4

Carbs 9

Protein 4

73. Bell Peppers and Kale Leaves

Preparation time: 5 minutes

Cooking time: 15 minutes

Servings: 4

Ingredients:

Two red bell peppers, cut into strips

Two green bell peppers, cut into strips

½ pound kale leaves

Salt and black pepper to taste

Two yellow onions, roughly chopped

¼ cup veggie stock

Two tbsp. tomato sauce

Directions:

Add all ingredients to a pan that fits your air fryer; mix well.

Place the pan in the fryer and cook at 360 degrees F for 15 minutes.
Divide between plates, serve, and enjoy!
Nutrition:
Calories 161
Fat 7g
Fiber 6g
Carbs 12g
Protein 7g

74.   Garlic Parsnips

Preparation time: 5 minutes
Cooking time: 15 minutes
Servings: 4
Ingredients:
1 pound parsnips, cut into chunks
One tbsp. olive oil
Six garlic cloves, minced
One tbsp. balsamic vinegar
Salt and black pepper to taste
Directions:
In a prepared bowl, add all of the ingredients and combine well.
Place them in the air fryer and cook at 380 degrees F for 15 minutes.
Divide between plates and serve.
Nutrition:
Calories 121
Fat 3g
Fiber 6g
Carbs 12g
Protein 6g

75.   Florets and Pomegranate

Preparation time: 5 minutes
Cooking time: 7 minutes
Servings: 4
Ingredients:
One broccoli head, florets separated
Salt and black pepper to taste
One pomegranate, seeds separated
A drizzle of olive oil
Directions:
In a prepared bowl, mix the broccoli with the salt, pepper, and oil; toss.
Put the florets in your air fryer and cook at 400 degrees F for 7 minutes.

Divide between plates, sprinkle the pomegranate seeds all over and serve.
Nutrition:
Calories 141 Fat 3
Fiber 4 Carbs 11 Protein 4

76.   Lime Broccoli

Preparation time: 5 minutes
Cooking time: 6 minutes
Servings: 4
Ingredients:
One broccoli head, florets separated
One tbsp. lime juice
Salt and black pepper to taste
Two tbsp. vegan butter, melted
Directions:
In a prepared bowl, mix well all of the ingredients.
Put the broccoli mixture in your air fryer and cook at 400 degrees F for 6 minutes.
Serve hot.
Nutrition:
Calories 151 Fat 4g
Fiber 7g Carbs 12g Protein 6g

77.   Green Cayenne Cabbage

Preparation time: 5 minutes
Cooking time: 12 minutes
Servings: 4
Ingredients:
One green cabbage head, shredded
One tbsp. olive oil
One tsp. cayenne pepper
A pinch of salt and black pepper
Two tsp. sweet paprika
Directions:
Mix all of the ingredients in a pan that fits your fryer.
Place the pan in the fryer and cook at 320 degrees F for 12 minutes.
Divide between plates and serve right away.
Nutrition:
Calories 124
Fat 6g
Fiber 6g
Carbs 16g
Protein 7g

78.   Tomato and Balsamic Greens

Preparation time: 5 minutes
Cooking time: 12 minutes
Servings: 4
Ingredients:
One bunch mustard greens, trimmed
Two tbsp. olive oil
½ cup veggies stock
Two tbsp. tomato puree
Three garlic cloves, minced
Salt and black pepper to taste
One tbsp. balsamic vinegar
Directions:
Combine all ingredients in a pan that fits your air fryer and toss well.
Place the pan in the fryer and cook at 260 degrees F for 12 minutes.
Divide everything between plates, serve, and enjoy!
Nutrition:
Calories 151
Fat 2g
Fiber 4g
Carbs 14g
Protein 4g

79.   Lime Endives

Preparation time: 5 minutes
Cooking time: 10 minutes
Servings: 4
Ingredients:
Four endives, trimmed and halved
Salt and black pepper to taste
One tbsp. lime juice
One tbsp. olive oil
Directions:
Put the endives in your air fryer, and add the salt, pepper, lemon juice, and vegan butter.
Cook at the temperature of 360 degrees F for 10 minutes.
Divide between plates and serve.
Nutrition:
Calories 100
Fat 3g
Fiber 4g
Carbs 8g
Protein 4g

80.   Oregano Artichokes

Preparation time: 10 minutes
Cooking time: 7 minutes
Servings: 4
Ingredients:
Four big artichokes, trimmed
Salt and black pepper to the taste
Two tbsp. lemon juice
¼ cup extra virgin olive oil
Two tsp. balsamic vinegar
One tsp. oregano, dried
2 garlic cloves, minced
Directions:
Season the artichokes with salt and pepper, fry them with half the oil and half the lemon juice, place them in the air fryer and cook for seven minutes at 360 degrees F.
Meanwhile, in a bowl, mix the rest of the lemon juice with vinegar, the remaining oil, salt, pepper, garlic and oregano and stir very well.
Arrange artichokes on a platter, drizzle the balsamic vinaigrette over them and serve.
Enjoy!
Nutrition:
Calories 200 Fat 3g
Fiber 6g Carbs 12g Protein 4g

81.   Green Veggies Mix

Preparation time: 10 minutes
Cooking time: 15 minutes
Servings: 4
Ingredients:
1-pint cherry tomatoes
1 pound green beans
Two tbsp. olive oil
Salt and black pepper to the taste
Directions:
In a bowl, mix cherry tomatoes with green beans, olive oil, salt and pepper, toss, transfer to your air fryer and cook at 400 degrees F for 15 minutes.
Divide among plates and serve right away.
Enjoy!
Nutrition:
Calories 162 Fat 6g
Fiber 5g Carbs 8g
Protein 9g

82.   Flavored Green Beans

Preparation time: 10 minutes
Cooking time: 15 minutes
Servings: 4
Ingredients:
1 pound red potatoes cut into wedges
1 pound green beans
Two garlic cloves, minced
Two tbsp. olive oil
Salt and black pepper to the taste
½ tsp. oregano, dried
Directions:
In a pan that fits in air fryer, combine potatoes with green beans, garlic, oil, salt, pepper and oregano, toss, introduce in your air fryer and cook at 380 degrees F for 15 minutes.
Divide among plates and serve.
Enjoy!
Nutrition:
Calories 211
Fat 6g
Fiber 7g
Carbs 8g
Protein 5g

83.   Beet Salad and Parsley Dressing

Preparation time: 10 minutes
Cooking time: 14 minutes
Servings: 4
Ingredients
Four beets
2 tbsp. balsamic vinegar
A bunch of parsley
Salt and black pepper
1 tbsp. extra virgin olive oil
One garlic clove
2 tbsp. capers
Directions:
Insert beets in the air fryer and cook them at 360°F for 14 minutes.
Combine parsley with garlic, pepper, salt, olive oil and capers in a bowl and mix thoroughly
Move beets to a cutting board peel them after cooling and slice. Transfer them to a salad bowl.
Sprinkle the parsley dressing all over after putting in vinegar
Serve.

Nutrition:
Energy (calories): 27 kcal
Protein: 0.37 g
Fat: 1.58 g
Carbohydrates: 2.94 g

84.   Beets and Arugula Salad

Preparation time: 5 minutes
Cooking time: 15 minutes
Servings: 4
Ingredients
One and ½ pounds beets
A sprinkle of olive oil
2 tbsp. orange zest
2 tbsp. cider vinegar
½ cup of orange juice
2 tbsp. brown sugar
Two scallions
2 tbsp. mustard
2 cups arugula
Directions:
Chafe beets with the orange juice and oil put in an air fryer and cook at 350° F for 10 minutes.
Move beet quarters to a bowl, put in arugula, orange Zest and scallions. Toss.
Blend sugar with mustard and vinegar in another bowl, beat well, and add to salad. Toss.
Serve.
Nutrition:
 Energy (calories): 95 kcal
Protein: 2.78 g
Fat: 0.58 g
Carbohydrates: 20.76 g

85.   Broccoli Salad

Preparation time: 5 minutes
Cooking time: 12 minutes
Servings: 4
Ingredients
One broccoli head, florets separated
1 tbsp. peanut oil
Six garlic cloves
1 tbsp. Chinese rice wine vinegar
Salt and black pepper
Directions:
Combine broccoli with salt, pepper and half of the oil in a bowl. Toss, put in an air fryer and

cook at 350° F for 8 minutes while shaking fryer halfway.

Get broccoli to a salad bowl, put the garlic, the rest of the peanut oil, and rice vinegar. Toss thoroughly.

Serve.

Nutrition:

Energy (calories): 42 kcal

Fat: 3.43 g

Carbohydrates: 2.64 g

86.   Brussels Sprouts And Tomatoes Mix

Preparation time: 5 minutes

Cooking time: 10 minutes

Servings: 4

Ingredients

1 pound Brussels sprouts

Salt and black pepper

Six cherry tomatoes halved

¼ cup green onions,

1 tbsp. olive oil

Directions:

Spice Brussels sprouts with pepper and salt, get them in an Air Fryer. Cook at 350° F for 10 minutes.

Move them to a bowl; add cherry tomatoes, green onions, pepper, salt and olive oil. Toss properly

Serve.

Nutrition:

Energy (calories): 85 kcal

Protein: 4.04 g

Fat: 3.77 g

Carbohydrates: 11.52 g

87.   Collard Green Mix

Preparation time: 5 minutes

Cooking time: 15 minutes

Servings: 4

Ingredients

One bunch collard greens

2 tbsp. olive oil

2 tbsp. tomato puree

One yellow onion

Three garlic cloves

Salt and black pepper

1 tbsp. balsamic vinegar

1 tbsp. sugar

Directions:

Blend oil, vinegar, garlic, tomato puree and onion in a bowl and beat.

Put in salt, pepper, collard greens and sugar. Toss, get it into the air fryer. Cook at 320° F for 10 minutes.

Share collard greens blend on plates

Serve.

Nutrition:

Energy (calories): 82 kcal

Protein: 0.46 g

Fat: 6.81 g

Carbohydrates: 5.24 g

88.   Herbed Eggplant and Zucchini Mix

Preparation time: 5 minutes

Cooking time: 13 minutes

Servings: 4

Ingredients

One eggplant, cubed

Three zucchinis, cubed

2 tbsp. lemon juice

Salt and black pepper

1 tbsp. dried thyme

1 tbsp. dried oregano

3 tbsp. olive oil

Directions:

Get a bowl, put in zucchinis, lemon juice, thyme pepper, salt, olive oil and oregano. Toss, put into the air fryer and cook at 360°F for 8 minutes.

Share in plates

Serve immediately.

Nutrition:

Energy (calories): 133 kcal

Protein: 1.79 g Fat: 10.47 g

Carbohydrates: 10.1 g

89.   Okra and Corn Salad

Preparation time: 5 minutes

Cooking time: 17 minutes

Servings: 6

Ingredients

1-pound okra

Six scallions

Three green bell peppers,
Salt and black pepper
2 tbsp. olive oil
1 tbsp. sugar
28 oz. canned tomatoes
1 cup of corn
Directions:
Heat oil over medium heat in the pan, put bell peppers and scallion, turn and cook for 5 minutes.
Get in okra, pepper, salt, tomatoes, sugar and corn, stir, then put into the air fryer—Cook at 360° F for 7 minutes.
Share okra blend on plates. Serve.
Nutrition:
Energy (calories): 209 kcal
Protein: 5.95 g Fat: 6.38 g
Carbohydrates: 36.07 g

90.   Crispy Potatoes and Parsley

Preparation time: 5 minutes
Cooking time: 15 minutes
Servings: 4
Ingredients
1-pound gold potatoes, cut into wedges
Salt and black pepper
2 tbsp. olive
Juice from ½ lemon
¼ cup parsley leaves
Directions:
Pat potatoes with pepper, salt, lemon juice and olive oil, put into the air fryer, then cook at 350° F for 10 minutes.
Share in plates, spray parsley on top.
Serve.
Nutrition:
Energy (calories): 100 kcal
Protein: 2.63 g Fat: 0.63 g
Carbohydrates: 21.84 g

91.   Swiss Chard Salad

Preparation time: 5 minutes
Cooking time: 18 minutes
Servings: 4
Ingredients
One bunch Swiss chard
2 tbsp. olive oil

One small yellow onion
A pinch of red pepper flakes
¼ cup pine nuts
¼ cup raisins
1 tbsp. balsamic vinegar
Salt and black pepper
Directions:
Heat pan and put olive oil over medium heat, put onions and chard, stir. Cook for 5 minutes.
Put pepper flakes, salt, pepper, raisins, vinegar and pine nuts, stir, bring into air fryer—Cook at 350° F for 8 minutes.
Share in plates. Serve.
Nutrition:
Energy (calories): 136 kcal
Protein: 1.76 g Fat: 12.6 g
Carbohydrates: 5.62 g

92.   Garlic Tomatoes

Preparation time: 5 minutes
Cooking time: 20 minutes
Servings: 4
Ingredients
Four garlic cloves
1 pound mixed cherry tomatoes
Three thyme springs
Salt and black pepper
¼ cup olive oil
Directions:
Mix in tomatoes with salt, garlic, black pepper, thyme and olive oil in a bowl. Toss to coat, bring into the air fryer. Cook at 360°F for 15 minutes.
Share tomatoes blend on plates
Serve.
Nutrition:
Energy (calories): 200 kcal
Protein: 1.56 g Fat: 13.78 g
Carbohydrates: 20.26 g

93.   Broccoli Hash

Preparation time: 10 minutes
Cooking time: 28 minutes
Servings: 2
Ingredients
10 oz. mushrooms
One broccoli head
One garlic clove

1 tbsp. balsamic vinegar
One yellow onion
1 tbsp. olive oil
Salt and black pepper
1 tbsp. dried basil
One avocado
A pinch of red pepper flakes
Directions:
Mix in mushrooms with onion, garlic, broccoli and avocado in a bowl.
Mix in oil, salt, pepper, vinegar and basil and beat properly.
Get this over veggies. Toss to coat, leave for 30 minutes. Put into air fryer's basket and then cook at 350° F for 8 minutes,
Share in plates.
Serve with pepper flakes over.
Nutrition:
Energy (calories): 280 kcal
Protein: 7.35 g Fat: 22.1 g
Carbohydrates: 19.45 g

94. Eggplant and Garlic Sauce

Preparation time: 5 minutes
Cooking time: 15 minutes
Servings: 4
Ingredients
2 tbsp. olive oil
Two garlic cloves
Three eggplants
One red chilli pepper
One green onion stalk
1 tbsp. ginger
1 tbsp. soy sauce
1 tbsp. balsamic vinegar
Directions:
Add eggplant slices to heated oil in the pan over medium heat and cook for 2 minutes.
Put in garlic, chilli pepper, green onions, soy sauce, ginger and Vinegar. Get into an air fryer and cook at 320° F for 7 minutes.
Share in plates.
Serve.
Nutrition:
Energy (calories): 186 kcal
Protein: 4.71 g Fat: 8.27 g
Carbohydrates: 27.84 g

95. Stuffed Baby Peppers

Preparation time: 5 minutes
Cooking time: 11 minutes
Servings: 4
Ingredients
12 baby bell peppers
¼ tbsp. red pepper flakes
6 tbsp. jarred basil pesto
Salt and black pepper
1 tbsp. lemon juice
1 tbsp. olive oil
Handful of parsley
Directions:
Mix in the pesto, salt, lemon juice, pepper flakes, black pepper, parsley and oil, beat properly and infuse bell pepper halves with the mix.
Put into the air fryer and then cook at 320° F for 6 minutes,
Assemble peppers on plates.
Serve.
Nutrition:
Energy (calories): 188 kcal
Protein: 25.86 g
Fat: 4.3 g
Carbohydrates: 14.52 g

96. Delicious Portobello Mushroom

Preparation time: 5 minutes
Cooking time: 17 minutes
Servings: 4
Ingredients
Ten basil leaves
1 cup baby spinach
Three garlic cloves
1 cup almonds
1 tbsp. parsley
¼ cup olive oil
Eight cherry tomatoes
Salt and black pepper
4 Portobello mushrooms
Directions:
Blend basil with garlic, spinach, parsley, almonds, fat, black pepper, salt and mushroom. Mix thoroughly.
Infuse each mushroom with the blend, put them in an air fryer and cook at 350°F for 12 minutes.

Share mushrooms on plates.

Serve.

Nutrition:

Energy (calories): 135 kcal

Protein: 1.21 g Fat: 13.8 g

Carbohydrates: 2.88 g

97.   Cherry Tomatoes Skewers

Preparation time: 10 minutes

Cooking time: 26 minutes

Servings: 4

Ingredients

3 tbsp. balsamic vinegar

24 cherry tomatoes

2 tbsp. olive oil

Three garlic cloves

1 tbsp. thyme

Salt and black pepper

For dressing

2 tbsp. balsamic vinegar

Salt and black pepper

4 tbsp. olive oil

Directions:

Mix in 2 tbsp. vinegar with three tbsp. oil, three garlic cloves, black pepper, thyme, salt in a bowl and beat properly.

Put tomatoes. Toss to coat and allow for 30 minutes.

Assemble six tomatoes on one skewer. Do the same with the remaining tomatoes.

Put into an air fryer and cook at 360°F for 6 minutes.

Mix in 2 tbsp. vinegar with salt, four tbsp. oil and pepper. Beat properly.

Assemble tomato skewers on plates.

Serve with dressing sprinkled over.

Nutrition:

Energy (calories): 210 kcal

Protein: 0.61 g Fat: 20.34 g

Carbohydrates: 6.53 g

98.   Green Beans and Tomatoes

Preparation time: 5 minutes

Cooking time: 20 minutes

Servings: 4

Ingredients

1-pint cherry tomatoes

1 lb. green beans

2 tbsp. Olive oil

Salt and black pepper

Directions:

Mix in green beans with cherry potatoes, olive oil, pepper and salt. Toss, put into the air fryer and cook at 400° F for 15 minutes.

Share in plates.

Serve immediately

Nutrition:

Energy (calories): 91 kcal

Protein: 1.46 g

Fat: 7.31 g

Carbohydrates: 6.34 g

99.   Pumpkin Oatmeal

Preparation time: 5 minutes

Cooking time: 20 minutes

Servings: 4

Ingredients:

Water (1.5 cups)

Pumpkin puree (.5 cup)

Stevia (3 tbsp.)

Pumpkin pie spice (1 tsp.)

Steel-cut oats (.5 cup)

Directions:

Set the Air Fryer at 360º Fahrenheit to preheat.

Toss in and mix the fixings into the pan of the Air Fryer.

Set the timer for 20 minutes.

When the time has elapsed, portion the oatmeal into bowls and serve.

Nutrition:

Calories 211

Protein 3 grams

Carbohydrates 1 gram

Fat 4 grams

100.   Yellow Squash - Carrots & Zucchini

Preparation time: 5 minutes

Cooking time: 30 minutes

Servings: 4

Ingredients:

Carrots (.5 lb.)

Olive oil (6 tsp. - divided)

Lime (1 sliced into wedges)

Zucchini (1 lb. sliced into .75-inch semi-circles)
Yellow squash (1 lb.)
Tarragon leaves (1 tbsp.)
White pepper (.5 tsp.)
Sea salt (1 tsp.)
Directions:
Set the Air Fryer at 400° Fahrenheit.
Trim the stem and roots from the squash and zucchini.
Dice and add the carrots into a bowl with two teaspoons of oil.
Toss the carrots into the fryer basket. Prepare for 5 minutes.
Mix in the zucchini, oil, salt, and pepper in the bowl.
When the carrots are done, fold in the mixture. Cook 30 minutes.
Stir the mixture occasionally. Chop the tarragon and garnish using and lime wedges.
Nutrition:
Protein: 7.4 grams
Carbohydrates: 8.6 grams
Fat: 9.4 grams
Calories: 256

101. Carrot Mix

Preparation time: 5 minutes
Cooking time: 30 minutes
Servings: 4
Ingredients:
Coconut milk (2 cups)
Steel-cut oats (.5 cup)
Shredded carrots (1 cup)
Agave nectar (.5 tsp.)
Ground cardamom (1 tsp.)
Saffron (1 pinch)
Directions:
Lightly spritz the Air Fryer pan using a cooking oil spray.
Warm the fryer to reach 365° Fahrenheit.
When it's hot, whisk and add the fixings (omit the saffron).
Set the timer for 15 minutes.
After the timer buzzes, portion into the serving dishes with a sprinkle of saffron.
Nutrition:
Protein: 3 grams
Carbohydrates: 4 grams
Fat: 7 grams
Calories: 202

CHAPTER 9:

Vegan Fruits

102. Lemon Cream Bars

Preparation time: 25 minutes

Cooking time: 22 minutes

Servings: 6

Ingredients

4 tablespoons coconut oil, melted

¼ teaspoon plus 1 pinch of kosher salt

1 teaspoon pure vanilla extract

½ cup plus 3 tablespoons granulated sugar

½ cup plus 2 tablespoons all-purpose flour

¼ cup freshly squeezed lemon juice

Zest of 1 lemon

½ cup canned coconut cream

4 tablespoons cornstarch

Powdered sugar, to taste

Directions:

Set the air fryer temp to 350ºF (180ºC).

In a prepared medium bowl, combine the coconut oil, ¼ teaspoon of salt, vanilla extract, and 3 tablespoons of sugar. Mix the flour until it forms a smooth dough. Transfer the mixture to a baking dish and gently press the dough to cover the bottom.

Place the dish in the fryer basket and bake until golden, about 10 minutes. Remove the crust from the fryer basket and set aside to cool slightly.

Using medium saucepan on the stovetop over medium heat, combine the lemon juice and zest, coconut cream, the pinch of kosher salt, and the remaining ½ cup of sugar,. Whisk in the cornstarch and cook until thickened, about 5 minutes. Pour the lemon mixture over the crust.

Place the dish in the fryer basket and cook until the mixture is bubbly and almost completely set, about 10 to 12 minutes.

Remove the dish from the fryer basket and set aside to cool completely. Transfer the dish to the refrigerator for at least 4 hours. Dust with the powdered sugar and then slice into 6 bars before serving.

Nutrition:

Energy (calories): 241 kcal

Protein: 1.88 g

Fat: 16.15 g

Carbohydrates: 23.8 g

103. Peanut Butter Cookies

Preparation time: 10 minutes

Cooking time: 10 minutes

Servings: 18 cookies

Ingredients

1 tablespoon ground flaxseed

3 tablespoons water

1 cup creamy peanut butter

¾ cup light brown sugar

²/3 cup all-purpose flour

1 teaspoon baking soda

½ teaspoon kosher salt

Directions:

In a prepared small bowl, combine the flaxseed and water in a small bowl. Mix well and then set aside for 5 minutes.

Using another large bowl, combine the peanut butter and brown sugar. Add the flaxseed mixture, flour, baking soda, and salt. Mix until a soft dough forms. Refrigerate the dough, for at least 20 minutes.

Set the air fryer temp to 330°F (166°C). Spray the fryer basket using vegan nonstick cooking spray.

To roll the dough into 18 equally-sized balls, use a small scoop or tablespoon. Use a fork to press a diagonal hash mark into each ball.

Working in batches, place 9 balls in the fryer basket and cook until slightly golden, about 5 minutes.

Before it serves, move the cookies to a wire rack to cool.

Nutrition:
Energy (calories): 223 kcal
Protein: 5.83 g
Fat: 9.25 g
Carbohydrates: 28.78 g

104.   Peach and Cherry Pies

Preparation time: 30 minutes
Cooking time: 20 minutes
Servings: 12 pies
Ingredients
Dough:
2 cups self-rising flour
¼ cup all-vegetable shortening
¾ cup almond milk
Filling:
¼ cup sugar
1 tablespoon cornstarch
3½ cups diced fresh peaches
½ cup dried cherries
½ cup sliced almonds
1 tablespoon lemon juice
¼–½ cup all-purpose white flour for work surface
Oil for misting or cooking spray
Directions:
Pour the flour into a prepared large bowl and, using a pastry blender, cut the shortening into it. Stir in the almond milk until a soft dough forms and set aside.

In a separate bowl, stir the filling ingredients together and set aside.

Divide the dough into 12 equal-size portions and roll them into balls.

On a sheet of wax paper, sprinkle 1 tablespoon of flour.

On the wax paper with flour, roll one ball of dough out to a circle about 4½ to 5 inches in diameter. Use additional flour as needed to prevent the dough from sticking.

Place a heaping tablespoon of filling on the dough.

Using a pastry brush or using your finger dipped in water, moisten the inside edge of the dough all around.

Fold the dough to make a half-moon shape, press to seal it, and use a fork to crimp the edges shut.

Repeat steps 6 through 9 to make 3 more pies.

Mist both sides of the pies with oil or cooking spray and place in the air fryer basket.

Cook at 360°F (182°C) for 18 to 20 minutes, until the crust lightly browns.

Repeat steps 6–12 twice more to make the remaining pies.

Nutrition:
Energy (calories): 200 kcal
Protein: 2.86 g
Fat: 4.8 g
Carbohydrates: 37.79 g

105.   Peach Yogurt Pudding Cake

Preparation time: 10 minutes
Cooking time: 35 minutes
Servings: 8
Ingredients
1 (8-ounce / 227-g) can diced peaches packed in juice, drained
Oil for misting or cooking spray
¼ cup silken tofu
2 tablespoons water
1 cup self-rising flour
¼ teaspoon baking soda
½ cup sugar
2 tablespoons oil
1 (5.3-ounce / 150 g) container vegan peach yogurt
¼ cup almond milk
¼ teaspoon almond extract

Directions:

Preheat the air fryer to 330°F (166°C).

Place the drained peaches in a single layer on several layers of paper towels, and cover with more paper towels to eliminate the excess moisture.

Spray the air fryer baking pan with oil or cooking spray.

In a prepared medium bowl, using a wire whisk, mix the silken tofu with the water.

Add the remaining ingredients, including the peaches, and whisk until well mixed.

Pour the batter into the air fryer baking pan and cook for 35 minutes or if the toothpick is inserted into the center of the cake comes out clean.

Let the cake rest for 10 minutes before removing it from the baking pan.

Nutrition:

Energy (calories): 147 kcal

Protein: 2.25 g

Fat: 4.24 g

Carbohydrates: 25.2 g

106. Apple Crisp with Lemon

Preparation time: 10 minutes

Cooking time: 30 minutes

Servings: 4

Ingredients

The Topping:

2 tablespoons coconut oil

¼ cup plus 2 tablespoons of whole-wheat pastry flour (or gluten-free all-purpose flour)

¼ cup coconut sugar

1/8 teaspoon sea salt

The Filling:

2 cups finely chopped (or thinly sliced) apples (no need to peel)

3 tablespoons water

½ tablespoon lemon juice

¾ teaspoon cinnamon

Directions:

To Make the Topping

In a bowl, combine the oil, flour, sugar, and salt. Mix the ingredients together thoroughly, either with your hands or a spoon. The mixture should

be crumbly; if it's not, place it in the fridge until it solidifies a bit.

To Make the Filling

In a 6-inch round, 2-inch deep baking pan, stir the apples with the water, lemon juice, and cinnamon until well combined.

Crumble the chilled topping over the apples. Bake or cook for about 30 minutes, or until the apples are tender and the crumble is crunchy and nicely browned. Serve immediately on its own or topped with nondairy milk, vegan ice cream, or nondairy whipped cream.

Nutrition:

Energy (calories): 139 kcal

Protein: 0.96 g

Fat: 6.97 g

Carbohydrates: 19.65 g

107. Plum Cake

Preparation Time: 10 minutes

Cooking Time: 30 minutes

Servings: 8

Ingredients:

4 plums pitted and chopped.

1 ½ cups almond flour

½ cup coconut flour

¾ cup almond milk

½ cup vegan butter, soft

¾ cup Silken Tofu

½ cup swerve

1 tbsp. vanilla extract

2 tsp. baking powder

¼ tsp. almond extract

Directions:

Prepare a bowl and mix all the ingredients and whisk well.

Pour this into a cake pan that fits the air fryer after you've lined it with parchment paper, put the pan in the machine and cook at 370°F for 30 minutes.

Cool the cake down, slice and serve

Nutrition:

Calories: 183

Fat: 4g

Fiber: 3g

Carbs: 4g

Protein: 7g

108. Baked Plums

Preparation Time: 5 minutes
Cooking Time: 20 minutes
Servings: 6
Ingredients:
6 plums; cut into wedges
10 drops of stevia
Zest of 1 lemon, grated
2 tbsp. water
1 tsp. ginger, ground
½ tsp. cinnamon powder
Directions:
In a pan that fits the air fryer, combine the plums with the rest of the ingredients, toss gently.
Put the pan inside the air fryer and cook at 360°F for 20 minutes. Serve cold
Nutrition:
Calories: 170 Fat: 5g
Fiber: 1g Carbs: 3g
Protein: 5g

109. Chocolate Strawberry Cups

Preparation Time: 5 minutes
Cooking Time: 10 minutes
Servings: 8
Ingredients:
16 strawberries; halved
2 cups chocolate chips; melted
2 tbsp. coconut oil
Directions:
In a pan which fits your air fryer, mix the strawberries with the oil and the melted chocolate chips, toss gently, put the pan in the air fryer and cook at 340°F for 10 minutes.
Divide into cups and serve cold
Nutrition:
Calories: 162 Fat: 5g Fiber: 3g
Carbs: 5g Protein: 6g

110. Fried Banana Slices

Preparation Time: 15 minutes
Cooking Time: 15 minutes
Servings: 8
Ingredients:
4 medium peeled ripe bananas, cut into 4 pieces lengthwise
1/3 cup rice flour, divided
4 tbsp. cornflour
2 tbsp. desiccated coconut
½ tsp. baking powder
½ tsp. vegan ground cardamom
A pinch of salt
Directions:
Preheat the Air fryer to 390 o F and grease an Air fryer basket.
Mix coconut, two tbsp. of rice flour, cornflour, baking powder, cardamom, and salt in a shallow bowl. Stir in the water gradually and then mix until a smooth mixture is formed.
Place the remaining rice flour in a second bowl and dip it in the coconut mixture.
Dredge in the rice flour and arrange the banana slices into the Air fryer basket in a single layer.
Cook for about 15 minutes, flipping once in between and dish out onto plates to serve.
Nutrition:
Calories: 260
Fat: 6g
Carbohydrates: 51.2g
Sugar: 17.6g
Protein: 4.6g
Sodium: 49mg

111. Pumpkin Bars

Preparation Time: 10 minutes
Cooking Time: 25 minutes
Servings: 6
Ingredients:
¼ cup almond butter
1 tbsp. unsweetened almond milk
½ cup coconut flour
¾ tsp. baking soda
½ cup dark sugar-free chocolate chips, divided
1 cup canned sugar-free pumpkin puree
¼ cup swerve
1 tsp. cinnamon
1 tsp. vanilla extract
¼ tsp. nutmeg
½ tsp. ginger
1/8 tsp. salt
1/8 tsp. ground cloves
Directions:
Preheat the Air fryer to 360 o F and layer a baking pan with wax paper.

Mix pumpkin puree, swerve, vanilla extract, milk, and butter in a bowl.

Combine coconut flour, spices, salt, and baking soda in another bowl.

Put together the two mixtures and mix well until smooth.

Add about 1/3 cup of the sugar-free chocolate chips and transfer this mixture into the baking pan.

Transfer into the Air fryer basket and cook for about 25 minutes.

Microwave sugar-free chocolate bits on low heat and dish out the baked cake from the pan.

Top with melted chocolate and slice to serve.

Nutrition:

Calories: 249 Fat: 11.9g

Carbohydrates: 1.8g

Sugar: 0.3g

Protein: 5g Sodium: 79mg

112. Strawberry Cobbler Recipe

Preparation Time: 10 minutes

Cooking Time: 25 minutes

Servings: 6

Ingredients:

3/4 cup sugar

6 cups strawberries; halved

1/2 cup flour

1/8 tsp. baking powder

1/2 cup water

3 ½ tbsp. olive oil

1 tbsp. lemon juice

A pinch of baking soda

Coconut oil

Directions:

In a bowl, mix strawberries with half of the sugar, sprinkle some flour, add lemon juice, whisk and pour into the baking dish that fits your air fryer and greased with Coconut oil.

In another bowl, mix flour with the rest of the sugar, baking powder and soda and stir well

Add the olive oil and then mix until the whole thing with your hands

Add 1/2 cup water and spread over strawberries

Introduce in the fryer at 355°F and bake for 25 minutes. Leave cobbler aside to cool down, slice and serve.

Nutrition:

Energy (calories): 203 kcal

Protein: 2.05 g

Fat: 8.42 g

Carbohydrates: 31.66 g

113. Cranberry Jam

Preparation Time: 5 minutes

Cooking Time: 20 minutes

Servings: 8

Preparation Time: 25 minutes

Ingredients:

2 lbs. cranberries

4 oz. black currant

3 tbsp. water

2 lbs. sugar

Zest of 1 lime

Directions:

In a pan that fits exactly on your air fryer, add all the ingredients and stir.

Place the pan in the fryer and cook at 360°F for 20 minutes. Stir the jam well, divide into cups, refrigerate and serve cold

Nutrition:

Energy (calories): 513 kcal

Protein: 0.22 g Fat: 0.18 g

Carbohydrates: 131.11 g

114. Apple-Toffee Upside-Down Cake

Preparation Time: 5 minutes

Cooking Time: 30 minutes

Servings: 9

Ingredients

¼ cup almond butter

¼ cup sunflower oil

½ cup walnuts, chopped

¾ cup + 3 tbsp. coconut sugar

¾ cup of water

1 ½ tsp. mixed spice

1 cup plain flour

1 lemon, zest

1 tsp. baking soda

1 tsp. vinegar

3 baking apples, cored and sliced

Directions:

Preheat the air fryer to 3900F.

In a skillet, melt the almond butter and three tbsp. of sugar. Pour the mixture over a baking dish that will fit in the air fryer. Arrange the slices of apples on top. Set aside.

In a mixing bowl, combine flour, ¾ cup sugar, and baking soda. Add the mixed spice.

In another bowl, mix the sunflower oil, water, vinegar, and lemon zest. Stir in the chopped walnuts.

Combine the wet ingredients to the dry ingredients until well combined.

Pour over the tin with apple slices.

Bake and cook for about 30 minutes or until a toothpick inserted comes out clean.

Nutrition:

Calories: 335

Carbohydrates: 39.6g

Protein: 3.8g

Fat: 17.9g

115.   Yummy Banana Cookies

Preparation Time: 5 minutes

Cooking Time: 20 minutes

Servings: 6

Ingredients

1 cup dates, pitted and chopped

1 tsp. vanilla

1/3 cup vegetable oil

cups rolled oats

ripe bananas

Directions:

Preheat the air fryer to 3500F.

In a prepared bowl, mash the bananas and add in the rest of the ingredients.

Let it rest inside the fridge for 10 minutes.

Drop a tsp. on cut parchment paper.

Place the cookies on parchment paper inside the air fryer basket. Make sure that the cookies do not overlap. Cook for about 20 minutes or until the edges are crispy.

Serve with almond milk.

Nutrition:

Calories: 382

Carbohydrates: 50.14g

Protein: 6.54g

Fat: 17.2g

116.   Raspberry Wontons

Preparation Time: 20 minutes

Cooking Time: 16 minutes

Servings: 12

Ingredients

For Wonton Wrappers:

½ cup Coconut sugar

18 ounces vegan cheese, softened

1 tsp. vanilla extract

1 package of vegan wonton wrappers

For Raspberry Syrup:

¼ cup of water

¼ cup sugar

1: 12-ounce package frozen raspberries

1 tsp. vanilla extract

Directions:

For wrappers: in a bowl, add the sugar, vegan cheese, and vanilla extract and whisk until smooth.

Place a wonton wrapper onto a smooth surface.

Place one tbsp. of vegan cheese mixture in the center of each wrapper.

With wet fingers, fold wrappers around the filling and pinch the edges to seal.

Set the air fryer's temperature to 350 degrees F. Lightly grease an air fryer basket.

Arrange wonton wrappers into the prepared air fryer basket in 2 batches.

Air fry for about 8 minutes.

Meanwhile, for the syrup: in a medium skillet, add water, sugar, raspberries, and vanilla extract over medium heat and cook for about 5 minutes, stirring continuously.

Remove from the heat and set aside to cool slightly.

Transfer the mixture into the food processor and blend until smooth.

Remove the wontons from the air fryer and transfer them onto a platter.

Serve the wontons with a topping of raspberry syrup.

Nutrition:

Calories: 325 Carbohydrate: 39.6g

Protein: 7.1g Fat: 15.5g

Sugar: 15.4g Sodium: 343mg

117. Fruit Sandwich

Preparation Time: 10 minutes

Cooking Time: 10minutes

Servings: 2

 Ingredients

2 slices of sandwich

Green apple

Banana

Maple syrup

Directions:

Slicing the apple and the banana finely

Fry the apple (to caramelize) and slices of bread for 6 minutes in Air Fryer at 160°F.

To Plate: Serve up the sandwich with banana slices and caramelized apple. Bathe with Maple syrup.

Nutrition:

Energy (calories): 47 kcal

Protein: 0.24 g

Fat: 0.15 g

Carbohydrates: 12.57 g

118. Candy Apple

Preparation Time: 5 minutes

Cooking Time: 10 minutes

Servings: 2

Ingredients

Apple

Salt.

Brown sugar.

Apple vinegar

Directions:

Peel the apple, remove the seed and cut into segments.

Season with the other ingredients, place them in a metal mould varnished with a little oil and

bring to the Air Fryer for 5 minutes at 180 °C. It is stirred so that it cooks evenly.

Nutrition:

Energy (calories): 47 kcal

Protein: 0.24 g

Fat: 0.15 g

Carbohydrates: 12.57 g

119. Caramelized Bananas

Preparation Time: 10 minutes

Cooking Time: 60 minutes

Servings: 2

Ingredients

Ripe bananas.

½ cup of maple syrup

Cinnamon powder

A little water

Directions:

Cut the peeled banana into pieces. Place them in a small pot with a little olive oil and sprinkle with the ingredient—Fry in Air Fryer for 58 minutes at 180°C. Serve up with bread, rice or vegetables.

Nutrition:

Energy (calories): 378 kcal

Protein: 1.98 g

Fat: 0.95 g

Carbohydrates: 96.93 g

120. Banana Rolls

Preparation Time: 10 minutes

Cooking Time: 60 minutes

Servings: 4

 Ingredients

3 ripe bananas

Optional English sauce

Agaragar prepared in water

Wheat flour

1 onion

200gr of soy meat

Olives

Sweet pepper

Garlic

Dressing

Directions:

Hydrate the meat for 10 minutes. Drain very well. Peel and chop the bananas in half in two slices each. To part, marinate the meat and fry with the garlic. Add the other minced Ingredients to the meat. Form circles with the pieces and fix them with the chopsticks. Fill with the meat; let it rest a little so that the liquid comes out. Seal with egg and a little wheat flour. Place in the Air Fryer for 48 minutes at 180ºC. Watch the cooking. Turn, so it cooks evenly.

Nutrition:

Energy (calories): 53 kcal

Protein: 5.3 g

Fat: 0.38 g

Carbohydrates: 8.33 g

121.   Fried Omelet of Ripe Bananas

Preparation Time: 10 minutes

Cooking Time: 8-12 minutes

Servings: 6

Ingredients

6 Ripe bananas

1 Cup of wheat

Grated vegan hard cheese

Sugar

Cinnamon

Directions:

Process or grind bananas and knead with flour and cheese to taste. Add sugar and cinnamon powder to taste. Knead very well and shape with your hand—Fry in Air Fryer for 8-12 minutes at 180ºC. Halfway through the cooking, turn around to cook on both sides.

Nutrition:

Energy (calories): 68 kcal

Protein: 2.64 g

Fat: 0.5 g

Carbohydrates: 14.39 g

122.   Sweet Corn Pies

Preparation Time: 10 minutes

Cooking Time: 6-10 minutes

Servings: 2

 Ingredients

1 ¼ cup of bread flour

¾ cup of water.

½ cup of shredded or molasses paper

2 tsp. of sweet anise

½ tsp. of salt

Directions:

Place the flour, put water, and salt in a bowl. Mix well until the dough is compact. Little by little, the paper and anise are added. Knead well, and 12 balls are formed. It is a shaped, thin corn cake. Fry in Air Fryer for 6-10 minutes at 160ºC. They eat with coffee, tea, alone or to taste.

Nutrition:

Energy (calories): 561 kcal

Protein: 10.63 g

Fat: 1.84 g

Carbohydrates: 126.13 g

123.   Banana Pie

Preparation Time: 10 minutes

Cooking Time: 5-10 minutes

Servings: 3

 Ingredients

3 Ripe bananas

1/2 cup flour

Beans

Red pepper

Onion

Coriander

Oil

Water

Salt

Directions:

For the filling, prepare a pot with beans, red pepper, onion, coriander and some spices. In a pot of water with sugar, cook the bananas peeled and cut into cubes. When softened, remove and ultimately crush the bananas. Mix with the flour. Form some balls with the dough and mash them well. Place a portion of the filling in the center and close the tortilla. Seal the pie with your hands and place it in the Air Fryer. Fry for 5 -10 minutes at 180ºC. Serve up.

Nutrition:

Energy (calories): 97 kcal

Protein: 2.86 g

Fat: 0.32 g

Carbohydrates: 20.73 g

124. Apple Fritters

Preparation Time: 10 minutes
Cooking Time: 10-15 minutes
Servings: 2
Ingredients
2 large apples
200 grams of flour
Salt
A ¼ liter of cider or beer
1 tsp. olive oil
Sugar
Directions:
First, peel the apples and remove the seeds. Cut into rings and sprinkle sugar. Add the flour to a bowl and add salt, oil, and beer. Mix. Sprinkle the apples in the mixture and place them in the Air Fryer tray with butter paper. Fry for 10 -15 minutes at 180ºC. Add sugar and Serve up hot.
Nutrition:
Energy (calories): 500 kcal
Protein: 10.91 g
Fat: 3.61 g
Carbohydrates: 107.11 g

125. Fried Apples

Preparation Time: 5 minutes
Cooking Time: 6 minutes
Servings: 2
Ingredients
2 apples
2/3 cups cornstarch
1 spoon of sugar
1/8 tsp. of cinnamon
½ cup of caramel sauce
Directions:
Peel and cut the apples. Mix with the cornstarch. Fry in the Air Fryer for 6 minutes at 180ºC. Flip

to be cooked on both sides. Spray cinnamon and sugar when serving.
Nutrition:
Energy (calories): 277 kcal
Protein: 1.59 g 3% Fat: 0.44 g
Carbohydrates: 68.78 g

126. Banana Salad

Preparation Time: 10 minutes
Cooking Time: 6-10 minutes
Servings: 2
Ingredients
2 large green bananas cut into squares
8 sweet peppers cut in squares
1 hot pepper
½ cup fresh cut coriander
The juice of 5 lemon
½ cup of olive oil
1 tsp. salt
2 cloves garlic crushed
Pepper
Directions:
In the Air Fryer mould, place the bananas with salt and the juice of 1 lemon. Cover and program it at 140ºC for 6 -10 minutes. Take out and let cool. Mix in a salad bowl the cooked bananas, chilli, coriander and spicy to your taste. In another bowl, mix the juice of 4 lemons, garlic, oil, salt and pepper to taste. Add to the previously made salad and Serve up fresh, or Reserve up in the fridge.
Nutrition:
Energy (calories): 695 kcal
Protein: 6.37 g
Fat: 55.13 g
Carbohydrates: 55.45 g

127. Salad of Rice and Avocados

Preparation Time: 10 minutes
Cooking Time: 10-15 minutes
Servings: 4
Ingredients
2 avocados in slices
1 cup of rice
1 can of drained peas
2 spring onions julienne
1 cucumber

1 tablet of vegetable broth
1 carrot in small cubes
Stuffed Olives
Olive oil
Lemon juice
Salt, pepper, and water
Directions:
In the mould of the Air Fryer, add the rice, a little oil, and salt. Mix and program it at 180°C for 10- 15 minutes. Let cool. Mix pepper, oil, lemon juice and the shredded pill. Mix all together all the ingredients with the rice and add the vinaigrette. Serve up fresh.
Nutrition:
Energy (calories): 276 kcal
Protein: 6.74 g Fat: 21.18 g
Carbohydrates: 28.1 g

128.   Lemon Artichokes

Preparation Time: 10 minutes
Cooking Time: 12-18 minutes
Servings: 4
 Ingredients
6 artichokes
Olive oil
1 tablet of vegetable broth
Parsley finely cut
Pepper
Juice and leftovers of 1 lemon
Directions:
Remove the first layers of the artichoke and garnish with lemon. Grease the mould of the Air Fryer and place the artichokes. Bathe with oil, lemon juice, and the shredded pill. Schedule at 180°C for 12-18 minutes. Serve up hot.
Nutrition:
Energy (calories): 121 kcal
Protein: 8.21 g Fat: 0.42 g
Carbohydrates: 27.43 g

129.   Orange Lava Cake

Preparation time: 10 minutes
Cooking time: 20 minutes
Servings: 3
Ingredients:
One tbsp. flax meal combined with two tbsp. water

Four tbsp. coconut sugar
Two tbsp. olive oil
Four tbsp. almond milk
Four tbsp. whole wheat flour
One tbsp. cocoa powder
½ tsp. Baking powder
½ tsp. orange zest, grated
Directions:
In a bowl, mix flax meal with sugar, oil, milk, flour, cocoa powder, baking powder and orange zest, stir very well and pour this into a greased ramekin that fits your air fryer.
Add ramekin to your air fryer, cook at 320 degrees F for 20 minutes and serve warm.
Enjoy!
Nutrition:
Calories 191
Fat 7 g
Fiber 8g
Carbs 13g
Protein 4 g

130.   Cinnamon Apples

Preparation time: 10 minutes
Cooking time: 10 minutes
Servings: 4
Ingredients:
Two tsp. cinnamon powder
Five apples, cored and cut into chunks
½ tsp. nutmeg powder
One tbsp. maple syrup
½ cup of water
Four tbsp. vegetable oil
¼ cup whole wheat flour
¾ cup old-fashioned rolled oats
¼ cup of coconut sugar
Directions:
Put the apples in a pan that fits your air fryer, add cinnamon, nutmeg, maple syrup and water.
Add oil mixed with oats, sugar and flour, stir, spread on top of the apples, introduce in your air fryer, cook at 350 degrees F for 10 minutes and serve them warm.
Enjoy!
Nutrition:
Calories 180 Fat 6g Fiber 8g
Carbs 19g Protein 12g

131. Carrot and Pineapple Cinnamon Bread

Preparation time: 10 minutes
Cooking time: 45 minutes
Servings: 6
Ingredients:
5 ounces whole wheat flour
¾ tsp. baking powder
½ tsp. baking soda
½ tsp. cinnamon powder
¼ tsp. nutmeg, ground
One tbsp. flax meal combined with two tbsp. water
Three tbsp. coconut cream
½ cup of sugar
¼ cup pineapple juice
Four tbsp. sunflower oil
1/3 cup carrots, grated
1/3 cup pecans, toasted and chopped
1/3 cup coconut flakes, shredded
Cooking spray
Directions:
In a bowl, mix flour with baking soda and powder, salt, cinnamon, nutmeg, and stir.
In another bowl, mix the flax meal with coconut cream, sugar, pineapple juice, oil, carrots, pecans and coconut flakes and stir well.
Put together the two mixtures and stir well until combined, pour into a springform pan greased with cooking spray, move to your air fryer and cook at 320 degrees F for 45 minutes.
Leave the cake to cool down, cut and serve it.
Enjoy!
Nutrition:
Calories 180 Fat 6g
Fiber 2g
Carbs 12g
Protein 4 g

132. Cocoa and Coconut Bars

Preparation time: 10 minutes
Cooking time: 14 minutes
Servings: 12
Ingredients:
6 ounces coconut oil, melted
Three tbsp. Flax meal combined with three tbsp. water
3 ounces of cocoa powder
Two tsp. vanilla
½ tsp. baking powder
4 ounces coconut cream
Five tbsp. coconut sugar
Directions:
In a blender, mix the flax meal with oil, cocoa powder, baking powder, vanilla, cream and sugar and pulse.
Pour this into a lined baking dish that fits your air fryer, introduce in the fryer at 320 degrees F, bake for 14 minutes, slice into rectangles and serve.
Enjoy!
Nutrition:
Calories 178
Fat 14g
Fiber 2g
Carbs 12g
Protein 5 g

133. Vanilla Cake

Preparation time: 10 minutes
Cooking time: 25 minutes
Servings: 12
Ingredients:
Six tbsp. black tea powder
2 cups almond milk, heated
2 cups of coconut sugar
Three tbsp. Flax meal combined with three tbsp. water
Two tsp. vanilla extract
½ cup of vegetable oil
Three and ½ cups whole wheat flour
One tsp. baking soda
Three tsp. baking powder

Directions:

In a bowl, mix heated milk with tea powder, stir and leave aside for now.

In a larger bowl, mix the oil with sugar, flax meal, vanilla extract, baking powder, baking soda and flour and stir everything well.

Add tea and milk mix, stir well and pour into a greased cake pan.

Introduce in the fryer, cook at 330 degrees F for 25 minutes, leave aside to cool down, slice and serve it.

Enjoy!

Nutrition:

Calories 180 Fat 4g

Fiber 4g Carbs 6g Protein 2g

134.   Sweet Apple Cupcakes

Preparation time: 10 minutes

Cooking time: 20 minutes

Servings: 4

Ingredients:

Four tbsp. vegetable oil

Three tbsp. Flax meal combined with three tbsp. water

½ cup pure applesauce

Two tsp. cinnamon powder

One tsp. vanilla extract

One apple, cored and chopped

Four tsp. maple syrup

¾ cup whole wheat flour

½ tsp. baking powder

Directions:

Heat a pan put the vegetable oil over medium heat, add applesauce, vanilla, flax meal, maple syrup, stir, take off the heat and cool down.

Add flour, cinnamon, baking powder and apples, whisk, pour into a cupcake pan, introduce in your air fryer at 350 degrees F and bake for 20 minutes.

Transfer cupcakes to a platter and serve them warm.

Enjoy!

Nutrition:

Calories 200 Fat 3g

Fiber 1g

Carbs 5g

Protein 4g

135.   Orange Bread with Almonds

Preparation time: 20 minutes

Cooking time: 40 minutes

Servings: 8

Ingredients:

One orange, peeled and sliced

Juice of 2 oranges

Three tbsp. vegetable oil

Two tbsp. flax meal combined with two tbsp. water

¾ cup coconut sugar+ 2 tbsp.

¾ cup whole wheat flour

¾ cup almonds, ground

Directions:

Grease a loaf pan with some oil, sprinkle two tbsp. of sugar and arrange orange slices on the bottom.

In a bowl, mix the oil with ¾ cup sugar, almonds, flour and orange juice, stir, spoon this over orange slices, place the pan in your air fryer and cook at 360 degrees F for 40 minutes.

Slice and serve the bread right away.

Enjoy!

Nutrition:

Calories 202

Fat 3g

Fiber 2g

Carbs 6g

Protein 6g

136.   Tangerine Cake

Preparation time: 10 minutes

Cooking time: 20 minutes

Servings: 8

Ingredients:

¾ cup of coconut sugar

2 cups whole wheat flour

¼ cup olive oil

½ cup almond milk

One tsp. cider vinegar

½ tsp. vanilla extract

Juice and zest of 2 lemons

Juice and zest of 1 tangerine

Directions:

In a prepared bowl, mix flour with sugar and stir.

In another bowl, mix oil with milk, vinegar, vanilla extract, lemon juice and zest, tangerine zest and flour, whisk very well, pour this into a cake pan that fits your air fryer, introduce in the fryer and cook at 360 degrees F for 20 minutes. Serve right away.

Enjoy!

Nutrition:

Calories 210

Fat 1g

Fiber 1g

Carbs 6g

Protein 4g

137. Maple Tomato Bread

Preparation time: 10 minutes

Cooking time: 30 minutes

Servings: 4

Ingredients:

One and ½ cups whole wheat flour

One tsp. cinnamon powder

One tsp. baking powder

One tsp. baking soda

¾ cup maple syrup

1 cup tomatoes, chopped

½ cup olive oil

Two tbsp. apple cider vinegar

Directions:

In a bowl, mix flour with baking powder, baking soda, cinnamon and maple syrup and stir well.

In another bowl, mix tomatoes with olive oil and vinegar and stir well.

Combine the two mixtures, stir well, pour into a greased loaf pan that fits your air fryer, introduce in the fryer and cook at 360 degrees F for 30 minutes.

Leave the cake to cool down, slice and serve.

Enjoy!

Nutrition:

Calories 203 Fat 2g

Fiber 1g Carbs 12g Protein 4 g

138. Lemon Squares

Preparation time: 10 minutes

Cooking time: 30 minutes

Servings: 6

Ingredients:

1 cup whole wheat flour

½ cup of vegetable oil

One and ¼ cups of coconut sugar

One medium banana

Two tsp. lemon peel, grated

Two tbsp. lemon juice

Two tbsp. Flax meal combined with two tbsp. water

½ tsp. baking powder

Directions:

In a bowl, mix flour with ¼ cup sugar and oil, stir well, press on the bottom of a pan that fits your air fryer, introduce in the fryer and bake at 350 degrees F for 14 minutes.

In another prepared bowl, mix the rest of the sugar with lemon juice, lemon peel, banana, baking powder, stir using your mixer and spread over baked crust.

Bake for 15 minutes more, leave aside to cool down, cut into medium squares and serve cold.

Enjoy!

Nutrition:

Calories 140

Fat 4g

Fibre 1g

Carbs 12g

Protein 1g

139. Dates and Cashew Sticks

Preparation time: 10 minutes

Cooking time: 15 minutes

Servings: 6

Ingredients:

1/3 cup stevia

¼ cup almond meal

One tbsp. almond butter

One and ½ cups cashews, chopped

Four dates, chopped

¾ cup coconut, shredded

One tbsp. chia seeds

Directions:

In a bowl, mix stevia with almond meal, almond butter, cashews, coconut, dates and chia seeds and stir well again.

Spread this on a lined baking sheet that fits your air fryer, press well, introduce in the fryer and cook at 300 degrees F for 15 minutes.

Leave the mix to cool down, cut into medium sticks and serve.

Enjoy!

Nutrition:

Calories 162

Fat 4g

Fibre 7g

Carbs 5g

Protein 6g

140. Grape Pudding

Preparation time: 10 minutes

Cooking time: 40 minutes

Servings: 6

Ingredients:

1 cup grapes curd

3 cups grapes

Three and ½ ounces maple syrup

Three tbsp. Flax meal combined with three tbsp. water

2 ounces coconut butter, melted

Three and ½ ounces of almond milk

½ cup almond flour

½ tsp. baking powder

Directions:

In a bowl, mix half of the fruit curd with the grapes, stir and divide into six heatproof ramekins.

In a prepared bowl, mix the flax meal with maple syrup, melted coconut butter, the rest of the curd, baking powder, milk and flour and stir well. Divide this into the ramekins and introduce in the fryer and cook at 200 degrees F for 40 minutes.

Leave puddings to cool down and serve!

Enjoy!

Nutrition:

Calories 230

Fat 22g

Fibre 3g

Carbs 17g

Protein 8 g

141. Coconut and Pumpkin Seeds Bars

Preparation time: 10 minutes

Cooking time: 35 minutes

Servings: 4

Ingredients:

1 cup coconut, shredded

½ cup almonds

½ cup pecans, chopped

Two tbsp. coconut sugar

½ cup pumpkin seeds

½ cup sunflower seeds

Two tbsp. sunflower oil

One tsp. nutmeg, ground

One tsp. pumpkin pie spice

Directions:

In a bowl, mix almonds and pecans with pumpkin seeds, sunflower seeds, coconut, nutmeg and pie spice and stir well.

Heat a pan put the sunflower oil over medium heat, add sugar, stir well, pour this over nuts and coconut mix and stir well.

Spread this on a lined baking sheet that fits your air fryer, introduce in your air fryer and cook at 300 degrees F and bake for 25 minutes.

Leave the mix aside to cool down, cut and serve.

Enjoy!

Nutrition:

Calories 252

Fat 7g

Fibre 8g

Carbs 12g

Protein 7g

142. Cinnamon Bananas

Preparation time: 10 minutes

Cooking time: 15 minutes

Servings: 4

Ingredients:

Three tbsp. coconut butter

Two tbsp. flax meal combined with two tbsp. water

Eight bananas, peeled and halved

½ cup of cornflour

Three tbsp. cinnamon powder

1 cup vegan breadcrumbs

Directions:

Heat a pan with the butter over medium-high heat, add breadcrumbs, stir and cook for 4 minutes and then transfer to a bowl.

Roll each banana in flour, flax meal and breadcrumbs mix.

Arrange bananas in your air fryer's basket, dust with cinnamon sugar and cook at 280 degrees F for 10 minutes.

Transfer to plates and serve.

Enjoy!

Nutrition:

Calories 214

Fat 1g

Fibre 4g

Carbs 12g

Protein 4 g

143. Coffee Pudding

Preparation time: 10 minutes

Cooking time: 10 minutes

Servings: 4

Ingredients:

4 ounces coconut butter

4 ounces dark vegan chocolate, chopped

Juice of ½ orange

One tsp. baking powder

2 ounces whole wheat flour

½ tsp. instant coffee

Two tbsp. Flax meal combined with two tbsp. water

2 ounces of coconut sugar

Directions:

Heat a pan with the coconut butter over medium heat, add chocolate and orange juice, stir well and take off the heat.

In a bowl, mix sugar with instant coffee and flax meal, beat using your mixer, add chocolate mix, flour, salt, baking powder, and stir well.

Pour this into a greased pan, introduce in your air fryer, cook at 360 degrees F for about 10 minutes, divide between plates and serve.

Enjoy!

Nutrition:

Calories 189 Fat 6g

Fibre 4g Carbs 14g

Protein 3 g

144. Blueberry Cake

Preparation time: 10 minutes

Cooking time: 30 minutes

Servings: 6

Ingredients:

½ cup whole wheat flour

¼ tsp. baking powder

¼ tsp. stevia

¼ cup blueberries

1/3 cup almond milk

One tsp. olive oil

One tsp. flaxseed, ground

½ tsp. lemon zest, grated

¼ tsp. vanilla extract

¼ tsp. lemon extract

Cooking spray

Directions:

In a bowl, mix flour with baking powder, stevia, blueberries, milk, oil, flaxseeds, lemon zest, vanilla extract and lemon extract and whisk well.

Spray a cake pan with cooking spray, line it with parchment paper, pour cake batter, introduce in the fryer and cook at 350 degrees F for 30 minutes.

Leave the cake to cool down, slice and serve.

Enjoy!

Nutrition:

Calories 210Fat 4gFibre 4g Carbs 10g

Protein 4g

145. Peach Cinnamon Cobbler

Preparation time: 10 minutes

Cooking time: 30 minutes

Servings: 4

Ingredients:

4 cups peaches, peeled and sliced

¼ cup of coconut sugar

½ tsp. cinnamon powder

One and ½ cups vegan crackers, crushed

¼ cup stevia

¼ tsp. nutmeg, ground

½ cup almond milk

One tsp. vanilla extract

Cooking spray

Directions:

In a bowl, mix peaches with coconut sugar and cinnamon and stir.

In a separate bowl, mix crackers with stevia, nutmeg, almond milk and vanilla extract and stir.

Spray a pie pan that fits your air fryer with cooking spray and spread peaches on the bottom.

Add crackers mix, spread, introduce into the fryer and cook at 350 degrees F for 30 minutes

Divide the cobbler between plates and serve.

Enjoy!

Nutrition:

Calories 201

Fat 4g

Fibre 4g

Carbs 7g

Protein 3g

146.   Easy Pears Dessert

Preparation time: 10 minutes

Cooking time: 25 minutes

Servings: 12

Ingredients:

Six big pears, cored and chopped

½ cup raisins

One tsp. ginger powder

¼ cup of coconut sugar

One tsp. lemon zest, grated

Directions:

In a pan that exactly on your air fryer, mix pears with raisins, ginger, sugar and lemon zest, stir, introduce in the fryer and cook at 350 degrees F for 25 minutes.

Divide into bowls and serve cold.

Enjoy!

Nutrition:

Calories 200 Fat 3g

Fibre 4g Carbs 6g

Protein 6g

147.   Vanilla Strawberry Mix

Preparation time: 10 minutes

Cooking time: 20 minutes

Servings: 10

Ingredients:

Two tbsp. lemon juice

2 pounds of strawberries

4 cups of coconut sugar

One tsp. cinnamon powder

One tsp. vanilla extract

Directions:

In a pan that exactly on your air fryer, mix strawberries with coconut sugar, lemon juice, cinnamon and vanilla, stir gently, introduce in the fryer and cook at 350 degrees F for 20 minutes

Divide into bowls and serve cold.

Enjoy!

Nutrition:

Calories 140

Fat 0g

Fibre 1g

Carbs 5g

Protein 2g

148.   Sweet Bananas and Sauce

Preparation time: 10 minutes

Cooking time: 20 minutes

Servings: 2

Ingredients:

Juice of ½ lemon

3 tbsp. agave nectar

1 tbsp. coconut oil

4 bananas, peeled and sliced diagonally

½ tsp. cardamom seeds

Directions:

Arrange bananas in a pan that fits your air fryer, add agave nectar, lemon juice, oil and cardamom, introduce in the fryer and cook at 360 degrees F for 20 minutes

Divide bananas and sauce between plates and serve.

Enjoy!

Nutrition:

calories 210 Fat 1g

Fiber 2g Carbs 8g

Protein 3g

149. Vegan Air Fryer Blueberry Apple Crumble

Preparation Time: 10 minutes

Cooking Time: 20 minutes

Servings: 4

Ingredients

1 medium apple, finely diced

½ cup frozen blueberries, strawberries, or peaches

¼ cup plus one tbsp. brown rice flour

2 tbsp. sugar

½ tsp. ground cinnamon

2 tbsp. non-dairy butter

Directions:

Preheat the air fryer set 5 minutes to 350 ° F. Mix the apple and frozen blueberries in a healthy baking pan or ramekin air fryer.

In a prepared small bowl, combine the flour, sugar, cinnamon, and butter. Spoon the flour mixture over the fruit. Sprinkle a little extra flour over everything to cover any exposed fruit— Cook at 350°F for 15 minutes.

Nutrition:

Energy (calories): 128 kcal

Protein: 2.18 g Fat: 4.43 g

Carbohydrates: 21.7 g

150. Vegan Pumpkin Bread Pudding

Preparation Time: 10 minutes

Cooking Time: 50 minutes

Servings: 4

Ingredients

1 16 ounces loaf French bread

½ cup raisins

1 ½ cup of soymilk or other non-dairy milk vanilla or plain

1 cup of pumpkin canned or cooked and pureed

¼ cup maple syrup

¼ cup dark brown sugar

1 tbsp. Ener-G Egg Replacer may substitute 2 ½ tsp. Starch (tapioca, potato, or corn starch) plus ½ tsp. baking powder

2 tsp. vanilla extract

1 ½ tsp. cinnamon

½ tsp. ginger powder

½ tsp. nutmeg

¼ tsp. allspice

1/8 tsp. ground cloves

¼ tsp. salt optional

Sauce

½ cup apple cider or juice

¼ cup maple syrup

1 tsp. cornstarch mixed with one tbsp. apple juice

1 ½ tbsp. brandy, rum, or bourbon add to taste up to ¼ cup

¼ cup chopped pecans or walnuts optional

Directions:

Cut or slice the bread into bite-sized pieces. If the bread looks moist or dense, spread it out on a cookie sheet and toast it for a few minutes in the oven. Place it in a large bowl and add the raisins.

Put the non-dairy milk into the blender along with the pumpkin, maple syrup, sugar, Ener-G, vanilla, spices, and salt. Blend until smooth. Pour it over the bread, using a silicone spatula to get out every drop. Stir well to coat all of the bread thoroughly. Set aside then soak for a few minutes while you ready the pan and preheat the oven.

Preheat oven to 350F. Line an 8x8-inch baking dish with parchment paper or foil lightly. Pour the bread pudding into the pan in an even layer. Bake for about 45 minutes or until the top is set and beginning to brown. Remove from oven and allow cooling for at least 15 minutes.

While the pudding is cooling, make the sauce. Place the apple cider and the maple syrup in a small saucepan over medium heat, and bring to a simmer, often stirring, until reduced to about half.

Carefully add the cornstarch mixture, bring it to a boil, and cook for another couple of minutes, continually stirring until the mix is no longer cloudy and thickens slightly. Remove from heat and add the brandy or other spirits a little at a time, to taste. Stir in the nuts. Poke a few holes in the top of the bread pudding with a toothpick, and pour the sauce over the top, distributing nuts evenly. Cut into squares and serve warm.

Nutrition:

Energy (calories): 1579 kcal

Protein: 21.89 g Fat: 102.42 g

Carbohydrates: 102.05 g

151.   Cranberry-Carrot Cake

Preparation Time: 10 minutes
Cooking Time: 40 minutes
Servings: 4
Ingredients
8-10 ounces fresh cranberries
1/3 cup natural granulated sugar
1 ¾ cups whole wheat pastry flour (or white whole wheat flour)
2 tbsp. ground flaxseeds
1 tsp. baking powder
½ tsp. baking soda
½ tsp. ground ginger
½ tsp. cinnamon
½ cup applesauce
1/3 cup maple syrup
2 tbsp. (liquid from canned or cooked chickpeas) aquafaba or plant milk of choice
1 tsp. vanilla extract
1 cup of grated carrot
Maple-Cream Cheese frosting optional (see recipe in Notes)
1/3 cup finely chopped walnuts optional
Confectioner's sugar optional
Directions:
Place the cranberries in a blade-fitted food processor and pulse on and off until chopped evenly and finely. Switch to a tub. Add the sugar, whisk thoroughly, and set aside.
Preheat oven to 350F.
In a large mixing bowl, combine the flour, flaxseeds, baking powder, baking soda, ginger, and cinnamon. Stir to combine thoroughly.
Make a hole in the center then add the applesauce, syrup, aquafaba/plant milk, and vanilla. Stir until the wet and dry ingredients are thoroughly combined, but don't over mix. Stir the batter with the cranberries and carrots.
Pour into a 9-inch circular cake pan with silicone. Springform pan or lightly oiled pan (see headnote). Bake for 35 to 40 minutes, or until the knife comes out clean inserted in the middle.
If using the walnuts, toast them in a small dry skillet over medium heat until they brown lightly.
If you have used a springform or other easy-to-release pan, release the pan once the cake has cooled to room temperature and spread the frosting evenly over the surface, allowing it to drip over the sides. Otherwise, in the pan, leave the cake and simply frost the top.
(If you don't wish to use the frosting, you can sprinkle the top with confectioners' sugar or just serve it plain.) With the optional walnuts, sprinkle evenly and then cut into wedges to serve.
Nutrition:
Energy (calories): 416 kcal
Protein: 9.37 g
Fat: 8.22 g
Carbohydrates: 81.3 g

152.   Vegan Gluten-Free Peach Cobbler

Preparation Time: 10 minutes
Cooking Time: 40 minutes
Servings: 4
Ingredients
Peaches
2 pounds peaches (about five large)
1 tsp. lemon juice
2 tbsp. sugar
¼ tsp. cinnamon optional
Dry
1 cup gluten-free baking flour blend
½ cup sugar
2 tbsp. tapioca starch (also called tapioca flour)
1 tbsp. baking powder
Pinch salt
Wet
¾ cup soy milk or other non-dairy milk
½ tsp. vanilla extract
Directions:
Bring several inches of water and let it boil in a large saucepan. Use a slotted spoon to lower each peach into the boiling water for about 20 seconds. Place on a cutting board or plate and set aside to cool. (This makes the peaches easy to peel.)
When the peaches are cool enough, peel them by piercing the skin with a knife and pulling it off. Slice the peaches into a large bowl. Add the lemon juice, two tbsp. Of sugar and cinnamon, if desired.

Preheat Air fryer set to 375 degrees F. Arrange the peaches in a deep 9-inch pie pan.

Mix the dry ingredients. Then add the wet ingredients, and stir just enough to eliminate large lumps. Pour over the peaches.

Bake for 35-45 minutes, covering loosely with aluminum foil if the top begins to get too brown. It's done with you can stick a toothpick in the middle and not have batter attached to it.

Allow cooling for a few minutes before serving.

Nutrition:

Energy (calories): 745 kcal

Protein: 6.81 g

Fat: 58.71 g

Carbohydrates: 51.99 g

153.   Apple Pie Oatmeal Cookies

Preparation Time: 10 minutes

Cooking Time: 30 minutes

Servings: 4

Ingredients

2 tsp. chia seeds or ground flax seeds

4 tbsp. of warm water

2 cup of regular or quick oats (use certified gluten-free if necessary)

¼ cup raisins

1 ½ tsp. pumpkin pie spice see Notes

½ tsp. baking soda

½ tsp. salt optional

1 large apple cored and chopped

2 ounces pitted and chopped dates (about four medjool dates or ¼ cup packed chopped dates)

1/8 cup water

1 tsp. apple cider vinegar

Directions:

Preheat the oven to 375.

In a prepared small bowl, combine the chia seeds (or ground flaxseed) with the warm water and set aside until thickened.

In a dry blender or food processor, grind one cup of the oats. Pour it into a mixing bowl and add the unground oats, pumpkin pie spice, baking soda, and salt. Stir in the raisins.

Place the apple, dates, 1/8 cup water, and apple cider vinegar in the blender. Blend until the consistency of apple sauce is about it. Pour it

together with the chia "egg" or egg replacer flax egg into the oat mixture and whisk to blend.

Fall through the rounded tbsp. Onto a baking sheet lined with parchment paper or a silicon mat. With a fork, flatten each cookie slightly. For about 12 minutes, bake. Until serving, cool on a wire rack.

Nutrition:

Energy (calories): 225 kcal

Protein: 5.86 g

Fat: 2.87 g

Carbohydrates: 46.23 g

154.   Pumpkin Oatmeal Cakes with Apple-Pecan Compote

Preparation Time: 10 minutes

Cooking Time: 30 minutes

Servings: 4

Ingredients

2 cups water

½ cup chopped dates about 3 ounces

¾ cups canned pumpkin

¾ tsp. cinnamon

¼ tsp. allspice

¼ tsp. powdered ginger

½ tsp. salt

1 tbsp. ground flaxseed

1 ½ cups steel-cut oats

1 ¼ cup plain coconut milk (the drinking kind, not canned) or other non-dairy milk

non-stick spray

Directions:

In a blender, put the water and dates and blend until the dates are finely chopped. Add the pumpkin, herbs, flaxseed and salt and blend until well mixed.

Heat a large saucepan and toast the oats, stirring periodically, for 1-2 minutes, until fragrant. The pumpkin mixture is carefully applied, standing back in case it spatters, and then the coconut milk. Stir well, reduce the heat to medium, and cook for about 30 minutes or until thick and chewy, stirring frequently.

Line an 11×7-inch baking dish with parchment paper or spray with non-stick spray. Spread the oats in the container, smoothing the top. Cool on the counter for one hour and then refrigerate until thoroughly chilled, at least an hour. Put onto a cutting board and cut into 16 triangles or rectangles.

Spray into a large non-stick frying pan with a light coating of vegan cooking spray and heat over medium-high heat. Add half of the oatmeal cakes and cook on each side until lightly browned, 2-3 minutes per side. Remove to a warm oven and repeat with the remaining patties. Keep warm until ready to serve.

Place two cakes on each dessert plate. Top with warm Apple-Pecan Compote, below.

Nutrition:
Energy (calories): 453 kcal
Protein: 15.37 g
Fat: 32.39 g
Carbohydrates: 45.8 g

155. Peach Oatmeal Bars

Preparation Time: 10 minutes
Cooking Time: 20 minutes
Servings: 4
Ingredients
2 cups old fashioned or rolled oats
¼ cup chopped dates
2 tbsp. chopped almonds
1 tbsp. chia seed or ground flax seeds
1 tsp. baking powder
1 tsp. cinnamon
1/8 tsp. pure stevia extract powder optional
¾ cup plus two tbsp. non-dairy milk I used vanilla soymilk
2 peaches about one ¼ cups, peeled and diced
1 tsp. vanilla
¼ tsp. almond extract
Directions:
Preheat oven to 350F. Line an 8×8- or 9×9-inch baking pan with parchment paper (this makes sure they don't stick and makes clean-up a breeze).

Combine dry ingredients (oats through stevia) in a large bowl. In a medium bowl, combine the remaining ingredients. Stir the wet ingredients into the dry, making sure that they are thoroughly combined. Spread into prepared pan. Bake for about 25 minutes. If you'd like a crunchier top, put the pan under the broiler for a

minute or two, observing to make sure they don't burn.

Remove from oven and allow to cool for at least 15 minutes. Remove from pan by lifting parchment paper. Cut into nine squares and enjoy.

Nutrition:
Energy (calories): 295 kcal
Protein: 10.76 g
Fat: 5.11 g
Carbohydrates: 72.51 g

156. Applesauce Ginger Cake with Maple Glaze

Preparation Time: 10 minutes
Cooking Time: 40 minutes
Servings: 4
Ingredients:
2 cups of white whole wheat flour or whole wheat pastry flour
1 cup sugar
2 tbsp. crystallized (candied) ginger, chopped small (about ¾ ounce)
1 tbsp. cornstarch
2 tsp. baking soda
1 ½ tsp. ginger powder
½ tsp. salt
½ tsp. cinnamon
1/8 tsp. cloves
2 ¼ cups unsweetened applesauce
1 tbsp. lemon juice
1 tsp. vanilla extract
Glaze
¼ cup maple syrup
1 tsp. cornstarch
1 pinch ginger powder
Additional candied ginger for serving optional
Directions:
Preheat oven at temperature of 350 degrees F. Lightly oil a bundt pan or 9×9-inch baking pan.

Mix all the dry ingredients; then add the applesauce, lemon juice, and vanilla extract. Stir until combined but don't over-stir. Pour into a pan and then bake for 45-60 minutes. By inserting a toothpick into the center test it; it's done when the toothpick comes out perfectly clean.

Remove from air fryer oven and let it cool for 10 minutes. Invert onto a cake dish.

Prepare the glaze: Combine the maple syrup, one tsp. cornstarch, and a generous pinch of powdered ginger in a small saucepan and mix well. Bring and let it boil over medium-high heat, continuously stirring. 1 minute to simmer. Remove from heat and allow to thicken and cool. (In order to speed up the cooling, you should put the pan in a bowl of cold water.)

When the glaze has thickened but is still pourable, drizzle it over the cake. Serve immediately, garnished with strips, if desired, of candied ginger.

Nutrition:

Energy (calories): 451 kcal

Protein: 6.8 g

Fat: 0.8 g

Carbohydrates: 105.08 g

CHAPTER 10:

Vegan Dessert

157. Vanilla Cupcakes

Preparation Time: 5 minutes
Cooking Time: 15 minutes
Servings: 4
Ingredients:
2 cups wheat flour
1 ½ cup almond milk
½ tsp. baking powder
½ tsp. baking soda
2 tbsp. butter
1 tbsp. maple syrup
3 tbsp. vanilla extract
2 tsp. vinegar
muffin cups
Directions:
Combine the Ingredients: except milk to create a crumbly blend. Add this milk to the mixture and make a batter and pour into the muffin cups. Preheat the fryer to 300 F and cook for 15 minutes.
Check whether they are done using a toothpick.
Nutrition:
Calories 161 Fat 5.6g Protein 7.2g

158. Delectable Pear Muffins

Preparation Time: 5 minutes
Cooking Time: 15 minutes
Servings: 4
Ingredients:
2 cups All-purpose flour

1 ½ cup almond milk
½ tsp. baking powder
½ tsp. baking soda
2 tbsp. vegan butter
2 tbsp. sugar
2 cups sliced pears
muffin cups
Directions:
Combine the Ingredients: except milk to create a crumbly blend. Add this milk to the mixture and make a batter and pour into the muffin cups. Preheat the fryer to 300 F and cook for 15 minutes.
Check whether they are done using a toothpick.
Nutrition:
Calories 114
Fat 4.8g
Protein 6.1g

159. Mini Rosemary Cornbread

Preparation Time: 15 minutes
Cooking Time: 25 minutes
Servings: 6
Ingredients:
¾ cup fine yellow cornmeal
½ cup sorghum flour
¼ cup tapioca starch
½ tsp. xanthan gum
2 tsp. baking powder
¼ cup granulated sugar
¼ tsp. salt
1 cup plain almond milk
3 tbsp. olive oil
2 tsp. fresh rosemary, minced
Directions:
In a prepared large bowl, mix the flour, cornmeal, starch, sugar, xanthan gum, baking powder, and salt.

Add the almond milk, oil, and rosemary. Mix until well combined.

Put the mixture into four greased ramekins evenly.

Press the "Power Button" of the Air Fry Oven and turn the dial to select the "Air Fry" mode.

Press the Time button and set the cooking time to 25 minutes.

Now push the Temp button and rotate the dial to set the temperature at 400 degrees F.

Press the "Start/Pause" button to start.

When the unit beeps to show that it is preheated, open the lid.

Arrange the pan in "Air Fry Basket" and insert it in the oven.

Place the ramekins onto a wire rack for about 10-15 minutes.

Carefully invert the bread onto a wire rack to cool completely before serving.

Nutrition:

Calories 220 Total Fat 8.5 g Carbs 35.5 g Fiber 2.8 g Sugar 8.6 g Protein 2.8 g

160.   Carrot Mug Cake

Preparation Time: 15 minutes
Cooking Time: 20 minutes
Serving: 1
Ingredients:
¼ cup whole-wheat pastry flour
1 tbsp. coconut sugar
¼ tsp. baking powder
1/8 tsp. ground cinnamon
1/8 tsp. ground ginger
Pinch of ground cloves
Pinch of ground allspice
Pinch of salt
2 tbsp. plus two tsp. unsweetened almond milk
2 tbsp. carrot, peeled and grated
2 tbsp. walnuts, chopped
1 tbsp. raisins
2 tsp. applesauce
Directions:
In a prepared bowl, mix the flour, sugar, baking powder, spices and salt.

Add the remaining ingredients and mix until well combined.

Place the mixture into a lightly greased ramekin.

Press the "Power Button" of Air Fry Oven and turn the dial to select the "Air Bake" mode.

Press the Time button and turn the dial to set the cooking time to 20 minutes.

Now push the Temp button and rotate the dial to set the temperature at 350 degrees F.

Press the "Start/Pause" button to start.

When the unit beeps to show that it is preheated, open the lid.

Arrange the ramekin over the "Wire Rack" and insert in the oven.

Place the ramekin onto a wire rack to cool slightly before serving.

Nutrition:

Calories 301 Total Fat 10.1 g Total Carbs 48.6 g Fiber 3.2 g Sugar 19.4 g Protein 7.6 g

161.   Simple Basil Tomatoes

Preparation Time: 10 minutes
Cooking Time: 10 minutes
Servings: 2
Ingredients:
3 tomatoes
Olive oil cooking spray
Salt and pepper to taste
1 tbsp. fresh basil, chopped
Directions:
Cut tomatoes in halves and drizzle them generously with cooking spray

Sprinkle salt, pepper, and basil

Press "Power Button" on your Air Fryer and select "Air Fry" mode

Press the Time Button and set time to 20 minutes

Push Temp Button and set temp to 320 degrees F

Press the "Start/Pause" button and start the device

Once the appliance beeps to indicated that it is pre-heated, arrange tomatoes in the Air Fryer cooking basket, let them cook

Once done, serve warm and enjoy!

Nutrition:

Calories: 34 Fat: 0.4 g Saturated Fat: 0.1 g
Carbohydrates: 7 g Fiber: 2 g
Sodium: 87 mg
Protein: 1.7 g

162. Cumin and Squash Chili

Preparation Time: 10 minutes
Cooking Time: 16 minutes
Servings: 4
Ingredients:
1 medium butternut squash
2 tsp. cumin seeds
1 large pinch chili flakes
1 tbsp. olive oil
1 and ½ ounces pine nuts
1 small bunch fresh coriander, chopped
Directions:
Take the squash and slice it
Remove seeds and cut into smaller chunks
Take a bowl and add chunked squash, spice and oil
Mix well
Pre-heat your Fryer to 360 degrees F and add the squash to the cooking basket in "AIR FRY" mode
Roast for 20 minutes, making sure to shake the basket from time to time to avoid burning
Take a pan and place it over medium heat, add pine nuts to the pan and dry toast for 2 minutes
Sprinkle nuts on top of the squash and serve
Enjoy!
Nutrition:
Calories: 339 Fat: 4 g
Saturated Fat: 1 g Carbohydrates: 40 g
Fiber: 17 g
Sodium: 525 mg
Protein: 17 g

163. Dates Pudding

Preparation Time: 5 minutes
Cooking Time: 10 minutes
Servings:
Ingredients:
3 tbsp. Coconut sugar
2 tbsp. custard powder
3 tbsp. unsalted butter
1 cup pitted and sliced dates
1 tbsp. sugar
Directions:
Boil the milk and sugar in a pan and add the icing cream, followed by the dates and mix until you get a thick mixture. Add the sliced fruit to the mixture—Preheat the fryer to 300 degrees Fahrenheit for five minutes. Put the dish in the basket and reduce the temperature to 250 degrees Fahrenheit. Cook for ten minutes and let cool.
Nutrition:
Calories 122
Fat 4.6g
Protein 6.3g

164. Mini Lava Cakes

Preparation Time: 10 minutes
Cooking Time: 20 minutes
Servings: 3
Ingredients:
¼ cup Vegan Buttermilk
Four tbsp. sugar
Two tbsp. olive oil
Four tbsp. almond milk
Four tbsp. flour
One tbsp. cocoa powder
½ tsp. baking powder
½ tsp. orange zest
Directions:
In a bowl, mix the flax egg with sugar, oil, milk, flour, salt, cocoa powder, baking powder and orange zest, stir very well and pour this into greased ramekins.
Add ramekins to your air fryer and cook at 320 degrees F for 20 minutes.
Serve lava cakes warm.
Enjoy!
Nutrition:
Calories 201
Fat 7
Fiber 8
Carbs 23
Protein 4

165. Pumpkin Pie

Preparation Time: 10 minutes
Cooking Time: 15 minutes
Servings: 9
Ingredients:
One tbsp. sugar
Two tbsp. flour
One tbsp. vegan butter

Two tbsp. water

For the pumpkin pie filling:

3.5 ounces pumpkin flesh, chopped

One tsp. mixed spice

One tsp. nutmeg

3 ounces of water

¼ cup vegan Buttermilk

One tbsp. sugar

Directions:

Put 3 ounces water in a pot, bring to a boil over medium-high heat, add pumpkin, vegan buttermilk, one tbsp. sugar, spice and nutmeg, stir, boil for 20 minutes, take off the heat and blend using an immersion blender.

In a bowl, mix flour with butter, one tbsp. sugar and two tbsp. water and knead your dough well.

Grease a pie pan that fits your air fryer with vegan butter, press dough into the pan, fill with pumpkin pie filling, place in your air fryer's basket and cook at 360 degrees F for 15 minutes. Slice and serve warm.

Enjoy!

Nutrition:

Calories 200

Fat 5

Fiber 2

Carbs 5

Protein 6

166. Coconut Pineapples & Vegan Yoghurt Dip

Preparation Time: 15 minutes

Cooking Time: 10 minutes

Servings: 4

Ingredients:

2 ounces of dried coconut flakes

One sprig of mint, finely chopped

½ medium size pineapples

8 ounces of vegan yogurt

Directions:

Heat the Air Fryer to 390°F.

Slice the pineapple into chips (sticks) and dip them into the diced coconut to allow the coconut to stick to them.

Place the sticks in the fryer basket and cook for about 10 minutes.

Stir the mint leaves into the vegan yogurt. Serve with pineapple sticks.

Nutrition:

Energy (calories): 118 kcal

Protein: 15.93 g

Fat: 4.59 g

Carbohydrates: 2.57 g

167. Stuffed Apple Bake

Preparation Time: 5 minutes

Cooking Time: 10 minutes

Servings: 4

Ingredients:

Four medium-sized apples, cored

Six tsp. of sugar

Four tbsp. of breadcrumbs

Two tbsp. of vegan butter

One tsp. of mixed spice

1½ ounce of mixed seeds Zest of

One lemon

Directions:

Score the apples' skin with a knife around the circumference to prevent them from dividing during baking.

Mix the sugar, breadcrumbs, vegan butter, zest, spice and mixed seeds in a bowl and stuff the apples with the mixture.

Heat the Air Fryer at 356°F and bake the stuffed apples for 10 minutes.

Nutrition:

Energy (calories): 117 kcal

Protein: 2.98 g

Fat: 8.4 g

Carbohydrates: 9.68 g

168. Berry and Apricot Crumble

Preparation Time: 10 minutes

Cooking Time: 20 minutes

Servings: 6

Ingredients:

2½ ounces of vegan butter

2¼ cups of apricot

½ pound of flour

Eight tbsp. of sugar

Six tsp. of lemon juice

5½ ounces fresh blackberries Salt to taste

Directions:

Cut the apricots into two and take out the stone, then cut into cubes.

Put them in a bowl and add two tbsp. of sugar, the blackberries and lemon juice and stir. Pour and spread the mixture evenly in an oven dish.

Place the flour in a prepared bowl and add six tbsp. of sugar, the vegan butter, salt, and a little water and mix thoroughly. Rub the mixture with your fingertips until crumbly.

Heat your Air Fryer to 390°F.

Spread the mixture on the fruits and press down lightly.

Put into the Air Fryer basket and bake for 20 minutes until the crumble appears golden.

Nutrition:

Energy (calories): 369 kcal

Protein: 6 g

Fat: 10.24 g

Carbohydrates: 66.78 g

169. Sponge Cake

Preparation Time: 10 minutes

Cooking Time: 20 minutes

Servings: 12

Ingredients:

3 cups flour

Three tsp. baking powder

½ cup cornstarch

One tsp. baking soda

1 cup olive oil

One and ½ cup of almond milk

1 and 2/3 cup sugar

2 cups of water

¼ cup lemon juice

2 tsp. vanilla extract

Directions:

In a bowl, mix flour with cornstarch, baking powder, baking soda and sugar and whisk well.

In another bowl, mix oil with almond milk, water, vanilla and lemon juice and whisk.

Combine the two mixtures, stir, pour in a greased baking dish that fits your air fryer, introduce in the fryer and cook at 350 degrees F for 20 minutes.

Leave the cake to cool down, cut and serve.

Enjoy!

Nutrition:

Energy (calories): 334 kcal

Protein: 3.32 g

Fat: 18.45 g

Carbohydrates: 38.6 g

170. Blueberry Pudding

Preparation Time: 10 minutes

Cooking Time: 25 minutes

Servings: 6

Ingredients:

2 cups flour

2 cups rolled oats

8 cups blueberries

One stick vegan butter, melted

1 cup walnuts, chopped

3 tbsp. maple syrup

2 tbsp. rosemary, chopped

Directions:

Spread blueberries in a greased baking pan and leave them aside.

In your food processor, mix rolled oats with the flour, walnuts, vegan butter, maple syrup and rosemary, blend well, layer this over blueberries, introduce everything in your air fryer and cook at 350 degrees for 25 minutes.

Leave dessert to cool down, cut and serve.

Enjoy!

Nutrition:

Calories 150

Fat 3g

Fibre 2g

Carbs 7g

Protein 4g

171. Cocoa and Almond Bars

Preparation Time: 30 minutes

Cooking Time: 4 minutes

Servings: 6

Ingredients:

¼ cup cocoa nibs

1 cup almonds, soaked and drained

2 tbsps. cocoa powder

¼ cup hemp seeds

¼ cup goji berries

¼ cup coconut, shredded

Eight dates, pitted and soaked

Directions:

Put almonds in your food processor, blend, add hemp seeds, cocoa nibs, cocoa powder, goji, coconut and blend very well.

Add dates, blend well again, spread on a lined baking sheet that fits your air fryer and cooks at 320 degrees F for 4 minutes.

Cut into equal parts and keep in the fridge for 30 minutes before serving.

Enjoy!

Nutrition:

Calories 140

Fat 6g

Fibre 3g

Carbs 7g

Protein 1g

172. Chocolate and Pomegranate Bars

Preparation Time: 120 minutes

Cooking Time: 10 minutes

Servings: 6

Ingredients:

½ cup almond milk

1 tsp. vanilla extract

One and ½ cups dark chocolate, chopped

½ cup almonds, chopped

½ cup pomegranate seeds

Directions:

Heat a pan with the almond milk over medium-low heat, add chocolate, stir for 5 minutes, take off heat add vanilla extract, half of the pomegranate seeds and half of the nuts and stir.

Pour this into a lined baking pan, spread, sprinkle a pinch of salt, the rest of the pomegranate arils and nuts, introduce in your air fryer and cook at 300 degrees F for 4 minutes.

Keep in the fridge for 2 hours before serving.

Enjoy!

Nutrition:

Calories 68

Fat 1g

Fibre 4g

Carbs 6g

Protein 1g

173. Tomato Cake

Preparation Time: 10 minutes

Cooking Time: 30 minutes

Servings: 4

Ingredients:

One and ½ cups flour

1 tsp. cinnamon powder

1 tsp. baking powder

1 tsp. baking soda

¾ cup maple syrup

1 cup tomatoes chopped

½ cup olive oil

2 tbsp. apple cider vinegar

Directions:

In a bowl, mix flour with baking powder, baking soda, cinnamon and maple syrup and stir well.

In another bowl, mix tomatoes with olive oil and vinegar and stir well.

Combine the two mixtures, stir well, pour into a greased round pan that fits your air fryer, introduce in the fryer and cook at 360 degrees F for 30 minutes.

Leave the cake to cool down, slice and serve.

Enjoy!

Nutrition:

Calories 153

Fat 2g

Fibre 1g

Carbs 25g

Protein 4 g

174. Berries Mix

Preparation Time: 5 minutes

Cooking Time: 6 minutes

Servings: 4

Ingredients:

2 tbsp. lemon juice

One and ½ tbsp. maple syrup

One and ½ tbsp. champagne vinegar

One tbsp. olive oil

1 pound strawberries, halved

One and ½ cups blueberries

¼ cup basil leaves, torn

Directions:

In a pan that fits your air fryer, mix lemon juice with maple syrup and vinegar, bring and let it boil over medium-high heat, add oil, blueberries, strawberries, stir, and introduce in your air fryer and cook at temperature of 310 degrees F for 6 minutes.

Sprinkle basil on top and serve!

Enjoy!

Nutrition:

Calories 163 Fat 4g

Fiber 4g Carbs 10g Protein 2.1g

175. Passion Fruit Pudding

Preparation Time: 10 minutes

Cooking Time: 40 minutes

Servings: 6

Ingredients:

1 cup Paleo passion fruit curd

Four passion fruits, pulp and seeds

Three and ½ ounces maple syrup

¾ cup of silken tofu

2 ounces ghee, melted

Three and ½ ounces of almond milk

½ cup almond flour

½ tsp. baking powder

Directions:

In a bowl, mix half of the fruit curd with passion fruit seeds and pulp, stir and divide into six heatproof ramekins.

In a bowl, whisk silken tofu with maple syrup, ghee, the rest of the curd, baking powder, milk and flour and stir well.

Divide this into the ramekins and introduce in the fryer and cook at 200 degrees F for 40 minutes.

Leave puddings to cool down and serve!

Enjoy!

Nutrition:

Calories 430 Fat 22g

Fiber 3g

Carbs 7g

Protein 8g

176. Pumpkin Cookies

Preparation Time: 10 minutes

Cooking Time: 15 minutes

Servings: 24

Ingredients:

Two and ½ cups flour

½ tsp. baking soda

1 tbsp. flaxseed, ground

3 tbsp. water

½ cup of pumpkin flesh, mashed

¼ cup maple syrup

2 tbsp. butter

1 tsp. vanilla extract

½ cup dark chocolate chips

Directions:

In a bowl, mix flaxseed with water, stir and leave aside for a few minutes.

In another bowl, mix flour with salt and baking soda.

In a third bowl, mix maple syrup with pumpkin puree, butter, vanilla extract and flaxseed.

Combine flour with maple syrup mix and chocolate chips and stir.

Scoop one tbsp. of cookie dough into a lined baking sheet that fits your air fryer, repeat with the rest of the dough, introduce them to your air fryer and cook at 350 degrees F for 15 minutes.

Leave cookies to cool down and serve.

Enjoy!

Nutrition:

Calories 140 Fat 2g

Fibre 2g

Carbs 7g

Protein 10g

177. Figs and Coconut Butter Mix

Preparation Time: 6 minutes

Cooking Time: 4 minutes

Servings: 3

Ingredients:

2 tbsp. coconut butter

12 figs, halved

¼ cup of sugar

1 cup almonds, toasted and chopped

Directions:

Put butter in a pan that fits your air fryer and melt over medium-high heat.

Add figs, sugar and almonds, toss, introduce in your air fryer and cook at 300 degrees F for 4 minutes.
Divide into bowls and serve cold.
Enjoy!
Nutrition:
Calories 170
Fat 4g
Fibre 5g
Carbs 7g
Protein 9g

178. Pears and Espresso Cream

Preparation Time: 10 minutes
Cooking Time: 30 minutes
Servings: 4
Ingredients:
Four pears, halved and cored
2 tbsp. lemon juice
1 tbsp. sugar
2 tbsp. water
2 tbsp. vegan butter
For the cream:
1 cup vegan whipped cream
1 cup vegan cream cheese
1/3 cup sugar
2 tbsps. espresso, cold
Directions:
In a bowl, mix pears halves with lemon juice, one tbsp. sugar, vegan butter and water, toss well, transfer them to your air fryer and cook at 360 degrees F for 30 minutes.
Meanwhile, in a bowl, mix vegan whipped cream with vegan cream cheese, 1/3 cup sugar and espresso, whisk well and keep in the fridge until pears are done.
Divide pears on plates, top with espresso cream and serve them.
Enjoy!
Nutrition:
Calories 211
Fat 5
Fibre 7
Carbs 8
Protein 7

179. Chocolate Chip Cookies

Preparation time: 10 minutes
Cooking time: 7 minutes
Servings: 6 cookies
Bake: 347°F
Ingredients
1 tbsp. refined coconut oil, melted
1 tbsp. maple syrup
1 tbsp. Nondairy milk
½ tsp. vanilla
¼ cup plus 2 tbsp. whole-wheat pastry flour or all-purpose gluten-free flour
2 tbsp. Coconut sugar
¼ tsp. sea salt
¼ tsp. baking powder
2 tbsps. vegan chocolate chips
Cooking oil spray this can be (sunflower, safflower, or refined coconut)
Directions
In a medium bowl, stir together the oil, maple syrup, milk, and vanilla. Add the flour, coconut sugar, salt, and baking powder. Stir just until thoroughly combined. Stir in the chocolate chips. Preheat the air fryer basket (with a 6-inch round, 2-inch deep baking pan inside) for 2 minutes. Then, spray the pan lightly with oil. Drop a tbsp.ful of the batter onto the pan, leaving a little room in between in case they spread out a bit—Bake for 7 minutes, or until lightly browned. Be careful not to overcook. Gently transfer to a cooling rack (or plate). Repeat as desired, making all of the cookies at once, or keeping the batter on hand in the fridge to be used later (it will keep refrigerated in an airtight container for about a week). Enjoy warm if possible!
Cooking Tip: These are my "safe" chocolate chip cookies because even if I eat the whole batch over a day or two, I don't feel too horrible about it. Of course, if you have tons of self-control around warm, gooey cookies (are you even human?), feel free to make it double or triple the batch. However, I enjoy keeping the batter on hand in the fridge to make up just a few when I need cookie love.
Nutrition
Calories: 71 Total fat: 3g Cholesterol: 0mg
Carbohydrates: 11g

Fibre: 1g
Protein: 1g

180. Oatmeal Raisin Cookies

Preparation time: 10 minutes
Cooking time: 7 minutes
Servings: 18 cookies
Bake: 347°F
Ingredients
¼ cup plus ½ tbsp. vegan margarine
2½ tbsp. non-dairy milk, plain and unsweetened
½ cup of organic sugar
½ tsp. vanilla extract
½ tsp. plus 1/8 tsp. ground cinnamon
½ cup plus two tbsp. flour (whole-wheat pastry, gluten-free all-purpose, or all-purpose)
¼ tsp. of sea salt
¾ cup rolled oats
¼ tsp. baking soda
¼ tsp. baking powder
2 tbsp. raisins
Cooking oil spray it can be (sunflower, safflower, or refined coconut)
Directions
In a medium bowl, using an electric beater, whip the margarine until fluffy.
Add in the milk, sugar, and vanilla. Stir or whip with beaters until well combined.
In a prepared separate bowl, add the cinnamon, flour, salt, oats, baking soda, and baking powder and stir well to combine. Add the dry mixture to the wet mixture and mix everything well with a wooden spoon. Stir in the raisins.
Preheat the air fryer basket (with your 6-inch round, 2-inch deep baking pan inside) for 2 minutes. Then, spray the pan lightly with oil. Drop tbsp.fuls of the batter onto the pan, leaving a little room in between each one as they'll probably spread out a bit—Bake for about 7 minutes, or until lightly browned.
Gently transfer to a cooling rack (or plate), being careful to leave the cookies intact. Repeat as desired, making all of the cookies at once, or keeping the batter on hand in the fridge to be used later (it will keep refrigerated in an airtight container for a week to 10 days).

Substitution Tip: You may substitute coconut oil for the margarine if you prefer. However, if you do this, add a pinch more salt, as the oil will be salt-free, unlike margarine. If you use the vegan margarine as directed, keep in mind that the "pure fat" variety will work best (as opposed to the whipped, lower-fat mixture). Finally, if you're trying to reduce the fat overall, applesauce can be substituted for part of these cookies' fat. However, I wouldn't replace it entirely, as the results can be overly sweet and a bit dry.
Nutrition
Calories: 78 Total fat: 4g
Cholesterol: 0mg Carbohydrates: 11g
Fibre: 1g
Protein: 1g

181. Easy Cinnamon Crisps

Preparation time: 2 minutes
Cooking time: 6 minutes
Servings: 4
Fry: 347°F
Ingredients
1 (8-inch) tortilla, preferably sprouted whole-grain
Cooking oil spray it can be (sunflower, safflower, or refined coconut)
2 tsp. coconut sugar
½ tsp. cinnamon
Directions
Cut the tortilla into eight triangles (like a pizza). Place on a large plate and spray both sides with oil.
Sprinkle the tops evenly with the coconut sugar and cinnamon. In short, spurts, respray the tops with the oil. (If you spray too hard for this step, it will make the powdery toppings fly off!)
Place directly in the air fryer basket in a single layer (its okay if they overlap a little, but do your best to give them space). Fry and cook for about 5 to 6 minutes, or until the triangles are lightly browned, but not too brown—they're bitter if overcooked. Enjoy warm if possible.
Nutrition
 Calories: 45 Total fat: 1g Cholesterol: 0mg
Carbohydrates: 8g Fibre: 1g
Protein: 1g

182. De-Light-Full Caramelized Apples

Preparation time: 4 minutes
Cooking time: 20 minutes
Servings: 2
Bake: 392°F
Ingredients
Two apples, any sweet variety
2 tbsp. water
1½ tsp. coconut sugar
¼ tsp. cinnamon
Pinch nutmeg
Dash sea salt
Cooking oil spray it can be (sunflower, safflower, or refined coconut)
Directions
Cut each apple in half (no need to peel) and then remove the core and seeds, doing your best to keep the apple halves intact—because ideally, you want apple halves, not quarters.
Place the apples upright in a 6-inch round, 2-inch deep baking pan. Add about two tbsp. of water at the bottom of the dish to keep the apples from drying out (the apples will sit in the water).
With sugar, cinnamon, and nutmeg, dust the tops of the apples evenly. Give each half a very light sprinkle of sea salt.
Spray the tops with oil (if you spray too hard, it will make the toppings fly off in a tragic whirlwind). Once moistened, sprinkle the tops again with oil. (This will keep them from drying out.)
Bake and cook for 20 minutes, or until the apples are very soft and nicely browned on top. Enjoy immediately, plain or topped with granola and ice cream.
Nutrition
Calories: 120
Total fat: 1g
Cholesterol: 0mg
Carbohydrates: 33g
Fibre: 6g
Protein: 1g

183. Cozy Apple Crisp

Preparation time: 10 minutes
Cooking time: 30 minutes
Servings: 4
Bake: 320°F
Ingredients
For the topping
2 tbsps. coconut oil
¼ cup plus 2 tbsps. whole-wheat pastry flour (or gluten-free all-purpose flour)
¼ cup of coconut sugar
1/8 Tsp. sea salt
For the filling
2 cups finely chopped (or thinly sliced) apples (no need to peel)
3 tbsp. water
½ tbsp. lemon juice
¾ tsp. cinnamon
Directions
To make the topping:
In a bowl, combine the oil, flour, sugar, and salt. Mix the ingredients thoroughly, either with your hands or a spoon. The mixture should be crumbly; if it's not, place it in the fridge until it solidifies a bit.
To make the filling:
In a 6-inch round, 2-inch deep baking pan, stir the apples with the water, lemon juice, and cinnamon until well combined.
Crumble the chilled topping over the apples. Bake for 30 minutes, or until the apples are tender and the crumble is crunchy and nicely browned. Serve immediately on its own or topped with nondairy milk, vegan ice cream, or non-dairy whipped cream.
Variation Tip: My daughter and I both love this dessert but disagree on what constitutes the best crumble topping. I prefer the one that's written in the recipe above. However, she prefers a more decadent version that includes vegan margarine and regular sugar. If you'd like to try her performance (and she strongly suggests you do), replace the coconut oil with vegan margarine and the coconut sugar with organic white sugar.
Ingredient Tip: I'm often asked what type of apples work best in this recipe. And in all honesty, I don't have an impressive answer—I

tend to search out the best-looking organic apples at the store. As long as they're not overly tart, most varieties will work wonderfully.

Nutrition

Calories: 172 Total fat: 7g

Cholesterol: 0mg Carbohydrates: 29g

Fibre: 4g Protein: 1g

184. Apple Puffs with Vanilla Caramel Sauce

Preparation time: 20 minutes

Cooking time: 10 minutes

Servings: 6 puffs

Bake: 320°F

Ingredients

For the filling:

Two medium apples, cored and finely diced (no need to peel)

2 tsp. cinnamon

2 tbsps. coconut sugar

1/8 tsp. sea salt

Cooking oil spray it can be (sunflower, safflower, or refined coconut)

Six large (13-inch x 17-inch) sheets of phyllo dough, thawed (see Ingredient Tip)

For the vanilla caramel sauce:

A 6-inch segment of a vanilla bean

½ cup plus one tbsp. maple syrup

¼ cup plus two tbsp. refined coconut oil (or vegan margarine)

¼ cup of coconut sugar

½ tsp. of sea salt

Directions

To make the filling:

In a prepared medium bowl, combine the apples, cinnamon, coconut sugar, and salt and set aside.

Spray the air fryer basket with oil spray and set aside. Gently unwrap the phyllo dough. Remove six sheets and carefully set them aside. Wrap the remaining phyllo in airtight plastic wrap and place back in the fridge.

To assemble the puffs:

Remove one large sheet of phyllo and place it on a clean, dry surface. Spray with the oil. Fold it into thirds (the long way, so that you form a long, skinny rectangle). As you go, spray each portion of dry phyllo so the exposed phyllo continually gets lightly coated with oil—this will give you a more flaky (vs. dry) result.

Place 1/3 cup of the apple mixture at the base of the phyllo rectangle. Fold the bottom of the phyllo up and over the mixture. Continue to fold up toward the top, forming it into a triangle as you go. Once you have an apple-filled triangle, place it in the air fryer basket and spray the top with oil.

Repeat with the remaining phyllo and apple mixture. Note: You'll probably only be able to fit three puffs in your air fryer at a time because you don't want them to overlap. If you don't wish to make a second batch right now, store the phyllo-wrapped, uncooked puffs in an airtight container and put in the fridge and air-fry them within a day or two.

Bake for 10 minutes, or until very golden-browned.

To make the sauce:

Make a lengthwise cut down the vanilla bean with a sharp knife and pry it open. Scrape out the insides with a table knife and place in a small pot. Add the maple syrup, oil, coconut sugar, and salt to the pot and set to medium-low heat, stirring very well to combine. After the sauce comes to a boil, reduce the heat to low and simmer gently for 3 to 5 minutes or slightly thickened.

Transfer the apple puffs to a plate and top with the caramel sauce. Enjoy while warm.

Ingredient Tip: Phyllo (aka filo) dough is easy to use, so don't be intimidated! There are just a few things you need to know: First, be sure to thaw frozen packages in the fridge overnight. I don't find it necessary to cover the unwrapped dough with damp towels, as most recipes suggest—just have the filling ready to go, and then work quickly once you've opened the package. And of course, be very gentle when working with phyllo, as it tears easily—but if it does pull, just place another sheet on top (or "patch" it with additional phyllo), and no one will ever know!

Nutrition

Calories: 366 Total fat: 16g

Cholesterol: 0mg Carbohydrates: 58g

Fibre: 3g

Protein: 2g

185. Strawberry Puffs with Creamy Lemon Sauce

Preparation time: 20 minutes
Cooking time: 10 minutes
Servings: 8 puffs
Bake: 320°F
Ingredients
For the filling
3 cups sliced strawberries, fresh or frozen (1½ pints or 24 ounces)
1 cup sugar-free strawberry jam (sweetened only with fruit juice)
1 tbsp. arrowroot (or cornstarch)
Cooking oil spray it can be (sunflower, safflower, or refined coconut)
Eight large (13-inch x 17-inch) sheets of phyllo dough, thawed (see Ingredient Tip)
For the sauce
1 cup raw cashew pieces (see Cooking Tip)
¼ cup plus 2 tbsp. raw agave nectar
¼ cup plus 1 tbsp. water
3 tbsp. fresh lemon juice
2 tsp. (packed) lemon zest (see Cooking Tip)
2 tbsp. neutral-flavoured oil (sunflower, safflower, or refined coconut)
2 tsp. vanilla
¼ tsp. of sea salt
Directions
To make the filling:
In a medium bowl, add the strawberries, jam, and arrowroot and stir well to combine. Set aside.
Spray the air fryer basket using oil spray and set aside.
To assemble the puffs:
Gently unwrap the phyllo dough. Remove eight sheets and carefully set them aside. Re-wrap the remaining phyllo in airtight plastic wrap and place it back in the fridge.
Remove one large sheet of phyllo and place it on a clean, dry surface. Spray with the oil. Fold it into thirds so that it forms a long, skinny rectangle. As you go, spray each portion of dry phyllo so the exposed phyllo continually gets lightly coated with oil.
Place about 1/3 cup of the strawberry mixture at the base of the phyllo rectangle. Fold the bottom of the phyllo up and over the mixture. Continue to fold up toward the top, forming it into a triangle as you go. Once fully wrapped, place it in the air fryer basket and spray the top with oil. Repeat with the remaining phyllo and strawberry mixture. Note you'll probably only be able to fit three puffs in your air fryer at a time because you don't want them to overlap.
Bake for 10 minutes, or until beautifully golden-browned.
To make the sauce:
Place the cashews, agave, water, lemon juice and zest, oil, vanilla, and salt in a blender. Process until completely smooth and velvety. (Any leftover sauce will keep nicely in the fridge for up to a week.)
Transfer the strawberry puffs to a plate and drizzle with the creamy lemon sauce. If desired, garnish with sliced strawberries. Enjoy while warm.
Cooking Tip: If your blender isn't a high-speed one (such as Vitamix or Blendtec), you'll need to soak the cashews in sufficient water to cover them for several hours so they'll be soft enough to blend. Then simply drain off the water. Even those of us with high-speed blenders should take care to scrape down the sides and mix very thoroughly to achieve an ultra-smooth, non-grainy result.
Nutrition
Calories: 295 Total fat: 14g
Cholesterol: 0mg Carbohydrates: 38g
Fibre: 2g Protein: 6g

186. Gooey Lemon Bars

Preparation time: 15 minutes
Cooking time: 25 minutes
Servings: 6
Bake: 347°F
Ingredients
For the crust:
¾ cup whole-wheat pastry flour
2 tbsp.Coconut sugar
¼ cup refined coconut oil, melted
For the filling:
½ cup of organic sugar
One packed tbsp. lemon zest (see Cooking Tip)

¼ cup fresh lemon juice

1/8 tsp. of sea salt

¼ cup unsweetened, plain applesauce

1¾ tsp. arrowroot (or cornstarch)

¾ tsp.of baking powder

Cooking oil spray it can be(sunflower, safflower, or refined coconut)

Directions

To make the crust:

In a small bowl, stir the flour, Coconut sugar, and oil together until well combined. Place in the refrigerator.

To make the filling:

In a medium bowl, add the sugar, lemon zest and juice, salt, applesauce, arrowroot, and baking powder. Stir well.

To assemble the bars:

Spray a 6-inch round, 2-inch deep baking pan lightly with oil. Remove the crust mixture from the fridge and gently press it into the pan's bottom to form a crust. Place inside the air fryer and bake for 5 minutes, or until it becomes slightly firm to the touch.

Over the crust, scrape and spread the lemon filling. Bake for about 18 to 20 minutes or until golden brown on top. Remove and leave to cool in the refrigerator for an hour or more. Cut into pieces until firm and cooled, and serve. To get each piece out, you could use a fork, as the pan is a little small for typical spatulas.

Cooking Tip: Don't let the idea of zesting a lemon scare you away if it's new to you! All you'll need is a fine grater or Microplane. The most important thing to remember is to gently zest only the yellow outer peel of the lemon because if you zest the white parts beneath that, it will taste bitter—and you're going for tart, not bitter. This tip applies to zesting limes and oranges as well, and once you get the hang of it, you'll find citrus zest adds a pop of flavour to a wide range of dishes!

Nutrition

Calories: 202 Total fat: 9g

Cholesterol: 0mg Carbohydrates: 30g

Fiber: 2g

Protein: 1g

187. Raspberry Lemon Streusel Cake

Preparation time: 15 minutes

Cooking time: 45 minutes

Servings: 6

Bake: 311°F

Ingredients

For the streusel topping:

2 tbsps. organic sugar

2 tbsps. neutral-flavoured oil (sunflower, safflower, or refined coconut)

¼ cup plus 2 tbsps. whole-wheat pastry flour (or gluten-free all-purpose flour)

For the cake:

1 cup whole-wheat pastry flour

½ cup of organic sugar

One tsp. baking powder

1 tbsp. lemon zest

¼ tsp. sea salt

¾ cup plus 2 tbsps unsweetened nondairy milk (plain or vanilla)

2 tbsps. neutral-flavoured oil (sunflower, safflower, or refined coconut)

1 tsp. vanilla

1 cup fresh raspberries

Cooking oil spray it can be (sunflower, safflower, or refined coconut)

For the icing:

½ cup Coconut sugar

1 tbsp. fresh lemon juice

½ tsp. lemon zest

½ tsp. vanilla

1/8 tsp. sea salt

Directions

To make the streusel:

In a small bowl, stir together the sugar, oil, and flour and place in the refrigerator (this will help it firm up and be more crumbly later).

To make the cake:

In a medium bowl, place the flour, sugar, baking powder, zest, and salt. Stir very well, preferably with a wire whisk. Add the milk, oil, and vanilla. Stir using a rubber spatula or spoon, just until thoroughly combined. Gently stir in the raspberries.

Preheat the air fryer for 3 minutes. Spray or coat the insides of a 6-inch round, 2-inch deep baking pan with oil and pour the batter into the pan.

Remove the streusel from the fridge and crumble it over the top of the cake batter. Carefully place the cake in the air fryer and bake for 45 minutes, or if a knife inserted in the center comes out clean (the top should be golden-brown).

To make the icing:

In a prepared small bowl, stir together the coconut sugar, lemon juice and zest, vanilla, and salt. If the cake has cooled for about 5 minutes, slice into four pieces and drizzle each with icing. Serve warm if possible. If you have leftovers, it can keep in an airtight container in the fridge for several days.

Nutrition

Calories: 296
Total fat: 11g
Cholesterol: 0mg
Carbohydrates: 49g
Fibre: 4g
Protein: 3g

188. Pineapple Upside-Down Cake

Preparation time: 10 minutes
Cooking time: 30 minutes
Servings: 6
Bake: 320°F
Ingredients
1 cup whole-wheat pastry flour
1½ tbsp. ground flaxseed
½ tsp. Plus 1/8 tsp. baking soda
¼ tsp. sea salt
½ cup pineapple juice, fresh or canned
2 tbsp. melted coconut oil (plus more for greasing your pan)
¼ cup plus 2 tbsp. agave nectar
½ tbsp. fresh lemon juice
1 tsp. vanilla
1 to 2 tbsp. coconut sugar (for coating the pan)
Three pineapple rings (fresh or canned)
Creamy Lemon Sauce (optional)
Vanilla or coconut vegan ice cream (optional)
Vegan whipped topping (optional)
Directions
In a medium bowl, add the flour, flax meal, baking soda, and salt. Whisk very well. Add the pineapple juice, oil, agave, lemon juice, and vanilla. Stir just until thoroughly combined.

Preheat your air fryer for 2 minutes. Gently grease the bottom and sides of a 6-inch round, 2-inch deep baking pan with coconut oil. Sprinkle to the bottom of the pan evenly with the coconut sugar (just enough to coat the bottom of your pan lightly).

Put the pineapple rings on top of the sugar in a single layer (you may need to break up some of the calls to do this). Pour the batter on top of the pineapple rings.

Carefully place the pan into your preheated air fryer. Bake and cook for 25 to 30 minutes, or until a knife inserted into the center comes out clean. Note: Your cake may look done before the center is cooked through, so the knife test is where it's at here.

Carefully remove the pan and allow to cool on a plate or wire rack for 3 to 5 minutes. Use a knife around the edges of the pan. Place a container on top (so that the dish is against the exposed cake). Gently flip over, so the cake is upside-down on the scale. Next, gently pull the baking pan off the cake so that the pineapple rings remain on top. Cut and serve—plain, or with Creamy Lemon Sauce, vegan ice cream, or whipped topping.

Nutrition

Calories: 191
Total fat: 5g
Cholesterol: 0mg
Carbohydrates: 35g
Fibre: 4g
Protein: 2g

189. Blackberry Peach Cobbler

Preparation time: 10 minutes
Cooking time: 20 minutes
Servings: 4
Bake: 320°F
Ingredients
For the filling:
1½ cups chopped peaches (cut into ½-inch thick pieces)
1 (6-ounce) package of blackberries
2 tbsp. coconut sugar
2 tsp. arrowroot (or cornstarch)
1 tsp. lemon juice

For the topping:
2 tbsp. neutral-flavoured oil (sunflower, safflower, or refined coconut)
1 tbsp. maple syrup
1 tsp. vanilla
½ cup rolled oats
1/3 cup whole-wheat pastry flour
3 tbsp. coconut sugar
1 tsp. cinnamon
¼ tsp. nutmeg
1/8 tsp. sea salt
Directions
To make the filling:
In a 6-inch round, 2-inch deep baking pan, place the peaches, blackberries, coconut sugar, arrowroot, and lemon juice. With a rubber spatula, stir well until thoroughly mixed. Set aside.
To make the topping:
In a separate bowl, combine the oil, maple syrup, and vanilla. Stir well. Add the oats, flour, coconut sugar, cinnamon, nutmeg, and salt. Stir well until thoroughly combined. Crumble evenly over the peach-blackberry filling.
Bake and cook for 20 minutes, or until the topping is crisp and lightly browned. Enjoy warm if at all possible, because it's beyond incredible that way!
Ingredient Tip: The sweetness level of peaches can vary so much! If you're using very ripe and sweet peaches, you may not need as much coconut sugar. You can also substitute frozen peaches here, as it's not always easy to find them fresh unless they're in season. One 10-ounce bag of frozen peaches is what you'll need for this recipe, but make sure to thaw and chop them before using them.
Nutrition
Calories: 248
Total fat: 8g
Cholesterol: 0mg
Carbohydrates: 42g
Fibre: 6g
Protein: 3g

190. Baked Apples

Preparation time: 15 minutes
Cooking time: 10 minutes
Servings: 4
Ingredients
2 tbsp. Brown Sugar
Four pcs. Apples
40 grams of mixed seeds
50 grams Fresh Breadcrumbs
Zest of orange and olive oil
1 tsp. Mixed spice or cinnamon
Directions
Core the apples and score skin around using a sharp knife to prevent splitting.
Mix all the rest of the ingredients, carefully stuff the inside of the apples, and spread all remaining mix. Bake the apple at 180° for 10 minutes until the sugar caramelized.
Nutrition:
Energy (calories): 180 kcal
Protein: 2.58 g Fat: 5.46 g
Carbohydrates: 33.97 g

191. Blackberry – Apricot Crumble

Preparation time: 10 minutes
Cooking time: 10 minutes
Servings: 6-10
Ingredients
1 cup of flour with a dash of salt
18 oz. Fresh apricots
½ cup of sugar
5 tbsp. Cold butter
2 tbsp. Lemon juice
Directions
Divide the apricots into halves and the stones are removed. Then dice these and put them in a bowl. Add in the blackberries with 2 tbsp. Of sugar, mix with lemon juice and blend.

Scoop the fruit mixture into the oven dish and spread it out evenly. In a bowl, combine the flour and salt with the remaining sugar and add the butter and one tbsp. Of cold water. Using your hands, mix these with your hand to create a crumb mixture. Preheat the air fryer at the temperature of 390 degrees Fahrenheit. Lay the crumbly mixture evenly on top of the fruit mixture and press down lightly.

Place the dish into the basket and put it in the air fryer, and bake for 20 minutes or until the crumble turns into golden brown and the inside well was done. You can always test by picking it with a toothpick. If the flour no longer sticks to the toothpick, then it's cooked.

Nutrition:

Energy (calories): 214 kcal

Protein: 1.38 g Fat: 9.84 g

Carbohydrates: 32.46 g

192. French Toast with Berries

Preparation time: 5 minutes

Cooking time: 5 minutes

Servings: 2

Ingredients

1 tsp. Vanilla extract

Mixed Berries Spread with a squeeze of maple syrup

Two slices of bread (Thick)

Directions

Spread mixed berries spread on top of the bread. Put in the basket of the air fryer and cook over 180 degrees F for 5 minutes. Serve toast with toppings of your choice.

Nutrition:

Energy (calories): 59 kcal

Protein: 1.77 g Fat: 0.67 g

Carbohydrates: 10.15 g

193. Peanut Butter – Marshmallow Turnovers

Preparation time: 10 minutes

Cooking time: 5 minutes

Servings: 4

Ingredients

4 tbsp. Peanut butter

4 tbsp. Marshmallow fluff

Four sheets of Filo pastry, defrosted

2 oz. Butter, melted

1 Pinch of sea salt

Directions

Preheat the air fryer to 360 degrees Fahrenheit, then brush butter over one sheet of Filo pastry. Lay another Filo sheet on top and again, brush it with butter. Repeat the process for all of the remaining two pastry sheets.

Cut layers of Filo sheets into 4 pcs. of 3x12-inch strips

On the underside of a Filo strip, put 1 tbsp. of peanut butter and 1 tbsp. marshmallow fluff. Fold the sheet's tip to cover the filling while forming a triangular shape and fold the edges in a zigzag manner until the filling is fully wrapped inside. Use a touch of butter to seal the end of the turnover.

Place these turnovers in the cooking basket and cook in the air fryer for 3-5 minutes or until these turn golden brown and puffy.

Finish with a pinch of sea salt for a mixture of sweet and salty flavour.

Nutrition:

Energy (calories): 171 kcal

Protein: 1.94 g Fat: 12.15 g

Carbohydrates: 14.47 g

194. Pigs in a Blanket

Preparation time: 20 minutes

Cooking time: 15 minutes

Servings: 7

Ingredients

1 -8oz can crescent dough

20 Vegan franks (Smart Dogs meatless hot dog)

¼ cup Dijon mustard

¼ cup of silken tofu

Sesame seeds

Directions

Preheat air fryer to 330 degrees F.

Cut crescent rolls dough into three equal parts, making three strips from each roll. Brush with Dijon mustard each dough strips and place the vegan hotdogs on one end of the dough and roll it up.

Arrange these on the fryer and cook for approximately 8 minutes. Move the temperature

up to 390 degrees F and cook for another 3 minutes or until they turn golden brown.
Nutrition:
Energy (calories): 76 kcal
Protein: 2.7 g Fat: 2.58 g
Carbohydrates: 10.36 g

195. Toasted Bread Sandwich

Preparation time: 5 minutes
Cooking time: 6 minutes
Servings: 4
Ingredients
1 English muffin
Salt and pepper to taste
Directions
Place the muffin inside the air fryer.
Heat the air fryer to 200 degrees Centigrade or 395 degrees Fahrenheit for about 6 minutes.
Arrange the sandwich and serve.   Stuff your sandwich with any desired fillings.
Nutrition:
Energy (calories): 68 kcal
Fat: 0.59 g
Carbohydrates: 13.83 g

196. Banana Bread Pudding

Preparation Time: 10 minutes
Cooking Time: 50 minutes
Servings: 4
Ingredients
One 16-ounce loaf of French bread
½ cup raisins
1 ½ cup of unsweetened almond milk vanilla or plain (or other non-dairy milk)
1 cup mashed overripe bananas
¼ cup maple syrup
¼ cup dark brown sugar
2 tsp. cornstarch or potato starch

2 tsp. vanilla extract
1 ½ tsp. cinnamon
½ tsp. baking powder
½ tsp. nutmeg
¼ tsp. allspice
Sauce
½ cup apple cider or apple juice
¼ cup maple syrup
1 tsp. cornstarch mixed with 1 tbsp. apple juice
1 ½ - 2 tbsp. brandy, rum, or bourbon (see Notes below)
¼ cup chopped pecans or walnuts optional
Directions:
Break the bread or tear it into bits that are bite-sized. Spread it out on a cookie sheet if the bread looks sticky or dense and toast it in the oven for a few minutes. Place it and put the raisins in a large bowl.
In the blender, mix non-dairy milk with banana, maple syrup, sugar, cornstarch, vanilla, baking powder and spices. Blend until perfectly smooth. Spill it over the bread using a silicon spatula. Stir well to cover all of the bread thoroughly. Put aside for a few minutes to soak while you are cleaning the pan and preheating the oven.
Preheat the furnace to 350F. Using parchment paper or foil to cover an 8 to 8-inch baking dish thinly. Pour the bread pudding in an even layer into the tub. Bake for 45 minutes or until the top is set and begins to brown. Take it out of the oven and let it cool for at least 15 minutes.
Make the sauce while the pudding is cooling. In a small saucepan, put the apple cider and maple syrup over medium heat and bring to a simmer, sometimes stirring, until approximately half the volume is reduced. Add the cornstarch mixture carefully and stir constantly, bring it to a boil, and simmer for a few more minutes until the mixture is no longer cloudy.
Remove from the heat and add a little at a time, to sample the brandy or other spirits. Stir the nuts in. Poke a few holes with a toothpick at the top of the bread pudding and pour the sauce over the top, uniformly spreading the nuts. Slice into squares, then serve.
Nutrition: Energy (calories): 631 kcal
Protein: 14.44 g Fat: 7.59 g
Carbohydrates: 126.59 g

197. Apple Cinnamon Scuffins

Preparation time: 10 minutes
Cooking time: 15 minutes
Servings: 4
Ingredients:
2 cups oat flour
1 tsp. baking powder
1 cup rolled oats
½ tsp. baking soda
¼ tsp. salt
1 tsp. cinnamon powder
½ cup date paste
½ cup currants
½ cup dairy-free yogurt
½ cup almond milk
½ cups chopped red apples
Confectioner's sugar for sprinkling
Directions:
In a prepared bowl, combine all the dry ingredients. Then, in another bowl, mix the date paste, dairy-free yogurt, and almond milk.
Add the cinnamon mixture to the milk mixture and combine. After, fold in the apples.
In baking sheet that can fit into the air fryer, line with parchment paper, and drop large spoonful's of the batter on the sheet.
Sprinkle with confectioner's sugar and bake at 350 F for 12 to 15 minutes.
Remove when ready, allow cooling, and serve.
Nutrition:
Calories 105
Total Fat 1g
Total Carbs 15g
Fibre 4g
Net Carbs 11g
Protein 9g

198. Custard and Rhubarb Pie

Preparation time: 15 minutes
Cooking time: 38 minutes
Servings: 4
Ingredients:
One pie shell, unbaked
3 cups rhubarb, cut into small pieces
1 cup coconut cream
4 tbsp aquafaba, whisked
One ¼ cup sugar

2 tbsp. flour
½ tsp. salt
Directions:
Unwrap the pie shell and place the rhubarb in the crust. The pie shell's size should fit into your fryer basket.
In a bowl, whisk the remaining ingredients until properly combined and pour into the crust.
Preheat the air fryer.
Put the cake into the fryer basket and bake at 400 F for 8 minutes, then reduce the temperature to 350 F degrees and cook further for 30 minutes or until the custard sets but is fluffy in the middle.
Remove the pie, allow cooling, slice, and serve.
Nutrition:
Calories 215
Total Fat 10g
Total Carbs 28g
Fibre 3g
Net Carbs 25g
Protein 3g

199. Rose Meringue Kisses

The first time I learned of infusing rose into food, I couldn't wait to try my hands on it. Here is a simple, pink specialty that you'll love. Your little girls will enjoy making them with you.
Preparation time: 7 minutes
Cooking time: 40 minutes
Servings: 4
Ingredients:
¼ cup aquafaba
4 tbsp. caster sugar
½ tsp. rose water
Pink food colouring
Directions:
Pour the aquafaba into a bowl and whisk with an electric mixer until a soft peak forms.
Gradually, add the sugar while whisking until well-combined. Fold in the rose water and pink food colouring to achieve the intensity of pink color as desired.
Mix the combined mixture into a piping bag and squeeze out mounds on a cookie sheet that fits into the fryer basket.

Preheat the air fryer and bake the meringues at 200 F for 40 minutes or until the meringues are firm like a biscuit.

Remove to cool and serve.

Nutrition:

Calories 100

Total Fat 7g

Total Carbs 7g

Fiber 0g

Net Carbs 7g

Protein 2g

200. Three – Ingredient Shortbread Biscuits

Preparation time: 10 minutes

Cooking time: 12 minutes

Servings: 4

Ingredients:

1/3 cup melted vegan butter

3 tbsp. caster sugar

½ cup flour

Directions:

In a bowl, combine the ingredients until well mixed.

Place the flour on a chopping board and knead until smooth and pleasant.

Cut into finger bites and decorate with fork holes.

Preheat the air fryer and put the bites in the fryer basket—Bake at 350 F for 12 minutes.

Terrific turnout!

Nutrition:

Calories 245

Total Fat 15g

Total Carbs 26g

Fiber 2g

Net Carbs 24g

Protein 2g

201. Molten Chocolate and Peanut Butter Fondants

Preparation time: 15 minutes

Cooking time: 7 minutes

Servings: 4

Ingredients:

1 cup unsweetened vegan dark chocolate

4 tbsp. vegan butter, diced divided

5 tbsp. aquafaba

1/8 cup flour

½ cup confectioner's sugar, divided

1 tsp. salt

Directions:

Pour the chocolate, half of the vegan butter in a bowl and microwave until completely melted. Stir at every 10-seconds interval. Remove the bowl and allow slight cooling.

Add in the aquafaba and whisk while adding the flour and half of the sugar gradually. Set aside.

In another bowl, melt the remaining butter in the microwave and whisk with the peanut butter and the remaining confectioner's sugar.

Preheat the air fryer.

Grease four small ramekins with cooking spray and divide half of the chocolate into each.

Pour the peanut butter into each ramekin's center and pour the remaining chocolate on top to cover the peanut butter.

Place two ramekins in the fryer basket and bake at 300 F for 7 minutes.

Remove and cook the remaining batter.

Cool for a minute, turn the fondants over onto plates and enjoy the delight.

Nutrition:

Calories 504

Total Fat 39g

Total Carbs 29g

Fiber 1g

Net Carbs 28g

Protein 10g

202. Raspberry Mug Cakes

Preparation time: 5 minutes

Cooking time: 5 minutes

Servings: 4

Ingredients:

¼ cup flour

1 tsp. baking powder

5 tbsp. sugar

½ cup chopped dairy-free white chocolate, melted

4 tbsp. almond milk

3 tsp. melted vegan butter

1 tsp. vanilla extract

A pinch salt

½ cup raspberries

Directions:

In a bowl, mix all the ingredients except the raspberries until properly combined and pour into four mugs, leaving 1 – inch space on top for rising.

Divide the raspberries into the mugs and fold into the mixture.

Place 2 cups in the fryer basket and bake at 380 F for 5 minutes or until the cakes are set.

Remove and cook the remaining batter.

Allow cooling and serve.

Nutrition:

Calories 186

Total Fat 13g

Total Carbs 8g

Fiber 0g

Net Carbs 8g

Protein 9g

203.   Yogurt Soufflé

Preparation time: 25 minutes

Cooking time: 14 minutes

Servings: 2

Ingredients:

1 tbsp. unbelted vegan butter

¼ cup of sugar

1 cup dairy-free yogurt

A pinch salt

¼ tsp. vanilla extract

3 tbsp. flour

½ cup aquafaba

3 oz. dairy-free coconut heavy cream

Directions:

Coat two 6-oz ramekins with the vegan butter.

Pour in the sugar and swirl in the ramekins to coat the butter. Pour out the remaining sugar and reserve.

Melt the remaining vegan butter in a microwave and set aside.

In a bowl, whisk the butter, yogurt, salt, vanilla extract, flour, and half of the aquafaba. Set aside.

In another bowl, beat the remaining aquafaba with the coconut cream until foamy.

Fold the coconut cream mixture into the yogurt mix one-third portion at a time as you thoroughly combine.

Preheat the air fryer.

Share the mix into the ramekins with ½-inch space left on top.

Put the ramekins in the fryer basket and bake at 350 F for 14 minutes.

When ready, remove and serve.

Nutrition:

Calories 251

Total Fat 18g

Total Carbs 18g

Fiber 2g

Net Carbs 16g

Protein 4g

204.   Fried Oreos

Preparation time: 50 minutes

Cooking time: 10 minutes

Servings: 4

Ingredients:

16 Oreo cookies

1 cup eggless pancake mix

2/3 cup almond milk

3 tbsp. flax egg

2 tsp. olive oil

Confectioner's sugar for dusting

Directions:

Freeze the Oreo cookies for 45 minutes.

In a bowl, combine the remaining ingredients until combined evenly.

Preheat the air fryer and grease the fryer basket with cooking spray.

Get the cookies from the fridge and coat deeply in the batter so that you cannot see through the batter.

Place the cookies in the fryer basket and fry at 350 F for 10 minutes or until a biscuit forms.

Transfer the cookies to a plate, relaxed for a few minutes, and dust with the sugar.

Serve.

Nutrition:

Calories 98

Total Fat 2g

Total Carbs 4g

Fiber 0g

Net Carbs 6g

Protein 16g

205. Plum Cobbler

Preparation time: 5 minutes
Cooking time: 12 minutes
Servings: 2
Ingredients:
¼ cup of sugar
¼ cup flour
½ cup cornmeal
1 tbsp. baking powder
A pinch of salt
4 tbsp. melted vegan butter + extra for greasing
1 tsp. vanilla extract
4 tbsp. plant milk (non-dairy milk)
2 cups stewed plums
1 tsp. lemon juice
Directions:
In a bowl, mix the sugar, flour, cornmeal, baking powder, vegan butter, vanilla extract, and non-dairy milk until smoothly combined.

Grease a 3 x 3 baking dish with the remaining butter and pour in the plums with lemon juice. Stir to combine.
Spoon the flour mixture on top and use a spoon to level the mix.
Place the dish in the fryer basket and bake at 390 F for 12 minutes.
Remove after; allow cooling for a few minutes, and serve with vegan ice cream.
Nutrition:
Calories 180
Total Fat 14g
Total Carbs 10g
Fiber 2g
Net Carbs 8g
Protein 3g

CHAPTER 11:

Vegan Snacks

206. Banana Chips

Preparation time: 10 minutes
Cooking time: 10 minutes
Servings: 4
Ingredients:
Four bananas, peeled and sliced into thin pieces
A drizzle of olive oil
A pinch of black pepper
Directions:
Put banana slices in your air fryer, drizzle the oil, season with pepper, toss to coat gently and cook at 360 degrees for 10 minutes.
Serve as a snack.
Enjoy!
Nutrition:
Calories 100
Fat 7g
Fiber 1g
Carbs 20g
Protein 1 g

207. Cabbage Rolls

Preparation Time: 10 minutes
Cooking time: 25 minutes
Servings: 8
Ingredients:
2 cups cabbage, chopped
Two yellow onions, chopped
One carrot, chopped
½ red bell pepper, chopped
1-inch piece ginger, grated
Eight garlic cloves, minced
Salt and black pepper to the taste
1 tsp. coconut aminos
2 tbsp. olive oil
Ten vegan spring roll sheets
Cooking spray
2 tbsp. Cornflour mixed with 1 tbsp. water
Directions:
Heat a pan with the oil over medium-high heat, add cabbage, onions, carrots, bell pepper, ginger, garlic, salt, pepper and amino, stir, cook for 4 minutes take off the heat.
Cut each spring roll sheet and cut it into four pieces.
Place 1 tbsp. Veggie mix in one corner, roll and fold edges.
Repeat this with the rest of the rolls, place them in your air fryer's basket, grease them with cooking oil and cook at 360 degrees F for 10 minutes on each side.
Arrange on a plate and then serve as an appetizer.
Enjoy!
Nutrition:
Calories 150 Fat 3g
Fiber 4g Carbs 7g
Protein 2g

208. Tortilla Chips

Preparation Time: 10 minutes
Cooking time: 4 minutes
Servings: 4
Ingredients:
Eight corn tortillas, each cut into triangles
Salt and black pepper to the taste
1 tbsp. olive oil
Directions:
Brush tortilla chips with the oil, place them in your air fryer's basket and cook for 4 minutes at 400 degrees F
Serve them with salt and pepper sprinkled all over.
Enjoy!
Nutrition:
Calories 53g
Fat 1g
Fiber 1.5g
Carbs 10g
Protein 2 g

209. Chickpeas Snack

Preparation Time: 10 minutes
Cooking time: 20 minutes
Servings: 4
Ingredients:
15 ounces canned chickpeas, drained
½ tsp. cumin, ground
1 tbsp. olive oil
1 tsp. smoked paprika
Salt and black pepper to the taste
Directions:
In a bowl, mix chickpeas with oil, cumin, paprika, salt and pepper, toss to coat, place them in the fryer's basket, cook at 390 degrees F for 10 minutes, and transfer a bowl.
Serve as a snack
Enjoy!
Nutrition:
Calories 140
Fat 1g
Fiber 6g
Carbs 20g
Protein 6g

210. Rice Balls

Preparation Time: 10 minutes
Cooking time: 35 minutes
Servings: 6
Ingredients:
One small yellow onion, chopped
1 cup Arborio rice
1 tbsp. olive oil
1 cup veggie stock
Salt and black pepper to the taste
2 ounces tofu, cubed
¼ cup sun-dried tomatoes, chopped
One and ½ cups vegan breadcrumbs
A drizzle of olive oil
Marinara sauce for serving
Directions:
Heat a pan with 1 tbsp. oil over medium heat, add onion, stir and cook for 5 minutes.
Add rice, stock, salt and pepper, stir, and cook on low heat for 20 minutes, spread on a baking sheet and leave aside to cool down.
Transfer rice to a bowl, add tomatoes and half of the breadcrumbs and stir well.
Shape 12 balls, press a hole in each ball, stuff with tofu cubes, and mould them again.
Dredge them in the rest of the breadcrumbs, arrange all balls in your air fryer, drizzle the oil over them and cook at 380 degrees F for 10 minutes.
Flip them and cook for 5 minutes more.
Arrange them on a plate and then serve them as a snack.
Enjoy!
Nutrition:
Calories 137 Fat 12g
Fiber 1g
Carbs 7g
Protein 5g

211. Tofu Snack

Preparation Time: 30 minutes
Cooking time: 20 minutes
Servings: 4
Ingredients:
12 ounces firm tofu, cubed
1 tsp. sweet paprika
1 tsp. sesame oil

1 tbsp. coriander, chopped

2 tbsp. coconut aminos

Directions:

In a bowl, mix paprika with the oil, coriander and amino, whisk well, add tofu pieces, toss to coat and leave aside for 30 minutes.

Transfer tofu cubes to your air fryer's basket and cook at 350 degrees F for 20 minutes, shaking halfway.

Transfer them to a bowl and serve as a snack.

Enjoy!

Nutrition:

Calories 90

Fat 2g

Fiber 1g

Carbs 6g

Protein 1g

212.   Apple Chips

Preparation Time: 10 minutes

Cooking time: 15 minutes

Servings: 2

Ingredients:

One apple, cored and thinly sliced

½ tsp. cinnamon powder

1 tbsp. stevia

Directions:

Arrange apple slices in your air fryer's basket, add stevia and cinnamon, toss and cook at 390 degrees F for 10 minutes, turning them halfway.

Transfer to a bowl and serve as a snack.

Enjoy!

Nutrition:

Calories 90

Fat 0g

Fiber 4g

Carbs 12g

Protein 4 g

213.   Potato Chips

Preparation Time: 30 minutes

Cooking time: 30 minutes

Servings: 4

Ingredients:

Four potatoes, scrubbed, peeled and cut into thin strips

A pinch of sea salt

1 tbsp. olive oil

2 tsp. rosemary, chopped

Directions:

In a bowl, mix potato chips with salt and oil, toss to coat, place them in your air fryer's basket and cook at 330 degrees F for 30 minutes.

Divide them into bowls, sprinkle rosemary all over and serve as a snack.

Enjoy!

Nutrition:

Calories 200

Fat 4g

Fiber 4g

Carbs 14g

Protein 5g

214.   Easy Zucchini Chips

Preparation Time: 10 minutes

Cooking time: 30 minutes

Servings: 6

Ingredients:

Three zucchinis, thinly sliced

Salt and black pepper to the taste

2 tbsp. olive oil

2 tbsp. balsamic vinegar

Directions:

In a bowl, mix oil with vinegar, salt and pepper and whisk well.

Add zucchini slices, toss to coat well, introduce in your air fryer and cook at 350 degrees F for 30 minutes.

Divide zucchini chips into bowls and serve them cold as a snack.

Enjoy!

Nutrition:

Calories 100 Fat 3g

Fiber 2g

Carbs 6g

Protein 7g

215. Beets Chips

Preparation Time: 10 minutes
Cooking time: 20 minutes
Servings: 4
Ingredients:
Cooking spray
Four medium beets, peeled and cut into skinny slices
Salt and black pepper to the taste
1 tbsp. chives, chopped
Directions:
Arrange beets chips in your air fryer's basket, grease with cooking spray, season with salt and black pepper, cook them at 350 degrees F for 20 minutes, flipping them halfway, transfer to bowls and serve with chives sprinkled on top as a snack
Enjoy!
Nutrition:
Calories 80
Fat 1g
Fiber 2g
Carbs 6g
Protein 1g

216. Avocado Chips

Preparation Time: 10 minutes
Cooking time: 10 minutes
Servings: 3
Ingredients:
One avocado, pitted, peeled and sliced
Salt and black pepper to the taste
½ cup vegan breadcrumbs
A drizzle of olive oil
Directions:
In a bowl, mix breadcrumbs with salt and pepper and stir.
Brush avocado slices with the oil, coat them in breadcrumbs, place them in your air fryer's basket and cook at the temperature of 390 degrees F for 10 minutes, shaking halfway.
Divide into bowls and serve them as a snack
Enjoy!
Nutrition:
Calories 180 Fat 11g
Fiber 3g
Carbs 7g
Protein 4g

217. Veggie Sticks

Preparation Time: 10 minutes
Cooking time: 30 minutes
Servings: 4
Ingredients:
Four parsnips, cut into thin sticks
Two sweet potatoes, cut into sticks
Four carrots, cut into sticks
Salt and black pepper to the taste
2 tbsp. rosemary, chopped
2 tbsp. olive oil
A pinch of garlic powder
Directions:
Put parsnips, sweet potatoes and carrots in a bowl, add oil, garlic powder, salt, pepper, rosemary, and toss to coat.
Put sweet potatoes in your preheated air fryer, cook them for 10 minutes at 350 degrees F and transfer them to a platter.
Add parsnips to your air fryer, cook for 5 minutes and transfer over potato fries.
Add carrots, cook for 15 minutes at 350 degrees F, also transfer to the platter.
Serve as a snack.
Enjoy!
Nutrition:
Calories 140 Fat 0g Fiber 2g
Carbs 7g Protein 4g

218. Polenta Biscuits

Preparation Time: 10 minutes
Cooking time: 25 minutes
Servings: 4
Ingredients:
18 ounces cooked polenta roll, cold
1 tbsp. olive oil
Directions:
Cut polenta into medium slices and brush them with the olive oil.
Place polenta biscuits into your air fryer and cook at 400 degrees F for 25 minutes, flipping them after 10 minutes.
Serve biscuits as a snack.
Nutrition:
Calories 120 Fat 0g
Fiber 3g Carbs 7g Protein 3g

219.   Potato and Beans Dip

Preparation Time: 10 minutes

Cooking time: 10 minutes

Servings: 10

Ingredients:

19 ounces canned garbanzo beans, drained

1 cup sweet potatoes, peeled and chopped

¼ cup sesame paste

2 tbsp. lemon juice

1 tbsp. olive oil

Five garlic cloves, minced

½ tsp. cumin, ground

2 tbsp. water

Salt and white pepper to the taste

Directions:

Put potatoes in your air fryer's basket, cook them at 360 degrees F for 10 minutes, cool them down, peel, put them in your food processor and pulse well.

Add sesame paste, garlic, beans, lemon juice, cumin, water, oil, salt and pepper, pulse again, divide into bowls and serve cold.

Enjoy!

Nutrition

Calories 170

Fat 3g

Fiber 10g

Carbs 12g

Protein 11g

220.   Cauliflower Crackers

Preparation Time: 10 minutes

Cooking time: 25 minutes

Servings: 12

Ingredients:

One big cauliflower head, florets separated and riced

½ cup cashew cheese, shredded

1 tbsp. flax meal mixed with 1 tbsp. water

1 tsp. Italian seasoning

Salt and black pepper to the taste

Directions:

Spread cauliflower rice on a lined baking sheet that fits your air fryer. Introduce in the fryer and cook at 360 degrees F for 10 minutes.

Transfer cauliflower to a bowl, add salt, pepper, cashew cheese, flax meal and Italian seasoning,

stir well, spread this into a rectangle pan that fits your air fryer, press well, introduce in the fryer and cook at 360 degrees F for 15 minutes more. Cut into medium crackers and serve as a snack.

Enjoy!

Nutrition:

Calories 120

Fat 1g

Fiber 2g

Carbs 7g

Protein 3g

221.   Basil Crackers

Preparation Time: 10 minutes

Cooking time: 17 minutes

Servings: 6

Ingredients:

½ tsp. baking powder

Salt and black pepper to the taste

One and ¼ cups whole wheat flour

¼ tsp. basil, dried

One garlic clove, minced

2 tbsp. vegan basil pesto

2 tbsp. olive oil

Directions:

In a prepared bowl, mix flour with salt, pepper, baking powder, garlic, cayenne, basil, pesto and oil, stir until you obtain a dough, spread this on a lined baking sheet that fits your air fryer, introduce in the fryer at 325 degrees F and bake for 17 minutes.

Leave aside to cool down, cut crackers and serve them as a snack.

Enjoy!

Nutrition:

Calories 170 Fat 20g

Fiber 1g Carbs 6g Protein 7g

222.   Veggie Wontons

Preparation Time: 10 minutes

Cooking Time: 15 minutes

Servings: 10

Ingredients:

Cooking spray

½ cup white onion, grated

½ cup mushrooms, chopped

½ cup carrot, grated

¾ cup red pepper, chopped

¾ cup cabbage, grated

1 tbsp. chilli sauce

1 tsp. garlic powder

Salt and pepper to taste

30 vegan wonton wrappers

Water

Directions

Spray oil in a pan.

Put the pan over medium heat and cook the onion, mushrooms, carrot, red pepper and cabbage until tender.

Stir in the chilli sauce, garlic powder, salt and pepper.

Let it cool for a few minutes.

Add a scoop of the mixture on top of the wrappers.

Fold and seal the corners using water.

Cook in the air fryer set the temperature at 320 degrees F for 7 minutes or until golden brown.

Nutrition

Calories 290

Total Fat 1.5g

Sodium 593mg

Total Carbohydrate 58g

Protein 9.9g

Potassium 147mg

223.   Avocado Rolls

Preparation Time: 20 minutes

Cooking Time: 25 minutes

Servings: 5

Ingredients:

Ten rice paper wrappers

Three avocados, sliced

One tomato, diced

Salt and pepper to taste

1 tbsp. olive oil

4 tbsp. sriracha

2 tbsp. sugar

1 tbsp. rice vinegar

1 tbsp. sesame oil

Directions

Mash avocados in a bowl.

Stir in the tomatoes, salt and pepper.

Mix well.

Arrange the rice paper wrappers.

Scoop mixture on top.

Roll and seal the edges with water.

Cook in the air fryer at 350 degrees F for 5 minutes.

Mix the rest of the ingredients.

Serve rolls with the sriracha dipping sauce.

Nutrition

Calories 422 Saturated Fat 5.8g

Total Carbohydrate 38.7g

Dietary Fiber 8.8g Protein 3.8g

Potassium 633mg

224.   Fried Ravioli

Preparation Time: 15 minutes

Cooking Time: 8 minutes

Servings: 4

Ingredients:

½ cup panko breadcrumbs

Salt and pepper to taste

1 tsp. garlic powder

1 tsp. dried oregano

1 tsp. dried basil

2 tsp. nutritional yeast flakes

¼ cup aquafaba liquid

8 oz. frozen vegan ravioli

Cooking spray

½ cup marinara sauce

Directions:

Mix the breadcrumbs, salt, pepper, garlic powder, oregano, basil and nutritional yeast flakes on a plate.

In another bowl, pour the aquafaba liquid.

Dip each ravioli into the liquid and then coat it with the breadcrumb mixture.

Put the ravioli in the air fryer.

Spray oil on the ravioli.

Cook at 390 degrees F for 6 minutes.

Flip each one and cook for another 2 minutes.

Serve with marinara sauce.

Nutrition:

Calories 154

Total Fat 3.8g

Saturated Fat 0.6g

Total Carbohydrate 18.4g

Dietary Fiber 1.5g

Protein 4.6g

Potassium 154mg

225. Corn Fritters

Preparation Time: 15 minutes
Cooking Time: 10 minutes
Servings: 4
Ingredients:
¼ cup ground cornmeal
¼ cup flour
Salt and pepper to taste
½ tsp. baking powder
¼ tsp. garlic powder
¼ tsp. onion powder
¼ tsp. paprika
¼ cup parsley, chopped
One cup corn kernels mixed with 3 tbsp. almond milk
2 cups fresh corn kernels
4 tbsp. vegan mayonnaise
2 tsp. grainy mustard
Directions:
Mix the cornmeal, flour, salt, pepper, baking powder, garlic powder, onion powder, paprika and parsley in a bowl.
Put the corn kernels with almond milk in a food processor.
Season with salt and pepper.
Pulse until well blended.
Add the corn kernels.
Transfer to a bowl and stir into the cornmeal mixture.
Pour a small amount of the batter into the air fryer pan.
Pour another a few centimetres away from the first cake.
Cook in the air fryer set the temperature at 350 degrees for 10 minutes or until golden.
Flip halfway through.
Serve with mayo mustard dip.

Nutrition:
Calories 135
Total Fat 4.6g
Saturated Fat 0.2g
Cholesterol 0mg
Sodium 136mg
Total Carbohydrate 22.5g
Dietary Fiber 2.5g
Total Sugars 2.7g
Protein 3.5g
Potassium 308mg

226. Mushroom Pizza

Preparation Time: 15 minutes
Cooking Time: 10 minutes
Servings: 4
Ingredients:
Four large Portobello mushrooms, stems and gills removed
1 tsp. balsamic vinegar
Salt and pepper to taste
4 tbsp. vegan pasta sauce
One clove garlic, minced
3 oz. zucchini, chopped
Four olives, sliced
2 tbsp. sweet red pepper, diced
1 tsp. dried basil
½ cups hummus
Fresh basil, minced
Directions:
Coat the mushrooms with balsamic vinegar and season with salt and pepper.
Spread pasta sauce inside each mushroom.
Sprinkle with minced garlic.
Preheat your air fryer to 330 degrees F.
Cook mushrooms for 3 minutes.
Take the mushrooms out and top with zucchini, olives, and peppers.
Season with salt, pepper and basil.
Put them back in the air fryer and cook for another 3 minutes.
Serve mushroom pizza with hummus and fresh basil.
Nutrition
Calories 70 Total Fat 1.56 g
Total Carbohydrate 11 g Dietary Fiber 3.4 g
Protein 4.3 g

227.   Crispy Brussels Sprouts

Preparation Time: 5 minutes
Cooking Time: 1 minute
Servings: 2
Ingredients:
2 cups Brussels sprouts, sliced
1 tbsp. olive oil
1 tbsp. balsamic vinegar
Salt to taste
Directions:
Toss all the ingredients in a bowl.
Cook in the air fryer at 400 degrees F for 10 minutes. Shake once or twice during the cooking process.
Check to see if crispy enough.
If not, cook for another 5 minutes.
Nutrition:
Calories 100
Total Fat 7.3g
Total Carbohydrate 8.1g
Dietary Fiber 3.3g
Protein 3g

228.   Sweet Potato Tots

Preparation Time: 10 minutes
Cooking Time: 12 minutes
Servings: 10
Ingredients:
2 cups sweet potato puree
½ tsp. salt
½ tsp. cumin
½ tsp. coriander
½ cup breadcrumbs
Cooking spray
Vegan mayo
Directions:
Preheat your air fryer set to 390 degrees F.
Combine all ingredients in a bowl.
Form into balls.
Arrange on the air fryer pan.
Spray with oil.
Cook for 6 minutes or until golden.
Serve with vegan mayo.
Nutrition:
Calories 77 Total Fat 0.8g
Total Carbohydrate 15.9g Dietary Fiber 1.1g
Total Sugars 3.1g Protein 1.8g

229.   Popcorn Tofu

Preparation Time: 15 minutes
Cooking Time: 12 minutes
Servings: 4
Ingredients:
½ cup cornmeal
½ cup quinoa flour
1 tbsp. vegan bouillon
2 tbsp. nutritional yeast
1 tsp. garlic powder
1 tsp. onion powder
1 tbsp. mustard
Salt and pepper to taste
¾ cup almond milk
1 ½ cups breadcrumbs
14 oz. tofu, sliced into small pieces
½ cup vegan mayo
2 tbsp. hot sauce
Directions:
In the first bowl, mix the first eight ingredients.
In the second bowl, pour the almond milk.
In the third bowl, add the breadcrumbs.
Dip each tofu slice into each of the bowls starting from the flour mixture, then the almond milk, and finally, the breadcrumbs.
Cook in the air fryer set the temperature at 350 degrees F for 12 minutes, shaking halfway through.
Mix the mayo and hot sauce and serve with tofu.
Nutrition:
Calories 261
Total Fat 5.5 g
Total Carbohydrate 37.5 g
Dietary Fiber 4.8 g
Protein 16 g

230.   Black Bean Burger

Preparation Time: 10 minutes
Cooking Time: 25 minutes
Servings: 6
Ingredients:
One ¼ cup rolled oats
16 oz. black beans, rinsed and drained
¾ cup of salsa
1 tbsp. soy sauce
One ¼ tsp. chilli powder
¼ tsp. chipotle chilli powder

½ tsp. garlic powder

Directions:

Pulse the oats inside a food processor until powdery.

Apply all the remaining ingredients and pulse until well combined.

Transfer to a bowl and refrigerate for 15 minutes.

Form into burger patties.

Cook in the air fryer at 375 degrees F for 15 minutes.

Nutrition:

Calories 158

Total Fat 2 g

Total Carbohydrate 30 g

Dietary Fiber 9 g

Protein 8 g

CHAPTER 12:

Vegan Bread and Pizza

231. Beer Bread (Vegan)

Preparation time: 10 minutes
Cooking time: 45 minutes
Servings: 4
Ingredients:
225 g wheat flour
150 ml dark beer (or malt beer)
75 g sourdough
10 g yeast
1 tbsp. salt
For the rye sourdough:
75 g rye flour
75 ml water (lukewarm)
Direction:
For a successful beer bread, the sourdough must first be prepared! To do this, mix rye flour and lukewarm water into a dough and cover and leave to rest in a warm place for 12 hours.
As soon as the sourdough is left to rest, dissolve the yeast and salt in 3 tbsp. Of dark beer until bubbles form. Then add the sourdough, wheat flour and the remaining dark beer and knead for 8 minutes.
Cover again the dough and then let it rest in a warm place for 1-2 hours. Then either put the dough in the hot air fryer's baking pan without

further processing or shape it like a loaf and place it on the grid insert. Bake bread for 5 minutes at 200 ° C, then reduce the baking temperature to 180 ° C and bake for another 25 minutes.
Now and then, brush the bread with a little water to have excellent, shiny crust forms.
Nutrition:
Energy (calories): 326 kcal
Protein: 10.46 g
Fat: 1.31 g
Carbohydrates: 67.31 g

232. Fitness Bread (Vegan)

Preparation time: 10 minutes
Cooking time: 80 minutes
Servings: 1 bread
Ingredients:
150 g whole wheat flour
150 g wholemeal rye flour
1 tbsp. agave syrup, alternatively also maple syrup
25 g yeast
1 tsp. salt
1 tbsp. flaxseed oil
40 g chopped walnuts
35 g chopped pumpkin seeds
50 g dried fruit of your choice cut into pieces (dates, raisins, etc.)
Water for brushing
Directions:
Sieve wheat and rye flour and add salt. Dissolve the yeast in lukewarm water and mix in agave syrup. Add the flour and oil and knead everything into a soft dough. Then cover a clean kitchen towel with the dough and let it rest in a warm position for 30 minutes.

In the meantime, mix the chopped nuts and kernels with the dried fruit cut into pieces and, after the resting time, knead well into the dough. Place the dough in the baking pan of the air fryer and cover it for another 15 minutes. Then program the air fryer to 200 ° C and bake the loaf for 5 minutes. Then reduce the temperature to 180 ° C and bake for another 55 minutes. Brush the bread with a little water now and then to create a friendly, shiny crust.

Nutrition:
Energy (calories): 927 kcal
Protein: 27.26 g
Fat: 31.24 g
Carbohydrates: 147.53 g

233.   Wholegrain Bread (Vegan)

Preparation time: 10 minutes
Cooking time: 60 minutes
Servings: 1bread
Ingredients:
500 g whole wheat flour
150 g ready-made sourdough
100 g grain mixture
300 ml of lukewarm water
One packet of dry yeast
2 tbsp. salt
Directions:
Put the flour, sourdough, salt, water, dry yeast and 2/3 of the grain mixture in a prepared large bowl and knead into a dough. Cover the dough in the bowl with a clean kitchen towel and leave in a warm place for an hour.
Line the air fryer with parchment paper and place the loaf on top. Brush the loaf surface with water and carefully press the rest of the grain mixture into the loaf.
Bake bread for 10 minutes at 200 ° C, and then reduce the temperature to 150 ° C and bake for another 40 minutes. Let the bread cool down well before eating.
Nutrition:
Energy (calories): 542 kcal
Protein: 17.27 g
Fat: 5.02 g
Carbohydrates: 114.68 g

234.   Walnut Bread With Cranberries (Vegan)

Preparation time: 10 minutes
Cooking time: 40 minutes
Servings: 1bread
Ingredients:
500 g of wheat flour
One yeast cube
250 ml of lukewarm water
1 tbsp. salt
100 g walnuts
100 g cranberries, dried
Directions:
In a prepared bowl, mix the flour and salt and create a well in the middle. Pour the yeast into the well and pour lukewarm water over it. Let rest for 10 minutes.
Then add walnuts and cranberries and knead everything into a dough. Grease the bread pan and dust with flour. Alternatively line with baking paper.
Now cover the bread pan with a clean kitchen towel and let rise in a warm place for 60 minutes. Then bake for 30-35 minutes at 200 ° C.
Nutrition:
Energy (calories): 632 kcal
Protein: 16.72 g
Fat: 17.55 g
Carbohydrates: 102.2 g

235.   Mixed Bread Or Rolls Made From Rye And Wheat (Vegan)

Preparation time: 10 minutes
Cooking time: 40 minutes
Servings: 1bread
Ingredients:
150 g rye flour
150 g wheat flour
280 ml of lukewarm water
½ yeast cube
1 tbsp. salt
Directions:
Put salt, rye and wheat flour in a bowl and mix. Make a well in the middle and add the yeast cubes. Pour lukewarm water over and let it rest for 10 minutes so that the yeast dissolves. Then knead all the ingredients into a dough and cover

with a clean kitchen towel. Let it rest in a warm place for 30 minutes.

Now, shape a bread or four rolls out of the dough. Grease the baking pan of the air fryer, sprinkle with flour, alternatively line with baking paper. Now put the bread or rolls in the mould and bake at 200 ° C (rolls 25 minutes, bread for 35 minutes).

Nutrition:

Energy (calories): 357 kcal

Protein: 10.61 g

Fat: 1.25 g

Carbohydrates: 75.87 g

236. Spicy Sourdough Bread (Vegan)

Preparation time: 10 minutes

Cooking time: 40 minutes

Servings: 1bread

Ingredients:

500g flour

75 g ready-made sourdough

½ yeast cube

1 tbsp. salt

375 ml of water

½ tsp. rosemary

½ tsp. marjoram

½ tsp. tarragon

Directions:

Mix the flour with salt, rosemary, marjoram and tarragon. Crumble the yeast and dissolve in lukewarm water. Mix with the flour and herbs. Add the sourdough and knead everything into a dough. Cover with a clean kitchen towel and let rise for about an hour.

Grease the bread pan and then sprinkle with flour, or line with baking paper. Pour in the dough and let it rest for another 30 minutes. Now sprinkle the dough with a little flour and bake in the air fryer for 35 minutes at 200 ° C.

Nutrition:

Energy (calories): 1880 kcal

Protein: 54.06 g

Fat: 6.34 g

Carbohydrates: 391.03 g

237. Spelled Bread (Vegan)

Preparation time: 10 minutes

Cooking time: 45 minutes

Servings: 1bread

Ingredients:

500 g spelled flour

1 tbsp. salt

One yeast cube

250 ml of lukewarm water

One pinch of sugar

1 tsp. anise

Directions:

Put flour, salt and anise in a bowl and mix. Make a well in the middle and crumble the yeast into it. Pour a pinch of sugar over it. Cover the yeast and sugar with lukewarm water and let rest for 10 minutes so that the yeast dissolves.

Mix all ingredients in the bowl and knead into a dough. Cover with a clean kitchen towel and let rise in a warm place for about 60 minutes.

Line the breadbasket of the air fryer with baking paper or grease and dust with flour. Put the dough in the breadbasket of the Airfryer and bake for 30-35 minutes at 200 ° C.

Nutrition:

Energy (calories): 1827 kcal

Protein: 52.02 g

Fat: 5.23 g

Carbohydrates: 382.6 g

238. Vegan Cookies with Chocolate Sparks

Preparation time: 15 minutes

Cooking time: 15 minutes

Servings: 2

Ingredients

2 ½ cups of whole wheat flour

1 cup brown sugar

½ tsp. baking soda

¼ tsp. salt

½ cup unsweetened non-dairy milk

¼ cup of coconut oil

2 flax eggs

1 tsp. vanilla extract

¾ cup vegan chocolate chips

Directions:

Preheat the air fryer to 350ºF.

Mix all dry ingredients in a prepared large bowl (the flour, sugar, baking soda, and salt).

Add the liquid ingredients to the large bowl and stir until well combined.

Add the chocolate chips and stir until well combined. Let the dough rest in the fridge for 30 minutes to make it easier to handle.

Put one scoop of ice cream per cookie on a baking sheet lined with parchment paper and flatten them with your hands a little to shape them.

Bake for about 15 minutes or until they start to brown on the sides.

Nutrition:
Calories: 84.3
Carbohydrates: 11.8g
Fat: 2.7g
Protein: 2.1g
Sugar: 3.4g
Cholesterol: 0.5mg

239. Banana Chocolate Muffins

Preparation time: 5 minutes
Cooking time: 20 minutes
Servings: 1-2
Ingredients
1/3 cup oil
1/3 lb. brown sugar
Three ripe bananas
½ lb. flour
3 tsp. yeast
½ lb. chocolate and hazelnut cream
Directions:
Peel the bananas and chop them. Put them in a bowl and cook them with the help of a fork. Add the oil, sugar and stir until everything is integrated.

Add the flour with the yeast sifted and continue stirring until you obtain a homogeneous dough.

Arrange muffin capsules on the plate and fill them with the batter to 2/3 full. Pour 1 tsp of cocoa cream on top and stir with a toothpick to blend well.

Bake and cook the muffins for 20 minutes in the air fryer preheated to 360 degrees F until they are done. Remove and cool on a wire rack. Add more chocolate, if you like.

Nutrition:
Calories: 133.1
Carbohydrates: 26.3g
Fat: 2.9g
Protein: 2.4g
Sugar: 6.3g
Cholesterol: 13mg

240. Vegan Corn Bread

Preparation time: 10 minutes
Cooking time: 25 minutes
Servings: 9
Ingredients
1 cup white flour
1 cup polenta
½ cup brown sugar
¼ tsp of salt
½ tsp baking soda
1 tbsp. baking powder
¼ cup of melted butter
2 flax eggs
Vegan buttermilk
1/3 cup unsweetened non-dairy milk
Directions:
Preheat the air fryer to 400°F.

In a large bowl, add the white flour, cornmeal, sugar, salt, bicarbonate, yeast, and stir until they are integrated.

Put the rest of the ingredients to the bowl. Stir again until all the ingredients have been perfectly integrated.

Pour the dough into a pre-greased baking dish and bake for about 25 minutes or until done. Brown on the outside, and when you put a knife, it comes out clean.

Take the cornbread out of the oven and let it cool for a few minutes before slicing and serving. It can be good to eat hot or cold with vegan butter, maple syrup, jam, substitute for bread, or whatever you like.

The leftovers can also be kept in an airtight jar at room temperature or the fridge for about one week or in the freezer for 2 to 3 months.

Nutrition:
Calories: 68.7
Carbohydrates: 13.1g
Fat: 0.7g
Protein: 1.7g
Sugar: 2g
Cholesterol: 0mg

241. Vegan Banana Bread

Preparation time: 15 minutes
Cooking time: 65 minutes
Servings: 12
Ingredients
Three very ripe bananas
2 cups of whole wheat flour
¾ cup brown sugar
1 tsp. ground cinnamon
1 tsp. baking soda
¼ tsp. of salt
One flax egg
½ cup unsweetened non-dairy milk
1/3 cup coconut oil, melted
1 tsp. vanilla extract, optional
Directions:
Preheat the air fryer to 350°F.

Using a fork, you can mash the bananas. I recommend that you use cups or a scale to measure the amount of banana because the size of one to another can vary. Use 1 ½ cups. Reserve.

In a bowl, mix flour, sugar, cinnamon, baking soda and salt until they are well integrated.

Add the bananas, flax egg, milk, oil and vanilla extract. Stir until well-integrated.

Grease a pan or line with parchment paper and bake for about 60-70 minutes or until golden brown.

Take out the banana bread and leave it in the mould for at least 15 minutes, then you can move it to a wire rack. Ideally, let it cool completely before slicing it, but you can also have it hot if you want.

Nutrition:
Calories: 209.3
Carbohydrates: 43.4g
Fat: 3.1g
Protein: 2.9g
Sugar: 20.4g
Cholesterol: 0mg

242. Vegan Bread with Lentils and Unleavened Millet

Preparation time: 25 minutes
Cooking time: 45 minutes
Servings: 2-4
Ingredients
1 lb. coral lentils
½ lb. of millet
1 tbsp. of vinegar or lemon
1 tsp. salt
Water
Spices to taste (turmeric, ginger, pepper, etc.)
Directions:
Place the lentils and millet in a bowl. Cover them with water and then let stand for 12 hours. After that time, rinse the grains, discarding the soaking water.

Crush the lentils and millet with a mini primer or food processor to form a sticky dough. Add the vinegar or the lemon, the salt and the chosen spices and mix.

Let the dough rest in a bowl and then covered with plastic wrap or with a kitchen cloth at room temperature for two days. After that time, the dough begins to rise, and you will feel an acidic smell due to the grains' fermentation. Place the dough in a previously oiled bread pan or upholstered with vegetable paper.

Take in a preheated air fryer at 360° for about 30-40 minutes or until a toothpick is inserted and it comes out dry.

Nutrition:
Calories: 80
Carbs: 14g
Fat: 2g
Protein: 1g

243. Bread, Black Olives, Leek and Rosemary

Preparation time: 15 minutes
Cooking time: 30 minutes
Servings: 2
Ingredients
4 tbsp. of wheat flour
1/3 of tbsp. baking powder
2 ½ tbsp. water
1 tbsp. olive oil
Black olives
One piece of leek
Sesame seeds
Rosemary to taste
Salt to taste
Directions:
In a prepared bowl, mix all the dry ingredients: 4 tbsp. of wheat flour, 1/3 of a tbsp. of baking powder, three pinches of rosemary and another two pinches of salt.
Mix well and add 1 tbsp. Of olive oil. Mix again. Add 2 tbsp. And half of the water and mixture also until you get a slightly sticky dough. Flour a clean table and put the ball of dough on top.
Knead well, can add more flour if necessary, to be able to knead with your hands without sticking.
Roll, make a churro and cut it into seven equal pieces. Shape each cut into a ball. Make a churro of each ball and flatten it with the roller.
Put the bread on the baking tray with the paper, and decorate them with black olives, finely chopped leek.
Bathe each bagel with ½ tbsp. Of oil, and add a pinch more of salt and the sesame seeds.
Bake at 4000F for 30 minutes and ready!
Nutrition:
Calories: 138 Carbohydrates: 22g Fat: 3.7g
Protein: 3.6g Sugar: 1.6g Cholesterol: 0mg

244. Black Olive Bread and Rosemary in Olive Oil

Preparation time: 60 minutes
Cooking time: 40 minutes
Servings: 4
Ingredients
1 lb. Wheat flour
1 cup of water
4 tsp. fresh yeast
Pitted black olives
Garlic powder
Rosemary to taste
Parsley to taste
Olive oil
Salt to taste
Directions:
Mix the flour with the 4 tsp. of fresh yeast, a tsp. of garlic powder, ½ of parsley, and two rosemary. Mix very well. Mix the yeast and spices with the flour that will give flavour to the black olive bread
Next, add 3 tbsps. of olive oil. Mix well, ensuring that there are a few lumps as possible. Add 1 cup of water.
With a shovel, mix all the ingredients well and distribute the wet ingredients among the dry ones.
Mix well until the dough acquires a manageable texture. Flour the table and smear your hands with more flour.
Remove the dough from the bowl and knead with force and energy for 8 minutes.
Now, shape and mold the dough into a ball and place it on a baking sheet and its greaseproof paper.
Stretch with a roller's help gives it an elongated shape, with rounded edges and a thickness of more or less 1 cm. Note that it will double in size, approximately. Let it rise for 1 hour. on the tray with the baking paper and covered with a cloth.
After the hour, paint the surface with generous olive oil so that the base is well greased.
On top, decorate with the sliced black olives, rosemary, salt and more garlic powder.
Now, put it in the air fryer at 3600F for about 40 minutes.
When it begins to toast, after about 30 minutes, if the bread is drying, you can repaint the top of the black olive bread with more olive oil.
Nutrition:
Calories: 138 Carbohydrates: 22g
Fat: 3.7g Protein: 3.6g Sugar: 1.6g
Cholesterol: 0mg

245.   Homemade Chocolate Bread

Preparation time: 60 minutes
Cooking time: 40 minutes
Servings: 4
Ingredients
1 lbs. Of flour
2 tsp. fresh yeast
¾ cup vegetable milk
1 bar of dark chocolate
Orange peel
Lemon peel
3 tbsp. of vegetable margarine
Cinnamon powder
A vanilla flavored soy yogurt
Agave syrup or your favorite sweetener
Directions:
Put the flour in a large bowl.
Put the crumbled yeast with your hands. Beat with a fork until undo. Afterwards, cut a piece of orange peel and another lemon and let it marinate in the milk.
Add a minimum of ½ tsp. of cinnamon.
On the other hand, heat until the 3 tbsp. Of margarine is melted. When it is melted, add it to the flour and mix well. Add the yogurt, 2 tbsp. Of syrup and the flavoured vegetable milk, it has previously removed the lemon and orange peels and beaten with a fork to distribute the yeast well through the milk.
Knead well until the ingredients are properly mixed.
Take the chocolate bar and chop it with a knife into small cubes. Add everything to the dough and knead for 3 minutes, with force and energy.
Sprinkle a little amount of flour on the table, put the dough on top, and knead for five more minutes.
Now, make a 'churro' and cut it into parts. Take each of the cuts, knead it and roll it.
Place the buns on the baking tray with the baking paper on. Let it rise for 1 hour. Afterwards, paint them with a little agave syrup, and with a spoon, spread it well over the entire surface of the bread.
Put in the air fryer at 3600F for 35-45 minutes.
But check them after 35 minutes, try to be aware.

Nutrition:
Calories: 146
Carbohydrates: 2g
Fat: 5g
Protein: 2g
Sugar: 10g
Cholesterol: 0mg

246.   Breakfast Berry Pizza

Preparation time: 7 minutes
Cooking time: 15 minutes
Servings: 6
Ingredients
1 sheet of frozen puff pastry
1 Container of Vegan Strawberry Cream
6 Oz of fresh raspberries
6 Oz of fresh blueberries
6 Oz of fresh blackberries
8 Oz of fresh strawberries
½ Tsp. of vanilla bean paste
¼ Tsp. of almond extract
2 Tsp. of maple syrup
Directions:
Preheat your air fryer to about 390° F
Thaw 1 of your pastry sheets according to the directions on the pack
Cut your pastry into its half and make fine cuts, with a knife, right on the top of each of the pastry sheet or poke it with a toothpick
Repeat the same process with the remaining quantity of the pastry
Put the pastry sheet in a greased baking tray and put it in the basket if the air fryer; then close the lid
Set the timer set to 15 minutes and the temperature to 390° F
When the timer beeps; remove the pastries from the air fryer and set them aside to cool for 10 minutes; meanwhile, prepare the topping by mixing the Vegan Strawberry Cream into a large bowl
Add the raspberries and mash the strawberries; then mix it with the raspberries, the vanilla paste, the almond extract and the maple syrup.
Stir the mixture very well and when your crust becomes cool, pour the mixture over it with a spatula

Top with the berries and the fresh strawberries
Serve and enjoy your pizza!
Note:
Some people prefer making a salty breakfast while others instead prefer having a sweet breakfast and at the same time a healthy one. This sweet pizza will be the best choice you can ever make.
Nutrition:
Calories 247.8 calories
Fat 6.1 grams
Saturated Fats 2.1 gram
Total Carbs 21 grams
Protein 25.4 grams

247.   Whole Wheat Vegan Toast

Preparation time: 5 minutes
Cooking time: 10 minutes
Servings: 3
Ingredients
1 Loaf of sliced whole wheat bread
2 Ripe bananas
1 Can of coconut milk
2 Tsp. of vanilla
1 Tsp. of cinnamon
¼ Tsp. of salt
½ Cup of dry roasted pecans
Cooking spray
Directions
Start by cutting the whole-wheat bread into equal-sized slices
In a blender, mix the coconut milk, the pecan, the vanilla, the cinnamon, and the salt. Pour your obtained mixture into a deep bowl; then add the bread and let soak for about 2 minutes
Grease a baking tray and preheat your air fryer to about 350° F
Lay the soaked bread into the greased tray and put it in the basket of the air fryer
Close the lid and then set the timer to about 8 minutes and the temperature to 360°F
When the timer beeps, remove the bread toasts from the air fryer; then set it aside to cool for about 5 minutes
Serve and enjoy with maple syrup!
Note:

This whole wheat Vegan French toast is very decadent, creamy. Try it and enjoy the warmth. This recipe will make you addicted to it with its light taste. You can earn top this vegan toast with any topping of your choice.
Nutrition:
Calories per serving 110 calories
Fat per serving 0.9 grams
Saturated Fats 0.2 gram
Total Carbs per serving 21.1 grams
Protein per serving 4 grams

248.   Flat Bread with Olive and Rosemary

Preparation time: 15 minutes
Cooking time: 20 minutes
Servings: 5
Note:
With the crispiness of the pizza crust and the delicious taste of the pita bread, this recipe will offer you a magical combination of both types. This recipe is light and topped with spices; you will like it.
Ingredients
One and ½ tsp. of active dry yeast
One and ½ tsp. of unrefined cane sugar
½ Tsp. of kosher salt
One and ½ cups of all-purpose flour
One and ½ cups of whole spelt flour
1 Tbsp. of finely cut fresh rosemary leaves
2 Tbsp. of extra-virgin olive oil
2 Tbsp. of thyme
½ Cup of pitted and cut olive
Directions:
In a deep mixing bowl, mix a little bit of olive oil with a little bit of yeast, salt, sugar and pour in about 1 cup of water (Make sure the water is warm)
Set aside the mixture and let rest for about 11 minutes
Add in the flours and the chopped rosemary; then blend the ingredients on a deficient speed
Use the dough hook to knead your dough, and once you obtain a smooth one; divide it into about two balls
Put the dough balls over a floured baking paper and let rest for about 3 hours

Put the pizza over a greased baking tray and use your hands and fingers to spread it into a circle

Cover your bread with a kitchen towel and set it aside to rest for about 12 minutes

Brush the bread with olive oil and put it in the basket of the air fryer; close the lid and set the timer to about 10 minutes and the temperature to about 365° F

When the timer beeps, remove the bread from the air fryer and sprinkle a little bit of pepper, olive oil and salt

Serve and enjoy!

Nutrition:

Calories per serving – 156.4 calories

Fat per serving – 10.1 grams

Saturated Fats – 2.5 gram

Total Carbs per serving – 4.6 grams

Protein per serving – 6.1 grams

249. Cinnamon Sugar Toast

Preparation time: 10 minutes

Cooking time: 8 minutes

Servings: 2

Ingredients:

1/4 cup granulated sugar

11/2 tsp. ground cinnamon

2 tbsp. vegan butter, room temperature

4 slices gluten-free sandwich bread

Directions:

In a prepared small bowl, combine sugar and cinnamon.

Preheat the air fryer set the temperature at 375°F for 3 minutes.

Spread butter over bread slices. Evenly sprinkle buttered slices with cinnamon-sugar mix.

Place two bread slices in an ungreased air fryer basket and cook for 4 minutes. Transfer to a

large plate. Repeat with remaining pieces. Serve warm.

Nutrition:

Energy (calories): 193 kcal

Protein: 5.68 g

Fat: 7.54 g

Carbohydrates: 26.89 g

250. Salted Caramel Banana Muffins

Preparation time: 10 minutes

Cooking time: 14 minutes

Servings: 8

Ingredients:

1 cup gluten-free all-purpose flour

1/2 tsp. baking soda

1/3 cup granulated sugar

1/4 tsp. salt

1/3 cup mashed banana, about one large ripe banana

1/2 tsp. vanilla extract

1 Silken tofu

1 tbsp. vegetable oil

1/4 cup salted caramel chips

Directions:

Preheat the air fryer set the temperature at 375°F for 3 minutes.

In a prepared large mixing bowl, combine flour, baking soda, sugar, and salt. In a separate prepared medium bowl, combine mashed banana, vanilla, tofu, and oil.

Pour all wet ingredients into dry ingredients and gently combine. Fold in salted caramel chips. Do not overmix. Spoon mixture into eight silicone cupcake liners lightly greased with preferred cooking oil.

Place four muffins in an air fryer basket. Cook for 7 minutes, then transfer to a cooling rack. Repeat with remaining muffins. Serve warm or cooled.

Nutrition:

Energy (calories): 103 kcal

Protein: 1.77 g

Fat: 1.93 g

Carbohydrates: 19.71 g

251. Pizza Tofu Bites

These little bites of tasty protein are perfect for an after-school treat or a snack on the weekend. Marinating the tofu helps it soak up the flavours before air frying. Dipping the bites into a bowl of warmed marinara sauce will bring all the ingredients together.

Preparation time: 15 minutes
Cooking time: 20 minutes
Servings: 4
Ingredients:
For Marinade
1/3 cup vegetable broth
2 tbsp. tomato sauce
1 tbsp. nutritional yeast
1 tsp. Italian seasoning
1 tsp. granulated sugar
1/2 tsp. fennel seeds
1/2 tsp. garlic powder
1/4 tsp. salt
1/4 tsp. ground black pepper
14 oz firm tofu, cut into 3/4" cubes
For Breading
2/3 cup plain gluten-free bread crumbs
2 tsp. nutritional yeast
1 tsp. Italian seasoning
1/2 tsp. salt
For Dip
1 cup marinara sauce, heated
Directions:
To Make the marinade: Combine all Marinade ingredients in a gallon-sized plastic bag or large bowl. Toss tofu to coat. Refrigerate for 30 minutes, tossing tofu once more after 15 minutes.

To make Breading and Pizza Tofu Bites: Preheat air fryer to 350°F for 3 minutes.

In a shallow dish, combine Breading ingredients. Strain marinade from tofu cubes. Dredge in bread crumb mixture.

Place half of the tofu in an air fryer basket lightly greased with preferred cooking oil. Cook 5 minutes. Flip tofu. Brush with additional cooking oil—Cook an additional 5 minutes.

Transfer cooked tofu to a large plate. Repeat with remaining tofu. Serve warm with marinara dip on the side.

Nutrition:
Energy (calories): 422 kcal
Fat: 27.84 g
Carbohydrates: 26.85 g

252. Vegan Caprese Sandwiches

Usually, a classic Caprese salad is served with a crisp artisan bread so you can sop up the flavours. Now enjoy that delicious salad in sandwich form! Don't overlook the last drizzle of olive oil on the sandwich bread: it pulls all of those traditional flavours together.

Preparation time: 10 minutes
Cooking time: 10 minutes
Servings: 2
Ingredients:
2 tbsp. balsamic vinegar
4 slices gluten-free sandwich bread
2 ounces vegan mozzarella shreds
Two medium Roma tomatoes, sliced
Eight fresh basil leaves
2 tbsp. olive oil
Directions:
Preheat the air fryer and set the temperature at 350°F for 3 minutes.

Prepare sandwiches by drizzling balsamic vinegar on bottom bread slices: layer mozzarella, tomatoes, and basil leaves on top. Add top bread slices.

Brush outside the top and bottom of each sandwich lightly with olive oil. Place one sandwich in an ungreased air fryer basket and cook for 3 minutes. Flip and cook an additional 2 minutes—transfer the sandwich to a large serving plate and repeat with the second sandwich.

Serve warm.
Nutrition:
Energy (calories): 440 kcal
Protein: 17.93 g
Fat: 22.6 g
Carbohydrates: 41.19 g

253. Mini Mushroom-Onion Eggplant Pizzas

Preparation time: 5 minutes
Cooking time: 16 minutes
Servings: 4
Ingredients:
2 tsp. + 2 tbsp. olive oil, divided
1/4 cup small-diced peeled yellow onion
1/2 cup small-diced white mushrooms
1/2 cup marinara sauce
One small eggplant, sliced into 8 (1/2") circles
1 tsp. salt
1 cup vegan shredded mozzarella
1/4 cup chopped fresh basil
Directions:
In a prepared medium skillet over medium heat, heat 2 tsp. olive oil 30 seconds. Add onion and mushrooms and cook for 5 minutes until onions are translucent. Add marinara sauce and stir. Remove skillet from heat.
Preheat the air fryer at 375°F for 3 minutes.
Rub remaining olive oil over both sides of eggplant circles. Lay circles on a large plate and season top evenly with salt—top with marinara sauce mixture, followed by shredded mozzarella.
Place half of the eggplant pizzas in an ungreased air fryer basket. Cook 5 minutes.
Transfer cooked pizzas to a large plate. Repeat with remaining pizzas. Garnish with chopped basil and serve warm.
Nutrition:
Energy (calories): 111 kcal
Protein: 10.94 g Fat: 3.15 g
Carbohydrates: 11.74 g

254. Cauliflower Personal Pizza Crusts

Preparation time: 10 minutes
Cooking time: 30 minutes
Servings: 2
Ingredients:
1 cup cauliflower rice
1 1/2 tbsp. Tapioca starch
1/2 cup vegan grated mozzarella
One clove garlic, peeled and minced
1 tsp. Italian seasoning
1/8 tsp. salt
Directions:
Preheat and set the air fryer's temperature to 400°F for 3 minutes.
In a medium bowl, combine all ingredients.
Divide mixture in half and spread into two pizza pans lightly greased with preferred cooking oil.
Place one pan in an air fryer basket and cook for 12 minutes. Once done, remove the pan from the basket and repeat with the second pan.
Top crusts with your favourite toppings and cook an additional 3 minutes.
Nutrition:
Energy (calories): 86 kcal
Protein: 10.16 g Fat: 0.16 g
Carbohydrates: 11.33 g

255. Pizza Bombs

Preparation time: 5 minutes
Cooking time: 12 minutes
Servings: 9 pizza bites
Ingredients:
1/3 cup gluten-free all-purpose flour
1/4 tsp. salt
1/4 tsp. baking powder
1/2 cup small-diced pepperoni
2 ounces Tofutti, room temperature
1/4 cup vegan shredded mozzarella cheese
1/2 tsp. Italian seasoning
2 tbsp. Almond Milk
1 tsp. olive oil
1/2 cup vegan marinara sauce, warmed
Directions:
Preheat the air fryer at 325°F for 5 minutes.
In a small bowl, combine flour, salt, and baking powder. In a prepared medium bowl, combine the remaining ingredients, except vegan marinara sauce, mixing until smooth. Add dry ingredients to bowl and mix until well combined.
Form mixture into nine (1") balls and place on an ungreased pizza pan. It's okay if pizza balls are touching. Put the pan in air fryer basket and cook 12 minutes. Transfer balls to a large plate. Serve warm with vegan marinara sauce on the side for dipping.
Nutrition:
Energy (calories): 112 kcal Protein: 4.49 g
Fat: 3.94 g Carbohydrates: 14.85 g

CHAPTER 13:

Vegan Main Dishes

256. Cauliflower Rice

"The healthiest cauliflower rice to date! Just go ahead and make it. It's the perfect rice to go with any of the heavier dishes!"

Preparation time: 10 minutes

Cooking time: 20 minutes

Servings: 3

Temperature: 370degreesF

Ingredients:

For the tofu

Two carrots, diced

½ cup onion, diced

2 tbsp. soy sauce

1 tsp. turmeric

½ block firm tofu, crumbled

For the rice

3 cups riced cauliflower

2 tbsp. sodium soy sauce, reduced

½ cup broccoli, finely chopped

1 tbsp. rice vinegar

½ cup peas, frozen

Two garlic cloves, minced

One and ½ tsp. sesame oil, toasted

1 tbsp. ginger, minced

½ cup frozen peas

1 tbsp. rice vinegar

Directions:

Preheat and set the Air Fryer's temperature to 370 degrees F

Take a large bowl and add tofu alongside remaining tofu ingredients

Stir well to combine

Set in the Air Fryer to cook for 10 minutes

Take another bowl and add the remaining ingredients

Stir them well

Transfer into the Air Fryer and cook 10 minutes more

Serve and enjoy!

Nutrition

Calories: 153

Fat: 4g

Carbohydrates: 18g

Protein: 10g

257. Sweet Potato Cauliflower Patties

"In the mood for some patties? Just make them from cauliflower! They will be both healthy and fried!"

Preparation time: 15 minutes

Cooking time: 20 minutes

Servings: 1

Temperature: 400degreesF

Ingredients

2 cups cauliflower florets

2 tbsp. arrowroot powder

1 tsp. garlic, minced

One large sweet potato, peeled and chopped

¼ cup flaxseed, grounded

1 cup cilantro, packed

¼ tsp. cumin

2 tbsp. Ranch seasoning mix

¼ cup sunflower seeds

½ tsp. chilli powder

1 cup cilantro, packed

One green onion, chopped

Salt and pepper

Any dipping sauce for serving

Directions:

Preheat your Air Fryer and set the temperature at 400 degrees F

Add sweet potato, cauliflower, onion, garlic, and sizzle into your food processor

Blend until smooth

Mould the mixture into patties and place onto a greased baking sheet

Place into your freezer for 10 minutes

Then transfer into your Air Fryer

Cook for 20 minutes and flip after 10 minutes

Serve and enjoy!

Nutrition:

Calories: 85

Fat: 2.9g

Carbohydrates: 6g

Protein: 2.7g

258.   Breaded Mushrooms

"Take your normal mushrooms and turn them into this crispy treat for all ages! Your kids are going to love you for this!"

Preparation time: 15 minutes

Cooking time: 7 minutes

Servings: 2

Temperature: 360degreesF

Ingredients:

½ pound button mushrooms

1 cup almond meal

1 Flax-Egg

1 cup almond flour

3 ounces cashew cheese

Salt and pepper

Directions:

Preheat and set the Air Fryer's temperature to 360 degrees F

Take a shallow bowl and toss almond meal with cheese into it

Whisk flax egg in one bowl and spread flour in another

Wash mushrooms, then pat dry

Coat every mushroom with flour

Dip each of them in the flax egg first, then in breadcrumb

Spray with cooking oil and place back in the Air Fryer

Air fry these mushrooms for 7 minutes in your Air Fryer

Toss the mushrooms after 3 minutes

Once cooked, serve warm

Enjoy!

Nutrition:

Calories: 140

Fat: 9.2g

Carboh0ydrates: 6.9g

Protein: 9.3g

259.   Carrot & Potato Mix

Preparation time: 10 minutes

Cooking time: 16 minutes

Servings: 6

Ingredients:

Potatoes (2)

Carrots (3 lb.)

Yellow onion (1)

Dried thyme (1 tsp.)

Black pepper and salt (to your liking)

Curry powder (2 tsp.)

Coconut milk (3 tbsp.)

Vegan cheese (3 tbsp.)

Parsley (1 tbsp.)

Directions:

Cube/chop the parsley, carrots, and onions. Crumble the vegan cheese.

Warm the Air Fryer to reach 365° Fahrenheit.

Once it's heated, toss in the veggies, thyme, curry powder, salt, and pepper. Set the timer and air-fry for 16 minutes.

Stir in the milk and cheese.
Portion and serve.
Nutrition
Protein Count: 4 grams Carbohydrates: 1 gram
Fat Content: 4 grams Calorie: 241

260. Eggplant Fries

"Ditch the traditional eggplants and fry them up a bit for that added crunchy goodness!"
Preparation time: 10 minutes
Cooking time: 5 minutes
Servings: 4
Temperature: 360degreesF
Ingredients:
One eggplant, peeled and sliced
One flax-egg
½ cup cashew cheese
2 tbsp. almond milk
2 cups almond meal
Cooking spray
Black pepper
Salt
Directions:
Take a bowl and add flax egg, salt, and pepper to it
Whisk it well
Take another bowl, mix cheese and panko, then stir. Dip eggplant fries in the flax egg mixture, coat in panko mix. Grease the Air Fryer basket using vegan cooking spray
Place the eggplant fries in it
Cook for 5 minutes at 400 degrees
Serve and enjoy!
Nutrition:
Calories: 162 Fat: 5g
Carboh0ydrates: 7g Protein: 6g

261. Crispy and Salty Tofu

"While many people don't like the flavour of normally prepared tofu, Air Drying them completely changes everything!"
Preparation time: 5 minutes
Cooking time: 15 minutes
Servings: 4
Temperature: 392degreesF
Ingredients:
¼ cup chickpea flour

¼ cup arrowroot
1 tsp. salt
1 tsp. garlic powder
½ tsp. black pepper
One pack (15 ounces) tofu, firm
Cooking spray as needed
Directions:
Preheat your Air Fryer 392 Degrees F
Take a medium-sized bowl and add flour, arrowroot, salt, garlic, pepper, and stir well
Cut tofu into cubes, transfer cubes into the flour mix
Toss well
Spray tofu with oil and transfer to Air Fryer cooking basket
Spray oil on top and cook for 8 minutes
Shake and toss well, fry for 7 minutes more
Serve and enjoy!
Nutrition:
Calories: 148
Fat: 5g
Carboh0ydrates: 14g
Protein: 11g

262. The Easy Paneer Pizza

"Gone Vegan but missing pizza? This is the guilty-free pizza that you need for your vegan journey!"
Preparation time: 5 minutes
Cooking time: 9 minutes
Servings: 4
Temperature: 347degreesF
Ingredients:
Cooking oil spray as needed
One flour tortilla sprouted
¼ cup vegan pizza sauce
½ cup vegan cheese
Vegan-friendly topping of your choice
Directions:
Preheat your Air Fryer 347 Degrees F
Spray your Air Fryer cooking basket with oil, add tortilla to your Air Fryer basket and pour the sauce in the center
Evenly distribute your topping on top alongside vegan cheese

Bake for 9 minutes
Serve and enjoy!
Nutrition:
Calories: 210
Fat: 6g
Carboh0ydrates: 33g
Protein: 5g

263. Cauliflower Sauce and Pasta

"The vegan pasta for those who are missing the classic Alfredo pasta!"
Preparation time: 10 minutes
Cooking time: 18 minutes
Servings: 4
Temperature: 392degreesF
Ingredients:
4 cups cauliflower florets
Cooking oil as needed
One medium onion, chopped
8 ounces pasta of your choice
Fresh chives for garnish
½ cup cashew pieces
One and ½ cups of water
1 tbsp. nutritional yeast
Two large garlic cloves, peeled
2 tbsp. fresh lemon juice
One and ½ tsp. salt
¼ tsp. fresh ground black pepper
Directions:
Preheat your Air Fryer 392 Degrees F
Add cauliflower to your Air Fryer basket and spray oil on top. Add onion
Roast for 8 minutes and stir, roast for 10 minutes more
Cook the pasta according to package instructions
Take a blender and add roasted cauliflower and onions alongside cashews, water, yeast, garlic, lemon, garlic, salt, pepper and blend well
Serve pasta together with the sauce on top and a garnish of minced chives and scallions
Serve and enjoy!
Nutrition:
Calories: 341
Fat: 9g
Carboh0ydrates: 51g
Protein: 14g

264. Tamarind Glazed Sweet Potatoes

"If you like the tanginess of tamarind, these tamarind glazed potatoes are what you need!"
Preparation time: 5 minutes
Cooking time: 22 minutes
Servings: 4
Temperature: 395degreesF
Ingredients:
Five garnet sweet potatoes, peeled and diced
1/3 tsp. white pepper
A few drops of liquid stevia
1 tbsp. vegan butter, melted
2 tsp. tamarind paste
½ tsp. turmeric powder
One and ½ tbsp. lime juice
A pinch of the ground allspice
Directions:
Preheat and set the Air Fryer's temperature to 395 degrees F. Get a mixing bowl and add all ingredients into it.
Mix them until sweet potatoes are well coated.
Cook for 12 minutes
Pause the Air Fryer and toss again. Increase the temperature to 390 degrees F
Cook for 10 minutes more
Serve warm and enjoy!
Nutrition:
Calories: 103
Fat: 9.1g
Carboh0ydrates: 4.9g
Protein: 1.9g

265. Lemon Lentils and Fried Onion

"Fried onions alone might send you off a bit. Why add some lentils to the mix? It'll make the flavours pop out even more!"
Preparation time: 10 minutes
Cooking time: 30 minutes
Servings: 4
Temperature: 392degreesF
Ingredients:
4 cups of water
Cooking oil spray as needed
One medium onion, peeled and cut into ¼ inch thick rings
Salt as needed

½ cup kale stems removed

Three large garlic cloves, pressed

2 tbsp. fresh lemon juice

2 tsp. nutritional yeast

1 tsp. salt

1 tsp. lemon zest

¾ tsp. fresh pepper

Directions:

Preheat your Air Fryer to 392 degrees F

Take a large-sized pot and bring lentils to boil over medium-high heat

Adjust the heat into low and simmer for 30 minutes, making sure to stir after every 5 minutes

Once they are cooked, take your Air Fryer basket and spray with cooking oil, add onion rings and sprinkle salt

Fry for 5 minutes, shaking basket and fry for 5 minutes more

Remove the basket and spray with oil. Cook for 5 minutes more until crispy and browned

Add kale to the lentils and stir, add sliced greens

Stir in garlic, lemon juice, yeast, salt, pepper, and stir well

Top with crispy onion rings and serve

Enjoy!

Nutrition:

Calories: 220

Fat: 1g

Carboh0ydrates: 39g

Protein: 15g

266.   The Daily Bean Dish

"A traditional bean dish made using your Air Fryer! A healthy protein-packed meal at its best!"

Preparation time: 5 minutes

Cooking time: 8 minutes

Servings: 4

Temperature: 392degreesF

Ingredients:

One can (15 ounces) pinto beans, drained

¼ cup tomato sauce

2 tbsp. nutritional yeast

Two large garlic cloves, minced

½ tsp. dried oregano

½ tsp. cumin

¼ tsp. salt

1/8 tsp. ground black pepper

Cooking oil spray as needed

Directions:

Preheat your Air Fryer to 392 degrees F

Take a medium bowl and add beans, tomato sauce, yeast, garlic, oregano, cumin, salt, pepper and mix well

Take your baking pan and add oil, pour bean mixture

Transfer to Air Fryer and bake for 4 minutes until cooked thoroughly with a slightly golden crust on top

Serve and enjoy!

Nutrition:

Calories: 284

Fat: 4g

Carboh0ydrates: 47g

Protein: 20g

267.   Fine 10 Minute Chimichanga

"If you are a fan of Deadpool, you've heard of chimichangas! This is your time to make a Vegan one!"

Preparation time: 2 minutes

Cooking time: 8 minutes

Servings: 4

Temperature: 392degreesF

Ingredients:

One whole-grain tortilla

½ cup vegan refried beans

¼ cup grated vegan cheese

Cooking oil spray as needed

½ cup fresh salsa

2 cups romaine lettuce, chopped

Guacamole

Chopped cilantro

Directions:

Preheat your Air Fryer to 392 degrees F

Lay tortilla on flat surface and place beans on center, top with cheese and wrap bottom up over filling, fold insides

Roll all up and enclose beans inside

Spray Air Fryer cooking basket with oil and place wrap inside the basket, fry for 5 minutes, spray on top and cook for 2-3 minutes more

Move to a plate and serve with salsa, lettuce, and guacamole
Enjoy!
Nutrition:
Calories: 317
Fat: 6g
Carboh0ydrates: 55g
Protein: 13g

268.   Mexican Stuffed Potatoes

"Stuff your Mexican potatoes style! You'll keep coming back to them, wanting for more!"
Preparation time: 15 minutes
Cooking time: 40 minutes
Servings: 4
Temperature: 392degreesF
Ingredients:
Four large potatoes
Cooking oil spray as needed
One and ½ cups cashew cheese
1 cup black beans
Two medium tomatoes, chopped
One scallion, chopped
1/3 cup cilantro, chopped
One jalapeno, sliced
One avocado, diced
Directions:
Preheat your Air Fryer to 392 degrees F
Scrub potatoes and prick with a fork, spray outside with oil
Transfer to Air Fryer and bake for 30 minutes
Check potatoes at 30 minutes mark by poking them. If they are tender, they are ready. If not, cook for 10 minutes more
Once done, warm your cashew cheese and beans in separate pans
Once potatoes are cooked, cut them across top
Pry them open with a fork with just enough space to stuff the remaining ingredients
Top each potato with cashew cheese, beans, tomatoes, scallions, cilantro, jalapeno, and avocado
Serve and enjoy!
Nutrition:
Calories: 420 Fat: 5g
Carboh0ydrates: 80g
Protein: 15g

269.   The Great Taquito

"Refried beans and a mixture of creamy delight packed in a tortilla, these taquitos are Vegan and Guilt-free!"
Preparation time: 15 minutes
Cooking time: 15 minutes
Servings: 4
Temperature: 392degreesF
Prep Time: 5 minutes
Cook Time: 7 minutes
Ingredients:
Eight corn tortillas
Cooking oil spray as needed
1 (15 ounces) can vegan refried beans
1 cup shredded vegan cheese
Guacamole
Cashew cheese
Vegan sour cream
Fresh salsa
Directions:
Preheat your Air Fryer to 392 degrees F
Warm your tortilla and run them underwater for a second, transfer to Air Fryer cooking basket and cook for 1 minute
Remove to the flat surface and place equal amounts of beans at the center of each tortilla, top with vegan cheese
Roll tortilla sides up over filling, place seam side down in Air Fryer
Spray oil on top and cook for 7 minutes until golden brown
Serve and enjoy!
Nutrition:
Calories: 420
Fat: 5g
Carboh0ydrates: 80g
Protein: 15g

270.   The Cheesy Vegan Sandwich

Preparation time: 3 minutes
Cooking time: 12 minutes
Servings: 4
Temperature: 392degreesF
Ingredients:
Two slices sprouted whole grain bread
1 tsp. vegan margarine
Two slices of vegan cheese

1 tsp. mellow white miso

One medium-large garlic clove, minced

2 tbsp. fermented vegetables, kimchi or sauerkraut

Romaine lettuce

Directions:

Preheat your Air Fryer to 392 degrees F

Spread outside of bread with Vegan margarine, place sliced cheese inside and close sandwich back up

Transfer Sandwich to Air Fryer and cook 6 minutes, flip and cook for 6 minutes more

Transfer to plate and spread miso and garlic clove inside one of the slices, top with fermented veggies and lettuce

Close sandwich and cut in half

Serve and enjoy!

Nutrition:

Calories: 288

Fat: 13g

Carboh0ydrates: 34g

Protein: 8g

271. Sesame Crunchy Tofu

"Sesame dressed crunchy tofu! This is the vegan protein dish to beat!"

Preparation time: 10 minutes

Cooking time: 20 minutes

Servings: 4

Temperature: 392degreesF

Ingredients:

One pack (8 ounces) tofu, extra firm

One and ½ tbsp. tamari

½ tsp. granulated garlic

½ cup sesame seeds, raw and toasted

2 tsp. flour

1 tbsp. arrowroot

2 tbsp. sunflower oil

Cooking oil spray as needed

Directions:

Preheat your Air Fryer to 392 degrees F

Slice tofu into ½ inch thick slabs, then into triangles

Press tofu by placing the pieces in a fine layer on top of a paper towel, cover with more towels and gently press the moisture

Place pressed tofu on a plate, sprinkle evenly with tamari and garlic

Turn to coat well

Take a medium bowl; add sesame seeds, flour, and arrowroot

Add tofu and stir well, coat with sesame mixture

Add oil and stir to coat the tofu

Spray Air Fryer basket with oil, transfer tofu to a single layer and bake for 10 minutes

Remove, turn the pieces and cook for 10 minutes more until golden brown and crisp

Serve and enjoy!

Nutrition:

Calories: 183 Fat: 18g

Carboh0ydrates: 5g

Protein: 4g

272. Creamy Cauliflower and Broccoli

"One of the best Air Fryer salad you are ever going to taste! Cauliflower and broccoli mixed with cashew cheese. Creamy heaven!"

Preparation time: 5 minutes

Cooking time: 16 minutes

Servings: 6

Temperature: 390degreesF

Ingredients:

1-pound cauliflower florets

One tbsp. lemon zest, grated

Two and ½ tbsp. sesame oil

¾ tsp. sea salt flakes

½ cup cashew cheese

1-pound broccoli florets

½ tsp. cayenne pepper, smoked

Directions:

Preheat your Air Fryer and set the temperature at 390 degrees F

Prepare the cauliflower and broccoli using the steaming method

Drain it and add cayenne pepper, sesame oil, and salt flakes

Cook for 15 minutes

Check your vegetables halfway during cooking

Stir in the lemon zest and cashew cheese

Toss to coat well

Serve warm and enjoy!

Nutrition:

Calories: 133

Fat: 9.0g

Carboh0ydrates: 7g

Protein: 5.9g

273.   Roasted Chickpeas

"The mango powder here really helps to flavour up the chickpeas here while the cinnamon and cumin bring them all so needed heat! Lovely."

Preparation time: 2 minutes

Cooking time: 10 minutes

Servings: 4

Temperature: 390degreesF

Ingredients

¼ tsp. Mango powder, dried

½ tsp. Cinnamon powder

¼ tsp. cumin powder

3 cups chickpeas, boiled

1 tsp. Salt

¼ tsp. Coriander powder, dried

½ tsp. chilli powder

1 tsp. Olive oil

¼ tsp. rosemary

Directions:

Preheat and set the air fryer's temperature to 370 degrees F

Transfer chickpeas with olive oil in your Air Fryer basket

Cook for 8 minutes

Shake after every 2 minutes

Take a bowl and add chickpeas with all spices and toss to combine

Serve and enjoy!

Nutrition:

Calories: 214

Fat: 4.4g

Carboh0ydrates: 34.27g

Protein: 10.98g

274.   Rosemary Russet Potato Chips

"Rosemary flavoured russet potatoes, just one of the many ways of preparing your amazing potatoes!"

Preparation time: 10 minutes

Cooking time: 60 minutes

Servings: 4

Temperature: 330degreesF

Ingredients:

Four russet potatoes

½ tsp. salt

2 tsp. rosemary, chopped

1 tbsp. olive oil

Directions:

Rinse potatoes and scrub to clean

Peel and cut them in a lengthwise manner similar to thin chips

Take a bowl and put them into it and soak water for 30 minutes

Take another bowl and toss the chips with olive oil

Transfer them to the cooking basket

Cook for 30 minutes at 330 degrees F

Toss with salt and rosemary while warm

Enjoy!

Nutrition:

Calories: 322

Fat: 3.69g

Carboh0ydrates: 66g

Protein: 7.5g

CHAPTER 14:

Vegan Staples

275. Twice Baked Stuffed Idaho Potatoes

Preparation time: 20 minutes
Cooking time: 65 minutes
Servings: 4
Ingredients:
1 cup spinach, chopped, OR kale
1-2 tsp. of olive oil, optional
1/2 tsp. salt
1/4 cup unsweetened non-dairy milk
1/4 cup unsweetened vegan yogurt
1/4 tsp. pepper
2 Idaho® Russet Baking Potatoes, large-sized
2 tbsp. of nutritional yeast
Optional toppings:
1/4 cup vegan yogurt, unsweetened
Parsley, or chives, or your choice of fresh herb, chopped
Smoked salt and pepper
Directions:
Rub all sides of the potatoes with oil.
Preheat the air fryer to 390F, unless your air fryer model does not require preheating. When the air fryer is hot, put the potatoes in the basket and set the timer for 30 minutes. When the timer

beeps, flip the potatoes and set the timer for 30 minutes. Depending on potato size, you may have to add 10-20 minutes more of cooking time. The potatoes are done when a fork can be easily pierced into them. When the potatoes are already cooked, let them cool enough until you can handle them.
In a lengthwise manner, slice the potato into halves. Scoop out the middle portion carefully from each potato half, leaving enough for a stable shell of white part and skin.
Mashup the scooped-out potato and mix with the nutritional yeast, non-dairy milk, vegan yogurt, pepper, and salt until the mixture is smooth. Stir the spinach into the mixture and combine.
Put the potato mixture in the potato shells.
Depending on the potato size, you can fit 2-4 potato halves in the air fryer basket. Cook in batches, if needed.
Set the air fryer's temperature to 350 degrees F and set the timer for 5 minutes.
Serve. Top with your choice of toppings, if desired.
Nutrition:
Energy (calories): 210 kcal
Protein: 7.84 g
Fat: 3.35 g
Carbohydrates: 37.79 g

276. Falafel Balls

Preparation time: 30 minutes
Cooking time: 12 minutes
Servings: 3
Ingredients:
One can (15 ounces) chickpeas, drained and then rinsed, OR 2 cups cooked chickpeas
1 cup rolled oats
One lemon, freshly squeezed juice only

1 tbsp. flax meal
1 tsp. garlic powder
1 tsp. ground cumin
1/2 cup diced sweet onion
1/2 cup minced carrots
1/2 cup roasted salted cashews
1/2 tsp. turmeric
2 tbsp. olive oil
2 tbsp. soy sauce
Directions:

Put the olive oil into a large-sized frying pan and heat over medium-high heat. When the oil is hot, add the carrots and onions, and sauté for about 7 minutes or until softened. Transfer to a large-sized bowl.

Put the oats and cashews into a food processor. Process until the mixture resembles a coarse meal. With the carrot mixture, apply the oat mixture to the dish. Put the chickpeas into the food processor. Add the lemon juice and soy sauce and the puree until the combination is semi-smooth – chunks are alright. You may need to stop and drag the sides a couple of times to get the ingredients moving. Transfer the chickpea mixture into the bowl with the mix of oat and carrot.

Add the spices and the flaxseed to the bowl. Using a fork, mix all ingredients until well combined, mashing any large pieces of chickpeas in the process.

With your clean hands, divide the mixture into 12 portions and form the pieces into balls. In a single layer, arrange the balls in the air fryer basket.

Set the temperature to 370F and the timer for 12 minutes – shake the basket after 8 minutes.

Serve as desired – stuffed into pitas together with tahini dressing or serve with your preferred accompaniments.
Nutrition:
Energy (calories): 604 kcal
Protein: 18.44 g
Fat: 38.25 g
Carbohydrates: 64.59 g

277. Black Bean-Tomato Soup with Poblano Chili Rings

Preparation time: 20 minutes
Cooking time: 25 minutes
Servings: 6
Ingredients
For the soup:
4 cups black beans, cooked and puréed
3 Roma tomatoes, coarsely chopped
Three cloves garlic
2 1/2 cups vegetable broth
1/2 white onion, medium-sized, coarsely chopped
1 to 2 tbsp. corn oil
1 tsp. salt
One ancho chilli stemmed and then seeded
1 1/2 cups water
For the poblano chilli rings:
One poblano chilli, cut into 1/2-inch thick rings
1/2 cup garbanzo or white bean aquafaba
1/2 cup panko breadcrumbs, divided
1/2 tsp. salt, divided
For garnishing:
Poblano Chile Rings
Ripe Hass avocado, chopped
Tortilla strips or chips
Vegan sour cream, vigorously whipped
Directions:
For the poblano chilli rings:
Toss 1/4 cup panko breadcrumbs with 1/4 tsp. Salt in a shallow bowl. Do the same with the remaining panko breadcrumbs and salt in another shallow bowl. Set aside one of the bowls with the panko breadcrumb mixture.

Dredge the chilli slices in the aquafaba and then coat with the breadcrumb mixture. The panko mixture will initially stick to the rings well, but after the first half of the calls, it will begin to clump and no longer stick well. When this happens, use the second bowl of panko mixture. In a single layer, arrange the coated chilli slices in the air fryer basket – do not overlap. You may need to cook in batches.

Set the air fryer's temperature to 390 degrees F and the timer for 8 to 10 minutes – shake the basket after 5 minutes – you want the chillies soft, and the panko browned. Cook the next batches for about 6 to 8 minutes since the air fryer is already hot. Serve right away topped with your soup.

For the soup:

Put the ancho chilli, tomatoes, and water into a 3-quart pot and stir to combine. Turn the heat to medium heat and let simmer for about 10 minutes.

After 10 minutes, carefully transfer the soup to a blender. Add the onion and garlic into the blender and puree until smooth – hold down the blender's cover with a clean kitchen towel to prevent the top from exploding. If you want to achieve a completely smooth puree, press the puree through a strainer.

Wipe the pot clean. Put the oil into the pot and heat on medium-high flame or heat. Return the puree to the pot and cook for around 5 minutes, stirring slowly. After 5 minutes, turn the heat to medium. Add the pureed bean, salt, and broth. Simmer for 10 minutes, adding liquid if needed to make the soup creamy but not too thick. Serve garnished with poblano chilli rings and your preferred other garnishes.

Nutrition:

Energy (calories): 1046 kcal

Protein: 12.98 g

Fat: 98.89 g

Carbohydrates: 37.43 g

278. Seaweed Salad with Crispy Tofu and Veggies

Preparation time: 35 minutes

Cooking time: 18 minutes

Servings: 4

Ingredients:

One batch of crispy tofu (starch the tofu once the wakame is on the stove)

One cucumber, large-sized

1 Haas avocado, chopped

1/4 cup green onion, chopped

1/4 cup sesame seeds

1/4 cup shiitake sesame vinaigrette (I used Annie's Naturals)

Two carrots, peeled

Three strips of dried wakame

Directions:

Soak the wakame in water for 5 minutes. After soaking, drain and then chop the strips into the bite-sized piece. Boil a pot of water. When the water is boiling, put the wakame pieces and cook for 5 minutes. After cooking, drain the wakame pieces and put them in the refrigerator to chill.

Spiralize the carrots and cucumber. If you do not have sriracha, then just chop them.

Toss the cucumber and carrots with the chilled wakame. Top with tofu, avocado, green onion, and sesame seeds. Serve right away

Nutrition:

Energy (calories): 221 kcal

Protein: 5.58 g Fat: 19.05 g

Carbohydrates: 11.18 g

279. Thai-Inspired Barbecue Cauliflower

Preparation time: 15 minutes

Cooking time: 22 minutes

Servings: 4

Ingredients:

One large or two small head cauliflower

One lemon, zest only

One lime, zest only

1 tbsp. brown sugar

1/2 cup pumpkin seeds

Ten garlic cloves

1-2 tbsp. Sriracha

2 tbsp. curry powder

3 tbsp. arrowroot starch or cornstarch

3/4 cup coconut milk

Hot rice, for serving

Raw vegetables, for serving, optional

Sea salt, to taste

Directions:

Put the curry, cornstarch, garlic, coconut milk, zest, sugar, sriracha, and salt to taste into a small-sized blender, and then blend until the mixture smooth.

Slice the cauliflower into florets and then put it into a large-sized bowl. Add the curry mixture, toss to coat well, and let marinate for 10 minutes.

Put 1/2 of the marinated cauliflower into the air fryer basket. Set the temperature to 360F and set the timer for 15 minutes, basting every 5 minutes.

Adjust the temperature to 390F, set the timer for 5 to 8 minutes, and cook until crisp. When there are only 2 minutes of cooking, add 1/2 of the air fryer's pumpkin seeds.

Repeat the process with the remaining marinated cauliflower and pumpkin seeds.

Serve with raw veggies, such as celery sticks and carrots, or with hot rice.

Nutrition:
Energy (calories): 190 kcal
Protein: 8.17 g Fat: 9.51 g
Carbohydrates: 21.8 g

280. Stuffed Garlic Mushrooms

Preparation time: 10 minutes
Cooking time: 25 minutes
Servings: 4
Ingredients:
16 small-sized button mushrooms
For the stuffing:
1 1/2 slices white bread
1 1/2 tbsp. olive oil
One garlic clove, crushed
1 tbsp. parsley, flat-leafed, finely chopped
Ground black pepper, to taste
Directions:
Preheat the air fryer to 390F.

In a food processor, put the bread and process it into fine crumbs. Add the parsley, garlic, and season with pepper to taste. Mix until combined. When thoroughly incorporated, add stir in the olive oil.

Cut the mushroom stalks off and then fill the caps with the breadcrumb mixture, patting the breadcrumb mixture into the lids to make sure no loose crumbs get into the air fryer fan. Put the filled mushroom caps in the air fryer basket, slide the basket back into the housing, cook for about 7-8 minutes or until the mushroom caps are crispy and golden.

Nutrition:
Energy (calories): 82 kcal
Protein: 2.49 g
Fat: 5.47 g
Carbohydrates: 6.59 g

281. Sticky Mushroom Rice

Preparation time: 5 minutes
Cooking time: 20 minutes
Servings: 6
Ingredients:
1/2 cup frozen peas
1/2 cup soy sauce or tamari
1/2 tsp. ground ginger
16 ounces cremini mushrooms, wiped clean, OR large sized mushrooms cut into halves
16 ounces jasmine rice, uncooked
2 tsp. Chinese five-spice
Four cloves garlic, finely chopped
4 tbsp. maple syrup
4 tbsp. white wine or rice vinegar
Directions:
Start cooking the jasmine rice following instructions on the package to be ready and hot when the sauce cooks. Mix the soy sauce, maple syrup, garlic, five-spice, ground ginger, and white wine until combined. Set aside. Put the mushrooms in the air fryer basket. Turn the temperature to 350 degrees F and also set the timer for 10 minutes. Open the air fryer and shake the basket. Pour the soy sauce mixture over the mushroom and add the peas. Stir and cook for 5 minutes. Pour the mushroom mixture over the pot of rice and stir to mix. Serve.
Nutrition:
Energy (calories): 367 kcal Protein: 9.49 g
Fat: 5.4 g Carbohydrates: 79.96 g

282. Crispy Tofu

Preparation time: 35 minutes
Cooking time: 18 minutes
Servings: 2
Ingredients:
2 tbsp. soy sauce, OR tamari for gluten-free

2 tbsp. nutritional yeast

1/2 tsp. garlic powder

1 tsp. water

1 tsp. sesame oil

1 tbsp. brown rice flour

One package (8-ounce) firm tofu, rinsed, drained, and then cubed

Directions:

In a small-sized bowl, combine all of the dry ingredients. Add the wet ingredients and stir to combine.

Pour the mixture over the tofu cubes, toss to coat, and let marinate for 30 minutes.

After marinating, sprinkles drain excess marinade. Sprinkle the tofu with 1 tbsp. Rice flour and mix to coat. Transfer to the air fryer basket. Turn the temperature to 350 degrees F and set the timer for 18 minutes.

Nutrition:

Energy (calories): 102 kcal

Protein: 5.57 g

Fat: 5.3 g

Carbohydrates: 8.22 g

283.   Tofu and Cauliflower Rice

Preparation time: 12 minutes

Cooking time: 20 minutes

Servings: 3-6

Ingredients

For round 1:

1 cup carrot, diced, around 1 1/2-2 carrots

1 tsp. turmeric

2 tbsp. soy sauce, reduced-sodium

1/2 block tofu, firm or extra firm

1/2 cup onion, diced

For round 2:

1 and 1/2 tsp. of toasted sesame oil

Two cloves garlic, minced

1 tbsp. ginger, minced

1 tbsp. rice vinegar

1/2 cup broccoli, finely chopped

1/2 cup of frozen peas

2 tbsp. soy sauce, reduced-sodium

3 cups cauliflower rice, OR cauliflower minced into smaller the pea-sized pieces

Directions:

Crumble the tofu putting the crumbled pieces into a large-sized bowl. Add the rest of the round 1 ingredient and toss to combine.

Put into the air fryer basket. Set the temperature to 370F and set the timer for 10 minutes – shake once halfway through cooking.

While the tofu is cooking, put all of the round 2 ingredients in the same bowl to toss the tofu and toss to combine.

When the timer beeps after 10 minutes, add the round 2 ingredients into the air fryer basket, gently shake the contents. Set the timer for 10 minutes, then shake the basket after 5 minutes.

When the timer beeps, check the cauliflower. If the cauliflower rice is not cooked at this point, then add 2 to 5 minutes to the cooking time – shake and check every few minutes until done to your preference.

Nutrition:

Energy (calories): 119 kcal

Protein: 6.2 g

Fat: 5.72 g

Carbohydrates: 12.57 g

284.   Roasted Carrots

Preparation time: 10 minutes

Cooking time: 25 minutes

Servings: 4

Ingredients:

1 tsp. herbs de Provence

Two ounces or 4 tbsp. orange juice, about 1/2 medium-sized orange

2 tsp. olive oil

500 grams or 1 pound heritage carrots, or baby carrots

Directions:

Wash the carrots and slice into chunks; do not peel.

Toss the carrots with the oil and then toss with the dried herbs. Transfer to the air fryer basket.

Set the temperature to 180C and set the timer for 20 minutes.

When the timer beeps, transfer the carrots to the container you used to toss them with the oil and herbs. Add the orange juice and toss. Return the carrots to the air fryer basket. Set the timer for 5 minutes.

Serve while still hot.

Notes: If using baby carrots, roast them whole – no need to slice into chunks.

Nutrition:

Energy (calories): 71 kcal

Protein: 1.05 g

Fat: 2.49 g

Carbohydrates: 11.91 g

285. Lemony Green Beans

Preparation time: 10 minutes

Cooking time: 11 minutes

Servings: 4

Ingredients:

One lemon

1 pound green beans washed and then destemmed

1/4 tsp. oil

Black pepper, to taste

Pinch salt

Toasted nuts of choice, optional

Directions:

Except for the nuts, if using, toss the green beans with the rest of the ingredients. Transfer to the air fryer basket.

Set the Air fryer's temperature to 400F and set the timer for 10 to 12 minutes.

Sprinkle with nuts, if preferred. Serve.

Nutrition:

Energy (calories): 47 kcal

Protein: 1.64 g

Fat: 0.56 g

Carbohydrates: 9.12 g

286. Roasted Rosemary Potatoes

Preparation time: 2 minutes

Cooking time: 10 minutes

Servings: 4

Ingredients:

1 tbsp. olive oil

1 tsp. rosemary

Two potatoes, large-sized

Salt and pepper

Directions:

Peel the potatoes and slice them into shapes for roasting. Toss with 1 tbsp. olive oil

Put those potatoes in the air fryer basket. Set the temperature for 180C and set the timer for 10 minutes.

When cooked, transfer to a serving bowl. Sprinkle with the rosemary and season to taste with pepper r and salt. Toss to mix well. Serve.

Notes: Do not overcrowd the air fryer – fill it half full at the most to perfectly roast the potatoes.

Nutrition:

Energy (calories): 177 kcal

Protein: 3.9 g

Fat: 3.59 g

Carbohydrates: 33.38 g

287. Scrambled Broccoli and Tofu

Preparation time: 5 minutes

Cooking time: 30minutes

Servings: 3

Ingredients:

4 cups broccoli florets

One block tofu, chopped into 1-inch pieces

2 tbsp. soy sauce

2 1/2 cups red potato, chopped into 1-inch cubes, about 2 to 3 potatoes

1/2 tsp. onion powder

1/2 tsp. garlic powder

1/2 cup onion, chopped

1 tsp. turmeric

1 tbsp. olive oil

1 tbsp. olive oil

Directions:

Put the tofu in a prepared medium bowl and toss with the onion, garlic powder, onion powder, turmeric, olive oil, and soy sauce. Set aside and let marinate.

In a small-sized bowl, toss the potatoes with the remaining 1 tbsp.—olive oil. Transfer the potatoes to the air fryer basket. Set the air fryer's temperature to 400 degrees F and set the timer for 15 minutes – shake the basket about 7-8 minutes into the cooking.

When the 15 minutes are up, shake the basket again. Transfer the broccoli to a serving bowl.

Put the tofu, setting aside any marinade left in the bowl. Set the temperature to 370F and set the timer for 15 minutes.

Meanwhile, toss the broccoli with the reserved marinade. If there is not enough marinade, then add some soy sauce.

When there are only 5 minutes of cooking time left for the tofu, return the broccoli to the air fryer and continue cooking for the remaining 5 minutes.

Nutrition:
Energy (calories): 446 kcal
Protein: 18.83 g
Fat: 17.38 g
Carbohydrates: 59 g

288. Whiskey Garlic Tofu with Veggie Quinoa

Whiskey Garlic Tofu with Veggie is a sticky, sweet and savoury favourite for any meal. Have it with a sandwich, salad or wrap.
Preparation time: 10 minutes
Cooking time: 10 minutes
Servings: 2
Ingredients:
One block extra-firm tofu, pressed
¼ cup vegan coconut or maple sugar
¼ cup whiskey or bourbon
1 tbsp. apple cider vinegar
Two garlic cloves, finely minced
1 tsp. onion powder
Sea salt and black pepper, to taste
Directions:
If using an air fryer, line the basket with a round of baking parchment paper.
Once the tofu is pressed, slice it into half-inch slabs.
In a saucepan, combine the vegan sugar, whiskey or bourbon, garlic, vinegar and onion powder.
Stir continually, bringing to a boil, then reduce to a simmer. Simmer for about 10 minutes, stirring constantly.
Allow cooling.
Coat all the tofu slices and place them on a baking sheet lined with baking parchment paper.
Fry in the air fryer at 370 degrees Fahrenheit for 7 minutes.

Turn the tofu over and cook for another 3-4 minutes.
Serve over salad, mashed potatoes or with veggie quinoa.
Nutrition:
Energy (calories): 315 kcal
Protein: 23.98 g Fat: 15.52 g
Carbohydrates: 25.32 g

289. Potato Fritter Sliders

Potato Fritter Sliders (Vada Pav) are an Indian snack food made in potato heaven! They are perfect served alongside sweet or savoury chutneys and sauces.
Preparation time: 15 minutes
Cooking time: 15 minutes
Servings: 3
Ingredients:
For Potato Stuffing:
Three potatoes, boiled
1 tbsp. canola oil
Eight curry leaves
½ tsp. Black mustard seeds
1/8 tsp. asafetida
Four cloves garlic, minced
1-inch piece ginger, minced
One green Serrano chilli, minced
½ tsp. Salt
½ tsp. ground turmeric
2 tbsp. cilantro, finely chopped
1-2 tbsp. freshly squeezed lemon juice
For the Batter:
¾ cup gram flour
1/3 cup water
½ tsp. Cayenne pepper or red chilli powder
½ tbsp. Oil
½ tsp. salt
Other Ingredients:
Eight dinner rolls
2 tbsp. vegan butter
2 tbsp. tamarind chutney
2 tbsp. mint-cilantro dry chutney
2 tbsp. chilli-garlic dry chutney
Directions:
Mix all the batter ingredients to form a thick and smooth paste.
Rest the batter while you prepare the stuffing.

For the Stuffing:

Mash the boiled potatoes using a potato masher.

In a pan on the stovetop, heat the oil. Add the mustard seeds and then curry leaves and let the mustard seeds pop.

Add asafetida, ginger, garlic and minced green chilli for 30 seconds until they are fragrant.

Add the salt, cilantro, turmeric, and potatoes. Mix well. Add the lemon juice and mix well.

Take the potato stuffing off the heat and set it aside to cool.

For the Potato Fritters:

Form medium-sized balls with the potato stuffing in the palms of your hands.

Brush the oil on the air fryer grilling pan.

Mix the batter, dip the potato balls into the batter, coat evenly, and place it onto the air fryer grill pan.

Cook at 390 degrees Fahrenheit in the air fryer for 14 minutes, checking halfway through cooking.

Remove the cakes from the grill pan.

For the Sliders:

Slice the dinner rolls into two pieces.

Heat the butter in a pan adjust over medium heat and place the sliced dinner rolls on the pan.

Lightly toast the rolls and then apply tamarind and green chutney on both sides of the dinner rolls.

Sprinkle some chilli-garlic chutney on the rolls and place the patties in between the dinner rolls pressing gently.

Serve immediately.

Nutrition:

Energy (calories): 650 kcal

Protein: 15.15 g Fat: 19.95 g

Carbohydrates: 106 g

290. Korean Fried Tempeh

Spicy and slightly sweet, these utterly delicious and vegan Korean fried tempeh are perfect as they have no added oil. They're full of protein, lower in fat and an ideal appetizer served with white rice and veggies as a main course.

Preparation time: 10 minutes

Cooking time: 20 minutes

Servings: 2-4

Ingredients:

For the Tempeh:

200g tempeh, cut into medium-sized chunks

3 - 4 tbsp. Panko breadcrumbs

2 tbsp. vegan mayonnaise

For the Sauce:

2 tbsp. Gochujang Korean red chilli paste

1 tbsp. maple or agave syrup

Two cloves garlic, minced

1tbsp. water

1 tbsp. soy sauce

Salt and pepper, to taste

To Serve:

1 tbsp. sesame seeds

1 tsp. fresh chopped chives

Chive flowers (optional)

Directions:

To make the breaded tempeh, plate the vegan mayo and breadcrumbs into separate shallow bowls.

Mix few drops of water with the mayo to thin it out.

Dip each piece of tempeh in mayo and then in the breadcrumbs and place into the air fryer basket.

Cook the tempeh in the air fryer for 15 minutes, flipping the pieces over every 4-5 minutes until they becomes golden brown and crispy.

When the tempeh is just about cooked, add the sauce to a frying pan, mix to form a paste and cook on medium heat for 2 - 3 minutes until slightly thick, glossy and bubbling.

Add the breaded tempeh and stir gently until fully coated. Garnish with the chives and sesame seeds, then serve as a snack or with white rice and veggies of your choice.

Nutrition: Energy (calories): 235 kcal

Protein: 14.96 g Fat: 13.8 g

Carbohydrates: 17.48 g

291. Lemon Tofu Piccata

Preparation time: 30 minutes

Cooking time: 20 minutes

Servings: 4

Ingredients:

For the Marinade:

¼ cup fresh lemon juice

One clove garlic, minced

2 tbsp. parsley

½ tsp. black pepper

½ tsp. sea salt

For the Tofu:

One block extra-firm tofu, cut into eight rectangular cutlets

1 cup Panko breadcrumbs or vegan breadcrumbs

½ cup vegan mayo

For the Sauce:

¼ cup lemon juice

1 cup vegetable broth

2 tbsp. fresh parsley

One clove garlic, minced

2 tsp. potato starch or cornstarch

2 tbsp. capers

¼ tsp. black pepper

½ tsp. sea salt

To Serve:

One lemon, sliced into rounds

Directions:

To marinate the Tofu:

Mix all the marinade ingredients in a blender or food processor.

Puree to a pretty smooth mix. In a prepared shallow bowl or on a large plate, cover the tofu with the marinade and marinate for 15-30 minutes

To bread the Tofu:

Put the vegan mayo into a shallow bowl and the Panko breadcrumbs in another shallow bowl.

Dredge each tofu cutlet first in the mayo, then in the breadcrumbs, making sure to get an even coating.

To cook the Tofu:

Arrange the tofu cutlets in a single layer in the air fryer basket. Cook in batches at degrees, Fahrenheit for 20 minutes, shaking the cutlets gently after 10 minutes to prevent sticking.

Repeat in batches, if needed.

To make the Lemon Piccata Sauce:

While the tofu cooks, put all together the sauce ingredients, except the capers in a blender or food processor.

Puree until smooth, and then stir in the capers.

Pour the sauce into a small saucepan.

Let it boil and then reduce to a simmer, stirring for 5-7 minutes, until it thickens.

Serve:

Spoon a couple of tbsp. Of the sauce over the breaded tofu cutlets and garnish with the lemon and parsley.

Nutrition:

Energy (calories): 694 kcal

Protein: 11.95 g

Fat: 71.2 g

Carbohydrates: 10.27 g

292.   Bbq Lentil Meatballs

These air fryer BBQ Lentil Meatballs are flavorful and chewy on the inside and satisfyingly crunchy on the outside. They're merely addictive served with your favourite vegan BBQ sauce.

Preparation time: 5 minutes

Cooking time: 40 minutes

Servings: 2

Ingredients:

For the Lentil Meatballs:

2 cups vegetable stock

1 cup dry brown or green lentils

½ cup chopped dried mushrooms

2 tbsp. sunflower oil

1 cup white or yellow onion, finely diced

1 tbsp. tomato paste

One clove garlic, minced

3 tbsp. vegan BBQ sauce

½ cup wheat gluten

2 tbsp. water or vegetable stock

1 tbsp. Vegan Worcestershire or low-sodium soy sauce

½ tsp. smoked paprika

1 tsp. onion powder

1 tsp. Dried parsley

¼ tsp. Black pepper

½ tsp. salt to taste

For the Topping:

1 cup vegan BBQ sauce

Directions:

Over medium-high heat, a large pot brings the vegetable stock, lentils, and mushrooms to a boil. Adjust heat lower and simmer for 20 minutes, until the lentils are tender and the liquid absorbed. In a small pan, warm the oil over medium heat. Add the onions and sauté for 7 -

10 minutes, or until onions are just beginning to caramelize.

Next, adjust the heat to a medium-low and add the tomato paste and garlic. Sauté for another minute or so, and then set the pan aside.

In a food processor, place cooked lentil-mushrooms mixture, onion-tomato mixture, wheat gluten, vegan Bbq sauce, water, Worcestershire sauce, onion powder, parsley, smoked paprika, salt and pepper. Pulse until the mixture is well combined but still chunky.

Coat the air fryer basket with a light spray of cooking oil.

Moisten clean hands with water, then form roughly 2-tbsp. Worth of the mixture into lentil balls.

Put each ball inside the air fryer basket, leaving at least half an inch between them.

Coat the lentil balls with a light spray of cooking oil and cook at 350 degrees Fahrenheit for 12 minutes. Transfer the lentil meatballs to a plate or platter, then drizzle the vegan BBQ sauce over the top

Serve immediately with toothpicks, and enjoy!

Nutrition:

Energy (calories): 2172 kcal

Protein: 8.37 g

Fat: 237.43 g

Carbohydrates: 27.22 g

293. Cajun French fry Po'boy with Vegan Mushroom Gravy

This New Orleans features crispy French fries sandwiched inside of a baguette and smothered with gravy. This vegan version is also good and utterly delicious!

Preparation time: 20 minutes

Cooking time: 15 minutes

Servings: 4

Ingredients:

For the French fries:

Four medium Russet potatoes, cut in half, and then into planks

6 cups of boiling water for soaking the potatoes

2 tsp. olive oil (or use aquafaba)

1 tsp. Cajun seasoning

¼ tsp. granulated garlic

½ tsp. smoked paprika

¼ tsp. ground black pepper

½ tsp. salt

Mushroom Gravy Ingredients:

1 tbsp. olive oil (use water if the recipe is oil-free)

3 cups chopped mushrooms

2 tsp. vegan Worcestershire sauce

2 tsp. soy sauce (you may substitute for coconut aminos)

1 tbsp. tapioca starch

½ cup of water

To Serve:

French or Italian soft loaf

Lettuce

Sliced tomatoes

Vegan mayo

Favourite hot sauce

Directions:

To make the French Fries:

Place the fries in a bowl or saucepan.

Let the water boil and then pour over the fries, covering them.

Soak the potatoes in hot water for 15 minutes, and then drain over the sink.

Once dry, toss the fries in the oil (or aquafaba if using), paprika, garlic, Cajun seasoning, salt and black pepper.

Add the fries to the air fryer basket and cook at 350 degrees Fahrenheit for 5 minutes. Shake the basket and cook further for 5 minutes.

Raise the heat to 390 degrees Fahrenheit and cook for another 5 minutes.

Shake the basket and then cook a final 5 minutes.

To make the Mushroom Gravy:

While the potatoes are in the air fryer, heat 1 tbsp. Olive oil in a prepared large skillet over medium heat.

Add the mushrooms and sauté until they begin to release all their juices.

Stir in the Worcestershire sauce and soy sauce and cook for 2 minutes.

Add the water and stir in the tapioca starch.

Set the heat up to medium-high and cook until the sauce is thick.

To assemble the Po'Boy:

Slice the bread in half lengthways.

Toast the bread if preferred and spread it with vegan mayo and hot sauce.

Layer the baked fries at the bottom piece of the bread. Spread the mushroom mixture on top of the fries.

Serve dressed in lettuce, tomato, and mayo. Put the top piece of bread and enjoy!

Nutrition:

Energy (calories): 381 kcal

Protein: 10.49 g 19% Fat: 6.7 g

Carbohydrates: 73.41 g

294. Bbq Soy Curls

Serve them accompanied with potato salad & greens for utter deliciousness.

Preparation time: 13 minutes

Cooking time: 8 minutes

Servings: 2

Ingredients:

1 cup of soy curls

1 cup of warm water

1 tsp. canola oil

1 tsp. vegetarian stock base*

¼ cup vegan BBQ sauce

Directions:

Soak the soy curls in water and vegetable bouillon in a bowl for about 10 minutes.

Drain the soy curls on a sieve, and squeeze out all excess water.

Place then into a mixing bowl, and pull them apart into shreds resembling string cheese.

Air fry the soy curls at 400 degrees Fahrenheit for 3 minutes. Work in batches to prevent overcrowding and to allow the rings to crisp up properly.

Remove the soy curls put them back to the mixing bowl, toss in vegan BBQ sauce and stir.

Make sure all of the curls get coated.

Return to air fryer and cook at 400 degrees Fahrenheit for 5 minutes stopping twice to shake the pan.

Serve the curls with a vegan potato salad, mixed greens, and a non-dairy mac and cheese.

Nutrition:

Energy (calories): 102 kcal

Protein: 12.04 g Fat: 2.69 g

Carbohydrates: 9.31 g

295. Buttermilk Battered Tofu

Buttermilk Battered Tofu is exceptionally delicious and utterly crispy. Serve with mashed potatoes in a salad or a sandwich.

Preparation time: 20 minutes

Cooking time: 15 minutes

Servings: 2

Ingredients:

For the Tofu:

8 oz. block medium-firm tofu, cut lengthways into four slices

½ tsp. pepper

1 tsp. salt

For the Dry Ingredients:

1½ cups all-purpose flour

1/3 cup cornstarch

1 tbsp. paprika

2 tsp. cayenne

1 tbsp. onion powder

1 tbsp. garlic powder

1 tbsp. salt

For the Wet Ingredients:

2 tbsp. vegan egg powder, mixed with ½ cup ice cold water

One cup soymilk, mixed with 2 tsp. apple cider vinegar

1 tbsp. hot sauce

2 tbsp. bourbon

Cooking spray oil

For the Sambal Mayo:

1 tbsp. to ¼ cup sambal

½ cup vegan mayo

To Serve:

Hamburger buns

¼ red onion, sliced thinly

One jalapeño, thinly sliced

2 cups red or green cabbage

Bread and butter pickles

Vegan butter, for toasting the buns

Directions:

Tofu Preparation:

Place the tofu on a wire rack set inside a lined baking sheet. Season with salt and pepper and let chill for an hour.

Combine all the dry ingredients in a prepared medium-sized bowl.

Combine all the wet ingredients in a separate medium-sized bowl.

Coat the tofu in the dry mixture and place back onto the wire rack.

Pour 3 tablespoon of the wet mixture into the dry mixture and using your hands combine the two.

Dip the tofu into the wet mixture, then pack the moistened dry flour mixture firmly around each piece.

Place the battered tofu back on the wire rack and place it into the refrigerator to chill for 30 minutes.

Spray the tofu evenly with cooking oil spray.

Place into the air fryer set at the temperature of 400 degrees Fahrenheit and cook for 10 minutes.

Flip the slabs over halfway through cooking.

Add a little more spray over any areas that look dry and cook for an additional minute or two if needed.

The tofu should be a deep golden colour.

To Serve:

Spread vegan butter over both sides of the buns and toast in a cast iron pan until crispy.

Serve immediately, piled with the cabbage, red onion, jalapeño, sambal mayo and pickles.

Nutrition:

Energy (calories): 918 kcal

Protein: 34.5 g

63%

Fat: 32.68 g

Carbohydrates: 126.19 g

296. Rainbow Veggies

Rainbow Veggies made in the air fryer caramelize in a lovely way without overcooking. Toss them with your favourite vinaigrette, mixed with greens for a different salad.

Preparation time: 10 minutes

Cooking time: 20 minutes

Servings: 4

Ingredients:

One zucchini, finely diced

One red bell pepper, seeded and diced

One yellow summer squash, finely diced

½ sweet white onion, finely diced

4 oz. fresh mushrooms, cleaned and halved

1 tbsp. extra-virgin olive oil

Salt and pepper, to taste

Directions:

Preheat the air fryer according to the recommendations of the air fryer.

Place the red bell pepper, zucchini, mushrooms, squash and onion in a large bowl.

Add the olive oil, black pepper and salt, and toss to combine.

Place the vegetables in a single layer in the air fryer basket.

Air-fry, the vegetables for 20 minutes, stirring halfway through the cooking time.

Nutrition:

Total Calories: 69 kcal.

Carbohydrates 7.7g

Protein 2.6g

Fat 3.8g

Sodium 48mg

Cholesterol 0mg

297. Tofu with Carrots and Broccoli

With an air-fryer, Chinese take-out is simple and nutritious. In an orange sauce, the crispy tofu is tossed with plenty of vegetables. It's easy to make and has less oil in it. {Vegan, Adaptable to Gluten-Free}

Preparation time: 10 minutes

Cooking time: 15 minutes

Servings: 2

Ingredients:

For the Tofu:

1 14-oz. block extra-firm tofu, pressed and cubed

3 tbsp. cornstarch

1 tbsp. soy sauce

1 tbsp. sesame oil

For the Sauce:

Two cloves garlic, minced

2 tsp. cornstarch

2 tbsp. orange zest

3 tbsp. rice vinegar (or substitute with white vinegar)

½ cup of orange juice

1 tbsp. light soy sauce (you may substitute with tamari for a gluten-free recipe)

1 tbsp. Shaoxing wine

2 tbsp. sugar

¼ tsp. fine sea salt

For the Stir fry:

One head broccoli, chopped into bite-size pieces

Two carrots, julienned

Directions:

To prepare the Tofu:

Mix the tofu with soy sauce and sesame oil to mix.

Sprinkle half of cornstarch over the tofu and mix. Repeat and make sure all the tofu is well coated.

Set the air fryer's temperature at 390 degrees Fahrenheit (unless the model doesn't require it).

Once hot, add the coated tofu to the air fryer basket and cook for 5 minutes.

When done, shake or stir the tofu.

Cook again for a further 5 minutes and set aside.

To stir fry:

Mix all the stir fry sauce ingredients in a bowl.

Heat 1/4 cup of water in a large nonstick skillet over medium-high heat until the water boils.

Add the broccoli and carrots.

Cover then cook until the veggies are tender, about 1 to 2 minutes.

Let the water completely evaporate. Stir the sauce and then pour into the skillet.

Quickly stir for a few times until the sauce is thick and glossy.

Add the tofu and stir a few more times to mix well. Immediately transfer to a plate and serve to pipe hot over steamed noodles or rice.

Nutrition:

Total Calories: 298kcal

Carbohydrates: 32.4g Protein: 16g

Fat: 12.6g Potassium: 609mg

298.   General Tso's Cauliflower Tofu

Skip the takeout! This version of General Tso's Cauliflower Tofu is super delicious and, best of all, healthy.

Preparation time: 15 minutes

Cooking time: 20 minutes

Servings: 2

Ingredients:

For the primary chickpea binder:

½ cup chickpea flour

½ - 1 cup water or almond milk

A pinch of salt.

For the basic Panko breading:

1 cup Panko crumbs

1 - 2 tbsp. olive oil

A pinch of salt.

For the sauce:

3 tbsp. soy sauce or coconut aminos

2 tbsp. rice wine vinegar

2 tbsp. sherry

2 tsp. sesame oil

3 tbsp. agave nectar or sugar

1 tbsp. cornstarch

¼ cup veggie stock

Dried chilli or chilli flakes, to taste

Toasted sesame seeds

Green onion, sliced thinly

Directions:

To prepare the chickpea binder:

In a prepared shallow dish, combine the chickpea flour and then slowly add water to the mix.

Continuously stir, removing any lumps using a fork until you reach the consistency of thin pancake batter.

Stir in a pinch of salt and set aside.

To prepare the panko breading:

In a shallow dish, combine the breadcrumbs and oil.

Use your hands or an oil brush to make sure the oil is evenly distributed, and add in a salt pinch.

To bread:

Prepare the vegetables or tofu into pieces.

Add the pieces to the chickpea binder and coat them thoroughly.

Transfer the pieces to the breading mixture, lightly press the breadcrumbs onto the parts, and then remove them to a tray.

To Air-Fry and Stir Fry:

Preheat and set the air fryer's temperature to 400 degrees Fahrenheit.

Cook the tofu or veggies for 10 - 20 minutes. Turn them as they cook to ensure they brown evenly. They should come out golden brown and crispy.

Combine all of the sauce ingredients, right down to the chilli flake, in a bowl or measuring cup.

Stir until the cornstarch is well blended in.

Pour this mixture into a pan and on medium heat, and allow it to come to a simmer. Stir constantly.

If the sauce is thick and glossy, add the chilli.

Stir and allow to bubble for one more minute.

Turn off the heat and add the breaded and air fried pieces.

Mix well to combine.

Serve and garnished with sesame seeds and green onion.

Nutrition: Energy (calories): 554 kcal

Protein: 14.87 g Fat: 20.24 g

Carbohydrates: 77.46 g

299. Five Spice Tofu

Preparation time: 10 minutes

Cooking time: 20 minutes

Servings: 4

Ingredients:

1 12-oz block extra-firm tofu

2 tbsp. oil

For the Marinade:

1 tbsp. Chinese black vinegar + 1 tsp.

2 tsp. Chinese five-spice powder

2 tsp. garlic powder

1 tsp. Dark soy sauce

¼ cup maple syrup

½ tsp. salt or to taste

Directions:

Prepare the marinade ingredients and mix in a large bowl.

Drain the tofu.

Wrap up the tofu in a clean kitchen paper towel and squeeze to remove excess water.

This will cause the tofu to crumble into chunks.

Add tofu to the marinade and mix until all the marinade is well absorbed.

Drizzle the oil over the tofu and mix. Prepare the air fryer basket by spraying it with cooking oil spray. This will ensure the tofu doesn't stick.

Transfer the tofu to the air fryer basket and cook at 400 degrees Fahrenheit for 20 minutes, shaking the basket halfway through cooking.

Serve piping hot.

Nutrition: Energy (calories): 235 kcal 11%

Protein: 20.95 g Fat: 11.62 g

Carbohydrates: 15.82 g

300. Crumbed Tempeh

This vegan version of fish fingers is healthy and oil-free! Perfect for the kids, served with ketchup or mayo.

Preparation time: 5 minutes

Cooking time: 12 minutes

Servings: 2

Ingredients:

200g packet tempeh

3 - 4 tbsp. besan flour

½ tsp. of celery salt

1 tsp. smoked paprika

½ cup Panko breadcrumbs

Almond Milk

Directions:

Slice up the tempeh in 1cm strips.

Mix the besan flour, celery salt and paprika.

Dip the tempeh strip into the almond milk, then coat with the flour mix.

Put the tempeh back into the milk and then coat with the breadcrumbs.

Sprinkle a little extra celery salt and cook at 180 degrees Celsius for 12 mins.

Nutrition:

Energy (calories): 235 kcal

Protein: 20.95 g

Fat: 11.62 g

Carbohydrates: 15.82 g

301. Fried Lasagna

Tofu ricotta filled lasagna noodles coated in bread crumbs, and herbs feature hearty Italian flavours that truly delight. Serve alongside marinara sauce for a flavour explosion.

Preparation time: 15 minutes

Cooking time: 15 minutes

Servings: 2

Ingredients:

6 Lasagna sheets

4 oz. block extra-firm tofu

2 tbsp. nutritional yeast

Two cloves garlic

2 tbsp. lemon juice

2 tsp. Olive oil

½ tsp. salt

A pinch of black pepper

1 cup vegan bread crumbs

1 cup almond milk

1 tsp. Apple cider vinegar

½ tsp. Garlic powder

½ tsp. Dried parsley

½ tsp. dried oregano

Directions:

Boil the lasagna sheets according to packet instructions and set aside.

Squeeze some liquid out of the tofu over the sink. It will crumble.

Add the crumbled tofu, nutritional yeast, garlic, olive oil, lemon juice, salt and pepper to a food processor.

Pulse until everything comes together and is smooth, but with some texture.

Once the lasagna sheets are cool, take one sheet, pat it dry and place it flat on a plate. Spread the whole sheet with about 1-2 tbsp, of the tofu ricotta mixture. Spread evenly in a thin layer.

Fold one side part of the lasagna sheet to the center, and then fold the other side over.

Press down the end and seal in as much as possible.

Pour the almond milk and apple cider vinegar to one bowl, whisk and let sit for 1 minute to curdle slightly.

In another separate bowl, add the bread crumbs and dried herbs, stirring to combine.

Take one folded lasagna, dip it into the almond milk, and then put in the bread crumbs and coat thoroughly. Press the breadcrumbs gently onto the pasta, so they stick.

Place the lasagna pockets in the air fryer spray with cooking oil spray and air fry at 400 degrees Fahrenheit for 7-9 minutes. Flip them halfway through cooking and cook until they are brown and crispy. Enjoy!

Nutrition:

Energy (calories): 266 kcal

Protein: 16.16 g

Fat: 12.66 g

Carbohydrates: 24.26 g

302. Buffalo Tofu

This 3-ingredient Buffalo tofu is a quick, easy and delicious snack! It cooks in under half an hour, so perfect for a movie night or game day.

Preparation time: 60 minutes

Cooking time: 20 minutes

Servings: 2

Ingredients:

One block extra-firm tofu drained and pressed

1 cup hot sauce

¼ cup vegan butter, melted

To Serve:

Vegan ranch or blue cheese dressing

Directions:

Cut the tofu into squares.

Preheat and set the air fryer's temperature to 390 degrees Fahrenheit.

Whisk the hot sauce together with the melted butter to form the buffalo sauce.

Marinate the tofu in the buffalo sauce mixture for 30 - 60 minutes.

Once the air fryer is preheated, coat the basket lightly with cooking oil spray and use tongs and add the tofu to the air fryer basket. Reserve the marinade.

Air-fry for 20 - 30 minutes, checking and shaking the tofu after 10 minutes, and then each additional 5 minutes after that.

Check the tofu each time for the desired crispness.

Toss the tofu back into the reserved hot sauce and then transfer to a serving plate.

If desired, serve alongside vegan blue cheese or ranch dressing and enjoy!

Nutrition:

Energy (calories): 448 kcal

Protein: 24.74 g

Fat: 36.52 g

Carbohydrates: 13.3 g

Support for College Students

Nutritional Medicine Major

CHAPTER 15:

Short Testimonies And Events In Favor Of Veganism

This is Sandra Muller! (IG: @sanisnutrition)

I came across Sandra on Instagram and was very intrigued that she was a vegan in a nutritional medicine program. I knew that she was in a program that doesn't thoroughly teach material based on plant-based nutrition, so I reached out to her. We started talking about some of the struggles she faces and how she's coped with them. So, I thought she'd be a perfect fit for this section because I'm aware that a LOT of vegan college students are studying nutrition, medicine, agriculture, etc., and will face challenges along the way. Let her story be a small guide for those of you who plan on joining college curriculums that aren't entirely aligned with your lifestyle!

This is what Sandra had to say when I asked for her to share some of her experiences as a vegan in a college program that still teaches material that isn't 100% vegan-friendly:

"The moment I realized how much a vegan diet is benefiting my health, I knew I wanted to study food science and nutrition. I wanted to make my master's degree in nutritional medicine, so I could tell everyone how you can change their life with a plant-based diet. I tried to change the world!

But was I dreaming too big? Is it even possible to study food science and nutrition in a society that tells you to drink milk for strong bones because the dairy industry is paying them to? Well, let me tell you, I was scared before I started. I feared preachy professors telling me that you must eat meat to be healthy. And even though it's not easy to study food science as a vegan, it's worth it!!

I'm lucky to study at a university in a small town in Germany where everybody is open about veganism. They don't tell you to go vegan, but at least they don't tell you that veganism is dangerous or whatnot. Most professors even say a vegan diet is super healthy, and I recently realized that they couldn't tell you anything else anymore because scientists have proven that a vegan diet is optimum for human health, so they would be bad professors if they'd not listen to the newest discoveries in food science.

You'll always be confronted with meat and other animal product during your time studying, though, because you must learn about it. Me, for example, I've already spent a fair amount of time in the chemistry lab. During my first year, we had to run some tests on the stomach content and feces to analyze all the enzymes and bacteria working inside a digestive system similar to a human's digestive system. A few vegans I study with decided not to do it. Me, on the other hand, decided to do it because I wanted to learn something. My main tip here is to just go with it. Think about your goals and why you started studying in the first place, and think about all the not-so-pleasant things you have to do as necessary steps to change the world one day!

Trust me, your morals and beliefs will be questioned during your studies! You just have to keep a clear head and remember your goals. One day, nutritional medicine will be purely for plant-based nutrition, but until then, you just have to stay focused and learn what you need to know so that you can continue to spread the message about the vegan lifestyle!"

As you can see, Sandra is a motivated student with ZERO intentions of following the 'norm.' She's standing strong with her beliefs, even though she's faced with people who sometimes disagree with the vegan lifestyle. For those of you who plan on studying nutrition in college, PLEASE be prepared to stand up for your beliefs and remember to take nutritional advice with a grain of salt because we don't live in a world that teaches purely plant-based nutritional science, YET!

Marine Science and Biology Major

This is Cassie Gatchel! (IG: @xo_cassieg)

I've known Cassie for a long while. We attended the same public high school and were exposed to many of the same ideologies as a small town. After high school, Cassie went to Florida to study Marine Biology in college while I stayed in Ohio to study Engineering and Business.

We may have taken entirely different paths, but after almost three years of being exposed to broader aspects of life, we've both realized that our oceans are in desperate need of help. We've both realized that a lot of human habits are simply unsustainable. We are destroying ocean life through the way we eat and how we dispose of our waste into our precious bodies of water...

This is what Cassie replied with when I asked her to tell me about some of the shocking things she's learned since studying ocean life:

"As a double major in Marine Science and Biology at the University of Tampa, I've realized the effects of overfishing in the United States. And trust me, it's not just happening in the United States, it's happening all over the world. Today, some of the biggest issues within our world is coral bleaching, which is caused by overfishing and pollution within our waters.

Our oceans can't function without coral and that means our oceans will be in grave danger if this doesn't stop. By cutting fish out of your diet, you're capable of saving the oceans and the amazing things that inhabit it.

In addition to overfishing, the commercial fishing industry are STILL killing and selling shark meat at many public restaurants and grocery stores. This is another major issue that needs to be brought to people's attention.

One personal experience that I'd like to share with you is when I spent over a month diving and learning about Marine Science during the summer of 2016. One of our most important lessons was over coral bleaching, which we went out to learn about the issue hands-on. Before diving off the boat, we took the temperature and PH of the water (which was more acidic than it should've been) and talked about the effects of coral bleaching. When we got into the water, the once colourful coral was white, and in addition to that, there were very few fish/animals living in the water. By overfishing, not recycling, and polluting our seas, we are killing off coral reefs that have been around longer than dinosaurs. Significant changes need to be made, so I hope you take my message and think about lifestyle changes you could make to combat these catastrophes.

Conclusion:

A vegan is anyone who completely abstains from using and consuming all animal products and by-products (this means no eggs, butter, milk, cheese, meat and animal blood). Vegetarians are vegans who abstain from consuming animal flesh. A vegetarian is not necessarily a vegan because vegetarians still consume eggs. All vegans are vegetarians, but not all vegetarians are vegans. Vegan diet is the most effective way of correcting the world's dangerous eating habits and simultaneously improving the world we live in. Veganism is the most protective action against bad habits and a restrictive approach to life. There are many compassionate reasons to be vegan. The foremost reason is that we continue to support animals' consumption without completely abstaining from animal products. This indirectly supports animal cruelty and the exploitation of animals, which is unfathomable and inhumane. This Vegan cookbook will help educate you on why you should be a vegan and provide you with some great vegan recipes. It is our mission to help you forgo processed foods and embrace whole foods plant-based nutrition. We want to help you control your portion sizes and show you how to manage your health in a fun and delicious way. We urge you to read and use the cookbook. We wrote it in such a way that you can use it as a reference cookbook. You will find the recipes easy to use, healthy, delicious and 100% vegan. With the help of Air fryer, the vegan cookbook has become more comfortable. Nowadays, vegan cookbooks are focused on plant-based nutrition, which explains the air fryer's relevance is increasing day by day. Our recipes are both that yummy and healthy that you will be delighted to share them with your friends and family. We believe that vegan cooking is for everyone, and we want to take out the myths and scare tactics that you may have encountered in the past. Vegan cooking is fun, is delicious, and has no room for undercooked, bland, or boring food with lazy techniques. Airfryer is the answer to making the perfect vegan air fryer cooking. We want you to embrace your natural abilities as a compassionate, health-driven person. If you're looking for a new way of eating, we are here to help. Our excellent knowledge of Vegan cookbooks will help you in mastering Airfryer cooking.

Along with many others, we believe that this lifestyle has the most significant potential to save the world. It's exciting to be a vegan these days. People increasingly realize that it is not only about losing weight but about giving up toxic habits. It is about actually caring about other living creatures and not treating them as sub-human. Don't wait till tomorrow to start choosing your lifestyle and make a change. Improve yourself and start living a healthier life today. And that's what you can do by embracing vegan cooking with air fryer recipes Airfryer is one of the most trending's and must in 2017. It works by blasting hot air around a basket containing whatever food you want to cook. It doesn't use oil at all, so that you can cook things with a great crispy outer.

Printed in Great Britain
by Amazon

17233136R00088